# The BATTLE of BEGINNINGS

## Why Neither Side Is Winning the Creation-Evolution Debate

# Del Ratzsch

InterVarsity Press
Downers Grove, Illinois

InterVarsity Press® is the book-publishing division of InterVarsity Christian Fellowship®, a student movement active on campus at hundreds of universities, colleges and schools of nursing in the United States of America, and a member movement of the International Fellowship of Evangelical Students. For information about local and regional activities, write Public Relations Dept., InterVarsity Christian Fellowship, 6400 Schroeder Rd., P.O. Box 7895, Madison, WI 53707-7895.

All Scripture quotations, unless otherwise indicated, are taken from the HOLY BIBLE, NEW INTERNATIONAL VERSION®. NIV®. Copyright © 1973, 1978, 1984 by International Bible Society. Used by permission of Zondervan Publishing House. All rights reserved.

Cover illustration: Telegraph Colour Library/FPG International
ISBN 0-8308-1529-5

Printed in the United States of America ∞

**Library of Congress Cataloging-in-Publication Data**

Ratzsch, Delvin Lee, 1945-
   The battle of beginnings: why neither side is winning the
creation-evolution debate/Del Ratzsch.
      p.    cm.
   Includes bibliographical references.
   ISBN 0-8308-1529-5 (pbk.: alk. paper)
   1. Evolution—Religious aspects—Christianity.   2. Creation.
3. Creationism.   I. Title.
   BT712.R37    1996
   231.7'65—dc20                                              95-48958
                                                                CIP

17   16   15   14   13   12   11   10   9   8   7   6   5
10   09   08   07   06   05   04   03   02   01

## Preface

My upbringing had a strongly fundamentalist flavor, and my parents, like many fundamentalists, had a deep respect for reason, the mind and education. When science became an object of early love, my parents encouraged me in its pursuit. But despite the high regard in which science was held, it was clear that somehow secular scientists had gone badly off the rails concerning this Darwin fellow. And therein lay a tension, because entering my late teens I found myself very much attracted to the evolutionary picture of history, life and humans.

Some argued, of course, that Genesis, belief and evolution could be reconciled, but at some point along the way I think I ceased to want them to be reconcilable. Evolution, along with the new cosmologies and backed by the undentable prestige of science, became part of a gratifyingly sophisticated excuse for unbelief—a ticket out of an oppressive universe with a God who set boundaries and made demands, into one where we set the rules and the cosmos itself was the only limit. (It was this personal experience as much as anything that has convinced me that creation-evolution issues frequently run much deeper than mere scientific theory.)

Staying in that brave new universe proved, however, to be exceedingly difficult, and I didn't manage it. The original tension was still here when I returned, but there seemed little choice but to live with it, struggle with it, and occasionally set it aside and rest up from the latest skirmish.

I still do not claim to know what the proper resolution to the creation-evolution dispute is. But it has become clear to me that much of what flies past in the present dispute is confused at best, and that most lay Christians (including the young people who are frequently the targets of choice) have virtually no defenses when authoritatively presented with those confusions, whether in secular classrooms, popular media or church-sponsored conferences.

I have written this book to those audiences. It is not my aim to convince readers to accept any particular resolution of the issue, but rather to point out those things that should not convince one. That category—arguments that should not convince—constitutes an unfortunately high proportion of the popular artillery of both sides. But whatever decision one makes on this issue, it should not be driven by misconception.

Such a decision is not necessarily easy. One of the attractions of the popular caricatures that reign in this area is that they make confident choice appear supremely simple. Unfortunately, it seems to me, the more accurately one sees the issues, the more difficult is the resolution. If some on both sides come away from what follows suspecting that many of the popular offhand "refutations" (their own and opponents') don't work quite as advertised, then the book will have served a purpose.

In working on this project, I have become indebted to many people. The entire Calvin College philosophy department read and responded to several chapters. David Van Baak, Kelly Clark, Kurt Wise, Charles Hummel, Ed Larson, Terry Gray, Greg Hull and Stephen Meyer read and commented on the entire manuscript, as did James Hoover of InterVarsity Press. They have saved me from various earlier mistakes, although several of them probably think that other mistakes remain. I am also indebted to Ruth Goring of InterVarsity Press. In addition, I have special debts to Lois and the late Ken Konyndyk, Donna Kruithof and Calvin College, which provided me with sabbatical and other research support.

My family—Betsy, Dylan and Philip—put up with a lot. And I owe deep debts of many years to my first family, to whom this is dedicated: Mom, Dad (in memoriam), Burl and Phyllis.

# 1 INTRODUCTION

**S**ome public disagreements transcend the category of mere debate and become social institutions. Each side develops its own organizations, journals, networks, buzzwords, mythologies, heroes, conspiracy theories, horror stories, dire predictions, standards of orthodoxy, loyalty tests and so forth. The "creation-evolution" dispute currently has that status in American culture—and not for the first time, either.

Unfortunately, in such disputes the harder the lines are drawn, the less actual communication there is and, indeed, the less importance actual communication seems to have. "Dialogue" becomes little more than occasions for counting coup or for recruiting the undecided. And the less actual contact of competing ideas there is, the easier it is for favorite ideas—on both sides—to be credited within their respective camps with a status they really do not deserve. Indeed, each side can see the case as so utterly closed that the very existence of opponents generates near bafflement. For instance, on the one side, Henry Morris:

> Now the most amazing thing about this whole state of affairs is the absurdity and impossibility of the very concept of evolution! That a theory which is so utterly devoid of any legitimate scientific proof could have attained such a position of universal power and prestige in the name of science is surely a remarkable commentary on human nature. Whether the explanation lies in some monumental web of intellectual conspiracy

or merely in man's enormous capacity for egocentric self-deception, the simple fact is that the evolutionary philosophy is both totally false and almost totally successful.[1]

And on the other side, Richard Dawkins:

It is absolutely safe to say that if you meet somebody who claims not to believe in evolution, that person is ignorant, stupid or insane (or wicked, but I'd rather not consider that). . . . [This is] an area where half the country claims to believe an absurd and palpable falsehood. I say "claims" because a belief that is held in carefully nurtured ignorance of the alternative is hardly a belief to be taken seriously.[2]

In a climate defined by such perceptions, mythologies flourish. A major aim of this book is to challenge mythologies of various sides of the creation-evolution dispute.

The present dispute has many aspects—scientific, historical, philosophical, theological, political and legal, for example. What follows will focus primarily, although not exclusively, on two general areas. First, there is little to be gained from criticizing views that opponents do not hold, or from continuing to raise objections that the opposed theory has already been modified to accommodate. Unfortunately, both sides frequently miss the mark here. Creationists widely misunderstand both Darwin's theory and the theories of his contemporary descendants. Evolutionists widely misconstrue various creationist positions, and frequently raise objections that creationists themselves recognized and responded to decades ago. Thus, we will begin by looking at the historical rise of evolutionary theories (chapter two), followed by a closer look at Darwin's specific work and theory (chapter three). We will then look at some popular creationist objections to evolutionary theory (chapter four) and will see that many of them misconstrue the real theories in question.

After that, we will follow the historical development of the modern creationist movement from its roots in Seventh-day Adventism and its connections with modern fundamentalism (chapter five) to the views and writings of its most popular present spokesmen—Henry Morris, John Whitcomb, Duane Gish and Gary Parker (chapter six). We will then examine some of the more common objections to creationism, and will see that they, too, often rest upon misconstruals (chapter seven).

Second, both sides routinely accuse the other of not being genuinely scientific. Whether or not a theory is legitimate science depends in part, of course, on what science is—how it is structured, how it works, what it can and cannot assume, what it can and cannot include, what it can or cannot achieve. Those are all questions within philosophy of science, and the claims and objections from combatants on both sides involve substantial assumptions and presuppositions concerning philosophy of science. In order to assess those assumptions—and the accusations based on them—I will first show why a number of the most common popular-level views about science are mistaken (chapter eight), give a brief introduction to some current philosophy of science (chapter nine), then look specifically at the philosophies of science underlying much of the present creation-evolution debate. Many of the philosophy of science arguments and assumptions of both creationists (chapter ten) and evolutionists (chapter eleven) fail to withstand close scrutiny—as do the objections based on them. The attempts of both sides to achieve quick victory by decreeing that the other side fails to meet some favorite philosophical definition of science are nearly without exception unsuccessful.

Since Darwin's own time, some Christians have advocated a middle position in the dispute—that God is, as Scripture indicates, creatively responsible for the cosmos around us, but that evolution, as described by mainstream biologists, was God's chosen means of bringing the creation to its present state. As with most compromise positions, such theistic evolution takes flak from both flanks—in this case, both from creationists and from evolutionists who are unbelievers. In chapter twelve we look at some popular arguments against theistic evolution, concluding that whether or not theistic evolution is ultimately defensible, the critical arguments examined fail to establish much of anything.

Evaluation of the respective scientific cases is not part of my present intent. We will examine a number of the scientific arguments (including the widely disputed arguments involving the Second Law of Thermodynamics), but will do so only to the extent that they exhibit misunderstandings of theory or of philosophy of science.

Detailed analysis of scientific claims and cases is, of course, essential to the debate, but in many cases (not all) there will be little point in doing that until misconstruals, philosophical confusion, logical missteps and various other snarls have been sorted out first. Working toward that end is the major aim of this book.

One source of dispute has been the very meaning of the terms *creationist* and *evolutionist,* those meanings having undergone change historically. Although there are those who argue that all believers are creationists in virtue of affirming *some* doctrine of creation or other, that is not the way *creationist* is generally used at present. I take the present popular usage to refer to those who hold the following:

Whether or not God could have built evolutionary potentials into the creation, or could have brought about life and all its diversity by evolutionary means, he did not in fact do so. There are thus discontinuities in nature—e.g., non-life/life, reptile/mammal, animal/human—which cannot be crossed by purely natural means, each such discontinuity requiring separate supernatural creative action.[3]

That definition would include young-earth creationists, old-earth creationists and progressive creationists, but would not include theistic evolutionists. However, since young-earth creationists have been the primary focus of recent debate, I will normally use *creationist* to refer to that group. (In some cases, antievolutionary work by people outside creationism has been completely adopted by that group, and I will discuss some of those people and their work in this creationist context.[4])

I will use the term *evolutionist* to include all who accept a broad evolutionary picture of the origin of life and its diversity. That will include both theists and naturalists. However, naturalistic evolutionists—specifically naturalistic anticreationists—will frequently be the focus of discussion concerning *evolutionist* objections to creationism. The naturalistic claims of such groups are not, of course, shared by theistic evolutionists, although various other objections to creationism often are.

In this book, then, I will not present a positive case either for biological evolution (theistic or otherwise) or for creationism. I do not pretend to know which is correct. But I will try to make the general case that large numbers of the critical arguments from each side against the other do not come to much—either because they are themselves defective or because no one holds the views against which they are directed.

I hope that what follows will convince some on both sides that key aspects of the dispute are not quite as transparently trivial as the popular propaganda from their own side might suggest.

But of course, maybe it will just make everybody on both sides mad.

# 2 DARWIN
## The Historical Context

The theory of evolution is in its broadest sense a theory about history—the history of life, of life's diversity and ultimately of the human species. Detailed development of the idea that the histories of the earth and of life might have had defining roles in shaping the character and diversity of life as we know it—that life itself grew rather than aged—is relatively new to the human race. There were hints of very general evolutionary ideas as early as ancient Greece, but well over 95 percent of recorded human history predates the 1859 publication of Darwin's *Origin of Species*. This chapter will look briefly at the background out of which Darwin's theory emerged.[1]

### The Geological Background

At the outset of the eighteenth century, the influence of Scripture was quite visible in European thought, including scientific thought. On the basis of one traditional interpretation of Scripture, it was widely believed that the earth was quite young, and was, in many respects, still in originally created form. There had, of course, been some alterations—the Fall had caused some changes, the flood still others. Yet traces of the original creation could be found in and around the earth's surface. Although the fairly young discipline of geology had begun trying to construct natural, scientific explanations of geological structures and events, much of early geological theorizing was done intentionally within the context of Scripture.

Both the scriptural record (with, e.g., the flood) and the geological record (with, e.g., its abrupt transitions between geological strata) seemed to suggest sharp discontinuities in historical and geological processes. At the turn of the eighteenth century, most theorizing in the newly emerging discipline was *catastrophist*—attempting to explain geological phenomena in terms of rapid, powerful and unique cataclysmic episodes (such as the biblical flood).

But monumental changes in the European intellectual landscape were in the works. Early in the seventeenth century, Descartes had made a profoundly influential case that the physical realm was a purely mechanical system of matter in mathematically describable motion. Then in the late seventeenth century, Newtonian physics made its entrance, and the scientific triumphs it generated assured its rapid dominance of large stretches of European thought by the mid-eighteenth century. Many of Newton's followers interpreted both Newton and Newtonian physics as implying (1) that nothing was truly scientific except empirical observation and what could be logically supported by those observations and (2) that (as Descartes had argued) nature was nothing but a vast, self-regulating physical machine. Although Newton himself held neither of those positions, they were nonetheless widely believed to have the authority of both Newton and his science behind them.

But how could one *scientifically* investigate the earth's past? Direct scientific observation of the past and its processes is, of course, impossible. Apparently the best alternative is an *indirect* approach—observing the indirect *results* of past processes and events (mountains, strata, formations, etc.) and then attempting to interpret those observations in some sensible and scientifically informative way.

In his 1785 *Theory of the Earth* James Hutton (1726-1797) proposed an approach to geology that conformed to both of the "Newtonian" principles above—a geology that was thus supposed to be as truly scientific as was Newtonian physics. In Hutton's system, the geological realm was essentially a Newtonian-style system of matter in motion. It was, moreover, a steady-state, self-balancing system. Some geological processes (such as volcanoes) built, and some (such as erosion) destroyed, but the two types were in an overall stable, ongoing balance. Hutton stipulated that in order to scientifically explain any geological feature, one was permitted to refer only to ongoing, natural processes involved in the maintaining of that balance. Given that science was supposed to rest solely on empirical observation, geological theories could only make reference to processes that not only continued in action *now* but were presently *observable.* Hutton further contended that geological processes operating now did so at the same strength and intensity as in the past. Such processes were not weaker now than they had been when the world was young and vigorous, as many of his contemporaries thought.

This combination of ideas—that the same geological processes operating at the same intensity characterized the earth's entire history and that this history exhibited a steady-state balance—came to be known as *uniformitarianism,* and was Hutton's most significant contribution to geology. (It is not, however, what geologists today mean by *uniformitarianism.* More later.)

Hutton's views had several unpopular implications. For instance, if the earth's history was a balanced steady-state history, then not only had there been no geological catastrophes (such as a universal flood), but earth's history had no overall direction over time (such as from hotter to cooler, from a smoother to a more wrinkled surface), as most catastrophists believed. But perhaps most significantly, if one had to explain all present aspects of the earth's surface in terms of familiar everyday processes, then the earth certainly appeared to be vastly older than previously thought. One does not, for instance, get beds of sedimentary stone thousands of feet thick very quickly from ordinary, gradual processes. Hutton himself concluded that the earth was ancient indeed, but his old-earth views attracted few followers during his own time and were widely rejected as contrary to the teachings of religion.

Hutton's basic idea of uniformitarianism was not greeted enthusiastically either, and catastrophism remained the reigning view into the early nineteenth century. The issue was not simple natural-supernatural dispute—some catastrophists were now looking for natural, rather than supernatural, explanations for the catastrophes their view required. But under the press of accumulating investigations, the discipline, although remaining catastrophist, was more or less converted during the first two decades of the nineteenth century to belief in an old earth, an earth with a history in the millions of years. That change was led in a significant degree by such clergyman-geologists as John Playfair (1748-1819), William Conybeare (1787-1857), William Buckland (1784-1856), Adam Sedgewick (1785-1873) and the unordained but ecclesiastically influential Hugh Miller (1802-1856).

So by the third decade of the nineteenth century, the earth's history was seen as consisting of successive, unimaginably long geological epochs. The geological record was now a display of deep time as well as of events and processes. Each epoch left characteristic geological features and strata, each epoch ending abruptly and being replaced by an entirely different epoch with different features and strata. There were sharp discontinuities between the epochs, which indicated the occurrence of the catastrophes that constituted the boundaries of the successive epochs.

During the transition from young- to old-earth views, geological theorizing was still widely carried out within the general outline of biblical history, harmony being achieved, for instance, through interpretation of the Genesis "days" of creation as standing for geological epochs. However, by the 1830s attempts to reconcile geological theory and Scripture, previously almost universal, were no longer a routine expectation in geological works. Hutton himself, for instance, had not even mentioned Scripture.

So whereas at the beginning of the eighteenth century the general geological project had been to explain scriptural and observed geological events within the context of scriptural history, by mid-nineteenth century that had frequently (although not universally) ceased to be a concern. Geology was widely taken to have an autonomous inner integrity of its own. It was to provide natural explanations in its own terms and on its own terms, with no requirement that geological theories provide for an initially idyllic earth, a flood or anything of that sort, unless empirical geological data supported such views.

### The Biological Background

One of the traditional tasks of the biologist has been to try to bring order out of the almost unmanageable welter of different sorts of living organisms. Indeed, such attempts are sometimes traced back to Adam's naming of the animals, giving rise to claims that taxonomy is the oldest profession. Efforts to classify organisms scientifically go back at least to Aristotle. The older classification schemes served well enough for a time, although there were vexing questions even early on. But the proliferation of newly discovered species resulting from world exploration in the sixteenth century put serious strains on the older systems of classification, and alternative methods of categorizing organisms began to appear.

A number of philosophical disputes also arose. One dispute concerned whether or not there even were such things as species. According to one side, there was a smooth gradation of forms in nature—an ascending "great chain of being"—with each niche being filled by some type of life-form. If that were the case, then there would be no genuine breaks in the continuity of forms, and any specification of some collection of organisms as a separate species would be purely arbitrary. In effect, the idea of species would be a mere mental construct, and would not represent anything real in actual nature. According to the other side, there were indeed genuine discontinuities in the biological realm, genuine divisions among plants and animals. Those divisions perhaps reflected original divinely created patterns and represented genuine species—species created as distinct from other species, unchanging, and not blurred into each other.

Another sticking point even among those who agreed on the propriety of classification concerned what the overall basis of a proper classification system should be. Some biologists selected some prominent aspect of living systems—mode of reproduction, teeth, habitat, diet, microscopic features, even usefulness to humans—and built their classification system around similarities, differences and degrees of that feature. Such systems were known as "artificial classifications." Others tried to classify organisms in some less restricted but more ambiguous and less rigorous "natural" manner—intuitive similarity, for example.

### The Fossil Connection

Running through the entire development of geology were persistent questions concerning the curiosities we now term *fossils*. The first questions, of course, were, What on earth were they? How did they get into such odd places? During the seventeenth century, fossils were widely thought to be just natural objects occurring in the earth, having no intimate connections with living organisms. Fossils often did resemble known organisms, but that was perhaps because nature tended to express particular patterns in various ways, and geological nature produced those patterns in minerals just as biological nature did in living tissue. Any suggestion that fossils might have organic origins was rejected by some antichurch Enlightenment figures— because otherwise Christians would claim support for their scriptural belief in the flood from marine fossils found on mountaintops. Some churches, on the other hand, displayed large fossil bones, claiming that they were organic—in particular that they were the remains of Old Testament giants and hence support for the accuracy of Scripture.

By the eighteenth century, however, fossils were almost universally acknowledged to be of organic origin. That in its turn generated further perplexities. As more fossil data accumulated, a number of patterns within the fossil record began to emerge. For one thing, not only was there a broad consistency to the order in which various strata lay in different places, but each specific stratum typically had its own characteristic body of fossils. In 1790 William Smith (1769-1839) developed the technique of identifying particular strata in different places by reference to the characteristic type of fossils ("index" fossils) contained therein. How was that orderliness to be explained? Early on, the flood was often invoked to explain the death, location and burial of the fossilized organisms, but surely, Smith argued, the violent forces of the flood shouldn't have left things so nicely sorted. According to Scripture the springs had "burst" from the deep and the flood had "destroyed" the world.

Fossils made abrupt, seemingly instantaneous, entrances into and exits from the fossil record. Where did they come from, and where did they go? Had some of those unfamiliar types of organisms become extinct? But surely Noah's ark was intended to prevent extinctions, and besides, extinctions would leave gaps in the overall plan of nature. But by the late eighteenth century, increasing numbers of scientists had come to believe that the earth's past had seen numerous extinctions.

Perhaps most ultimately consequential, however, was the growing early-nineteenth-century conviction that there was a progression in the fossil record. Whatever the time scale in years might turn out to be, the older the strata, the stranger and, seemingly, simpler were the characteristic organisms fossilized within those strata. Once fossils were accepted as organic remains and once they were ordered geologically, it was insistently apparent that the plants and animals that had inhabited this planet had been different in different periods. Once biology was tied to geology via fossils, life acquired a history just as the earth's surface had, and that history was not static. There seemed to be some sort of progression.

If all that was true, there were serious implications for biology. If fossils were of organic origin, these strange forms would have to be coherently incorporated somewhere within some classification system. Some sort of sense would have to be made of appearances and disappearances in the fossil record. Some sort of understanding of the type and mechanics of the apparent historical progression would need to be sought. In general, the lot of the biologist would be made vastly more difficult.

### The Broader Intellectual Context

For whatever trouble it might cause some biologists, the apparent historical progression did fit in rather nicely with some prominent eighteenth- and nineteenth-century philosophical currents. Eighteenth-century thought had contained a strong dose of optimism concerning humans and the human prospect. That optimism carried over even more strongly into the nineteenth century, which increasingly anticipated new inventions, increasingly expected progress of all sorts.

The nineteenth-century concept of progress was significantly shaped by the German Idealists (such as Arthur Schopenhauer, G. W. F. Hegel, Friedrich von Schelling). The Idealists believed that reality was more properly viewed as *spirit* than as the material, Newtonian machine that the Enlightenment had tended to see. History was thus not the unvarying mechanical ticking of the machine but rather the gradual, progressive, evolutionary unfolding and development of some Absolute, some cosmic World Spirit. Material reality, as a manifestation of the evolving Absolute, was itself in a process of ascent. Progress on this view represented more than the eighteenth-century idea of the mere realization of already-present potential. It represented genuine *transformation*. When the historical succession implied by the fossil record penetrated into biological theorizing, one strategy for accounting for it drew on the dominant scientific old-earth catastrophism with its fixed and unchanging species. But another strategy was to link that historical succession with emerging currents of an evolutionary philosophy of progress.

The best-known evolutionary theory involving an innate biological principle of progress and ascent was that of the French invertebrate zoologist Jean-Baptiste Antoine de Monet, Chevalier de Lamarck (1744-1829), whose *Zoological Philosophy* was published in 1809. Lamarck did not fit into the German Idealist camp, but rather interpreted nature as a Newtonian-style system of matter in law-governed motion. However, among the principles that governed material reality he included an inner innate drive toward increased complexity, improvement and progress, which characterized all of life. That inner impetus was the motive force for an ongoing, persistent evolution of all forms of life steadily up the ladder of life-forms.

Lamarck's views were not always entirely consistent and were often presented unclearly. But the basic theme was that life in simplest form emerged from nonlife by natural and mechanical spontaneous generation; over time, by small steps, it ascended a ladder of increasing complexity, a climb that was driven by this internal, mechanical, material "power of progressively complicating organization." The basic path of ascent was straightforward and linear.

Although in principle such a process should have produced in nature a complete, smooth sequence roughly similar to the great chain of being, it was difficult to deny the presence of gaps in the actual chain as Lamarck knew it. How could those gaps be explained?

Lamarck believed that the earth was several million years old, and it seemed clear from the geological record that substantial changes in conditions on the earth had occurred during that time. But nature was a *system* with significant interaction among its components. In particular, organisms had to be adapted to prevailing conditions in order to remain viable. If conditions changed—as they apparently had—then the living forms present either had to change to remain adapted or else faced extinction. But Lamarck rejected the whole idea of extinction. Extinction seemed utterly contrary to the whole thrust of a Nature in which life embodied a principle of ascent. Thus, organisms *had* adapted. (Fossil remains of allegedly extinct forms merely represented organisms ancestral to present forms in their climb up the ladder.) Because organisms had had to adapt to varying conditions, the sequence had been distorted—hence the gaps, deviations and branches in the ladder of life as actually displayed in nature.

The adaptive changes in organisms demanded by changing conditions were brought about in large part by the organisms' struggle to survive. Organs that suddenly had new demands placed on them or that came under more extensive use because of changing conditions could, through the organisms' striving to survive, sometimes change to meet the new demands. In some cases, wholly new types of organs could even be grown. Once such changes had been achieved, those newly acquired characteristics could then be passed on to the next generation. Thus, the changes demanded by the environment could become permanent in that type of creature. But although essential to survival, such changes were really off the main track of evolution and disrupted the smooth, uniform gradations that the ladder of organisms otherwise should have displayed. (This "inheritability of acquired characteristics," which was simply a subsidiary detail of Lamarck's view and was widely accepted during this period, is often mistakenly presented as being the basis of his theory. It was not, and Lamarck did not even claim to have invented it.)

There were, again, unclarities in the theory (such as over the number of occurrences of spontaneous generation, over how many lines of ascent there actually were, over the possibility of occasional extinctions at the top and very bottom of the ladder), but the core idea was of life following an inevitable upward ascent along a linear hierarchy of increased complexity, with every form of life occupying some place on (or near) the main line on the scale.

A number of features of Lamarck's theory of evolution should have been attractive to early-nineteenth-century thinkers. It rather clearly incorporated an underlying principle of progress. It brought a naturalistic perspective to both the origin and the history of life, attributing both to continuing, ongoing natural processes. Yet Lamarck's theory did not catch on; it attracted no influential advocates until several decades later, when it was resurrected as a possible alternative to Darwin's theory. It was rejected for a number of reasons, a major one being the fierce opposition of one of the most influential scientists in France at that point: Georges Cuvier (1769-1832).

In the second and third decade of the nineteenth century Cuvier published a number of volumes involving the "principle of correlation"—the idea that living organisms were integrated, coherent systems and had to be analyzed as such. For instance, an animal that survived by running down and killing antelope had to be built for speed and quickness, had to have some way of dispatching the antelope once caught, had to have appropriate teeth, the right sort of stomach, and so forth. Its various parts had to be coordinated with each other and with the whole organism—it could not be simply a stitched-together collection of generic components. Cuvier concluded that since animals had to be coordinated and systematized wholes, gradual, bit-by-bit changes in species would be impossible—the resultant organisms would be unadapted and nonviable. Thus, sharp, inviolate boundaries limited the changeability of species.

Under Cuvier's influence, old-earth catastrophism dominated until about the 1830s. But effective as Cuvier's attacks were initially, they proved to be the last influential antievolutionary fling among professional biologists for a considerable time. It was a relatively short-lived fling as well. Both uniformitarianism and the "developmental hypothesis"—evolution—would soon return in force.

### Geology Again: Lyell

Old-earth catastrophism was the most influential geological view in 1830 when Charles Lyell (1797-1875) published the first volume of his three-volume *Principles of Geology*. Lyell's subtitle tells all: *Being an Attempt to Explain the Former Changes of the Earth's Surface by Reference to Causes*

*Now in Operation.* Lyell's intent was to turn Hutton's uniformitarian sketch into a genuinely scientific, detailed, empirical explanatory theory.

Following Hutton, Lyell laid down the normative stipulation that legitimate geological explanations should appeal only to presently observable processes operating at presently observable intensities. This was, of course, contrary to the common catastrophist beliefs that some past processes simply no longer operated and that processes which did still operate had been more powerful in the past. And Lyell also followed Hutton in claiming that while local geological conditions might change, overall the earth not only did not experience global catastrophes, but was a *steady state* system. (Lyell's version of uniformitarianism is, like Hutton's, quite different from that employed in contemporary geology. More later.)

Although he was a uniformitarian with respect to geology, at least until later in his life Lyell was unsympathetic to biological evolution. He severely criticized Lamarck's doctrine of the mutability (changeability) of species, citing, for example, the stability of particular species over millions of years in the fossil record, and he traced the basic characteristics of species back to the creation. Any apparent progression in fossils he attributed simply to imperfections in the fossil record. Lyell did highlight the importance of a "struggle for existence" and believed that competition between species occurred, but those struggles did not produce adaptation and change in species—only extinction of the less well adapted.

Although not everyone accepted Lyell's uniformitarianism immediately, his extensive demonstration of the power and plausibility of the uniformitarian explanation did have its effect. In a relatively short time Lyell's *Principles* contributed to the ultimate overthrow of catastrophism. But one of its deepest consequences involved a young naturalist who received a copy of volume 1 of the *Principles* as an embarkation gift on beginning a voyage on the British survey ship *Beagle:* Charles Darwin (1809-1882).

# 3 DARWIN'S THEORY
## A Brief
## Introduction

**T**he Beagle *sailed from England on December 27, 1831. It returned in* October 1836, and by that time Darwin had come to believe that Lyell was right concerning geological change having been slow and gradual over long ages. Also by that time—or shortly thereafter—Darwin had come to believe that species had undergone slow, gradual transformation as well. He had come, in short, to believe in biological evolution—or "descent with modification," as he initially termed it.[1]

What convinced him? On the *Beagle* voyage—and for decades afterward—Darwin collected an extensive catalog of observations, patterns and puzzles that, he argued, could be best understood, or even only understood, in evolutionary terms. The data involved geographical distribution of fossil species, changes in the fossil sequence, distribution of living species, relationships between fossil and living species in particular geographical areas, extinction patterns, island ecologies, the structure of classification systems, embryology, morphology, rudimentary and vestigial organs, the relative size and diversity of various genuses, and a host of other considerations, some general and some fairly technical. Two brief examples will suffice.

First, it was frequently found that although the fossils in specific geographical regions changed over geological time, the fossil species from different geological periods *within* a particular geographical region exhibited significant similarities. Further, the species currently living in a region typically exhibited similarities to some of the fossil species in that region. Thus, within specific geographical regions there was often a characteristic family resemblance among fossils and between fossils and living species.

But although that pattern held true within particular geographical regions, deep differences often occurred *between* geographical regions—between, say, species past and present in South America and those found in Australia. It seemed to Darwin that descent with modification—evolution—offered the only plausible explanation. If later species had evolved from earlier species in each of those regions, the resemblances within each region, past and present, would be easy to understand—they were actually related to each other. And if life had evolved differently in each region, due to unique regional conditions or for some other reason, then the striking differences between the two different regions, both past and present, would also be easily understood. One could, of course, believe that God had simply chosen to distribute created species in that manner, but that, thought Darwin, did not represent a genuine explanation of those patterns.

Second, islands typically have fewer species than are found in mainland areas of similar size, and an unusually high proportion of the species on a given isolated island system are unique and found nowhere else in the world. Further, on many islands entire orders of plants and animals (such as mammals) are missing, although other forms occupy the ecological niches usually filled by the missing orders. For instance, giant flightless birds fill the usual mammal niches in New Zealand; and on some other islands devoid of ordinary trees, plant orders that elsewhere produce only bushes actually produce trees.

On Darwin's evolutionary view, all these peculiarities (and others as well) fell neatly into place. Islands had been originally colonized by a few lucky migrating members of a few species, which had then by evolution diversified into previously vacant ecological niches (as birds had in New Zealand). The results of that evolutionary diversification were usually unique, because the original species were evolving into unusual niches they did not and could not compete for elsewhere. Again, one could claim that this was simply the way God had chosen to distribute various created species. But here again, Darwin argued, that wasn't really an explanation. The pattern, on that view, was simply arbitrary, whereas evolution made sense of it.

Once one had accepted biological evolution, the key question was, How had it occurred? What was the mechanism by which evolutionary change occurred? Darwin was not attracted to philosophical versions of evolutionary theory, according to which evolution was the inevitable result of drives toward improvement inherent within the evolving organisms themselves, or was the unfolding of latent cosmic progressiveness, or something else of that general sort. Species just did not seem to fall into the nice linear hierarchies such theories implied.

Darwin determined to try to find the *how* of evolution on a purely empirical basis of gradual, presently observable processes. Although the evolutionary idea that later species emerge out of earlier species was not itself inherently materialistic, Darwin (who despite an earlier period of training for the ministry began developing deist and eventually agnostic views) wished to produce a thoroughly mechanistic, materialistic theory of the *process* of the evolution of species.

The adaptation of organisms to their environment was generally recognized, and there had been earlier suggestions that perhaps the environment acted directly on organisms, molding them in ways appropriate to the particular environment in question. But Darwin couldn't reconcile that view to observed facts either. For instance, although one can find nearly identical environments in widely separated parts of the earth, the life-forms in the different places quite frequently are very different. That was the situation Darwin found when comparing, for example, the Cape Verde Islands (off the coast of Africa) with the Galápagos Islands (off the coast of South America). Despite strongly similar environments, the life in the former seemed closely related to African species, while that in the latter seemed closely related to South American forms. Resemblance seemed more closely linked to geographic proximity than to environmental similarity. Quite obviously, environmental determinism couldn't account for that. And creationism offered no explanation beyond God's just having chosen to distribute species in that manner—which was exactly the same thing the creation view would say no matter what the distribution pattern was. Darwin took that to be merely a *restatement* of the data—not a genuine explanation of the data.

Yet organisms were typically adapted to their environment, even if that was accomplished in different ways in different places. If in general the environment did not directly cause individual organisms to change appropriately, how did that adaptation arise? Although the question of how adaptations arise might appear to be a different question from that of how new species might arise, Darwin suspected that the questions were perhaps not distinct at all. Given gradual geological change, continued adaptation to slowly changing environments might over geological stretches of time result in the development of new species.

So Darwin set out to try to answer this cluster of questions concerning adaptation and speciation, using only empirical data and principles. That effort involved putting together over a period of years a massive data collection concerning the variations of organisms—past, present, foreign and domestic, wild and tame.

As noted by others before him (including his philosophical evolutionist grandfather Erasmus Darwin), domestic animal breeding sometimes produced new varieties within species. But diverging varieties, Darwin would argue, were really just species-in-the-making. If so, there was no deep principial distinction between varieties and species, but only a difference of degree. Once a variety became different enough from other varieties within its own species, it would become a species in its own right. The emergence of new varieties could be viewed simply as a step in the longer gradual process of the emergence of new species. Thus the crucial question was, How did new varieties emerge? What was the process by which domestic breeders produced "better" strains of domestic organisms?

Darwin eventually fastened on *selection* as the key to domestic (artificial) alteration of species. Individual organisms with the desired traits—the traits being bred for—were selectively bred so that the desired traits would be passed on to the next generation. Those lacking the desired trait were prevented from passing on their less desirable traits. Following repeated selections of this sort, in a few generations every individual in the domesticated group would have the chosen traits, having descended from several generations of ancestors all of whom had the characteristic in question.

This process depended crucially on (1) the occurrence of variations in individual organisms, (2) those variations then being heritable by offspring, (3) the breeder's consistently selecting those individuals with the new trait as breeding stock, and (4) the breeder's doing that for a sufficient number of generations for the trait to spread through and "take over" the flock, herd or whatever.

Exactly how variations arose Darwin did not profess to know, although he believed that the environment played some role in inducing them and thus in generating divergence among the varieties within a species. That new traits acquired by an organism could be passed on to succeeding generations Darwin, like Lamarck, accepted readily, even claiming that no one could doubt it.

But although Darwin was a bit unsure how frequent were spontaneous variations in the wild, it looked as though nature could produce gradual alterations in species, even to the point of producing new species, if some agency in nature could replace the breeder and consistently, selectively favor some direction of variation in order for the change to "take."

That was the situation in October 1838, when Darwin read *An Essay on the Principle of Population As It Affects the Future Improvement of Society, with Remarks on the Speculations of Mr. Godwin* (1798), by the Reverend Thomas Malthus (d. 1835). In it Malthus argued that a population inherently expands beyond the potential of food production expansion to match. The result, of course, is endemic starvation. Darwin said that upon reading Malthus he saw "at once" how to adapt Malthus's economics to his own biological quandary. Species typically produce many more young than the environment can support. Simple observations showed that. An "inevitable" consequence, argued Darwin, is competition for the limited resources the environment can provide—in short, a struggle for survival. The losers in that struggle die—or at least do not manage to reproduce and pass on their characteristics very successfully. The winners—those who are more successful in reproducing—thus have the edge in handing their traits on to the future. What is it that allows one organism to be successful and another not? Those having any sort of variation that gives them a competitive advantage will be the ones who do better, have more offspring and are more heavily represented in the next generation. This purely automatic, infallible mechanism does the selecting in nature. It is *natural* selection.

Thus, given the empirical facts of spontaneous, heritable, advantageous variations, of the overproduction of species and of the "pruning" of the relatively less fit in the consequent struggle for survival, variations that give an adaptive, reproductive advantage would over a number of generations become universal in the species. As that process occurred repeatedly, particularly among groups that had become isolated from the rest of their species, forms would gradually alter to the point that different groups derived from the same original ancestral stock would no longer be interfertile—they could no longer breed with each other. Since species were by now defined in terms of interbreedability, new species would have thus arisen from the "accumulation of innumerable slight variations."

## Uniqueness of Darwin's Theory

That, in rough form, was Darwin's theory of natural selection, his proposed mechanism (or at least a key mechanism) governing the origin of new species. The theory no longer depended so obviously on nineteenth-century optimism or on the inner, nearly spiritual stretching and exuberant growings of nature underlying philosophical evolutionism. Here was what Darwin had sought: a mechanism explaining biological evolution in terms of material, deterministic, mechanical, natural processes—a theory, in short, that could be advanced as a purely scientific, empirical theory. Evolution based on a mechanically operating natural selection was perhaps the most important uniqueness in Darwin's theory.

But there were other novel aspects to Darwin's views as well. First, his natural selection involved the extension of a kind of uniformitarianism into biology—the generating of species involved only the cumulative effects of ongoing, ordinary, natural processes. (This was obviously not a steady-state uniformitarianism, of course.) Life and its changes were to be seen as law-governed, just as the heavens and the surface of the earth were.

Second, for Darwin (in good nineteenth-century British political fashion) the individual was the handle on which natural selection got its grip—that is, the individual, with its unique variations, was what lived or died, reproduced or did not. In earlier views, the evolving species itself—or the Ideal Form of the species—had been the focus of evolutionary activity or evolutionary competition. Not for Darwin.

Third (in keeping with good nineteenth-century British economic theory), competition was given a key role. In fact, Darwin and other British biologists may have been consciously influenced by the doctrines of Adam Smith. Just as for Smith the economic competition of individuals was the ultimate source of greater economic good for the whole, for Darwin competition among individuals generated the evolution of species. And one implication of Malthusian economics was that competition and natural selection could occur among individuals of the same species—not just between different species.

A fourth innovation in Darwin's theory of natural selection involved the central role given to variations. For many biologists, attention properly focused on the uniformities within species. Those uniformities were what defined a species. What was important was the extent to which the individual organism mirrored the ideal type or the ideal conception of that kind of organism in the mind of God. Variations, in this light, were defects, departures from the ideal that obscured the purity of the true form. Only in penetrating past the obscuring variations to the true form could one achieve any genuine knowledge of species. But for Darwin, variations were the key to the whole process. Malthus had provided the executioner of the relatively less fit. New, favorable variations provided the architecture of the new, of the *evolution* of species.

Fifth, the variations appeared purely randomly—not in the sense of being undetermined by natural, physical laws (Darwin was a strict determinist) but in the sense that we were ignorant of the particular deterministic rules governing them and, more crucially, in the sense that utterly contrary to philosophical evolution their appearing or not or their being favorable or not was in no way a response to or tailored to the organism's needs. If an organism varied in a favorable way, typically that variation would be preserved. If it varied in an unfavorable way, that variation typically would be eliminated. But both were matters unrelated to anything other than sheer biological law.

Further, the evolution produced by a mechanical natural selection had no preferred, preset, preordained goal. If fitness were served by "retrogression" or even "degeneration," natural selection would favor that direction. Evolution did in general move from a simpler past to a qualitatively different, more complex future; in that sense Darwin did accept the catastrophist idea of a movement over history rather than Lyell's steady-state history. Yet Darwin's movement did not have the abrupt changes of the catastrophists; it had the continuity of Lyell. But it did not reflect any cosmically significant direction. Which variations perished and which were preserved was a purely arbitrary function of mechanical factors affecting life, death and reproductive success. Those factors and their effects were as massively varied as were the earth's environments and the organisms trying to make a living within them. A variation spectacularly successful in one environment might be a writ of execution in another. Or, depending on what form and faculties one's ancestors had bequeathed, an indispensable function performed one way by one species might get done vastly differently by another. Thus there apparently was a branching tree, rather than a line of descent. And given that organisms were systems (Cuvier's insight), seemingly small variations could have enormous ramifications for the makeup and behavior of the organism as a whole. As different variations accumulated in different ways, groups previously (in principle) interfertile ceased to be so—and now two species existed where formerly there was only one.

## Darwin's *The Origin of Species*
Darwin was cautious, realizing that his theory and especially the materialist

principles he associated it with would be controversial, and did not rush into print. This was, after all, to be a thoroughly empirical theory, and Darwin spent nearly twenty years amassing a staggering quantity of observational data from a wide variety of fields. (His investigations of barnacles were so absorbing and protracted that one of his sons, visiting a friend's house for the first time, asked the friend where his father "did his barnacles." Wasn't that what fathers *did?*)

Although Darwin set down the general outline of natural selection in an unpublished, 231-page paper in 1844, he was still busily collecting data in 1858 when he received a manuscript from Alfred Russel Wallace (1823-1913) entitled "On the Tendency of Varieties to Depart Indefinitely from the Original Type." Wallace had independently arrived at a similar theory by an extremely similar route, having, for instance, studied both isolated island fauna and the writings of Malthus, just as Darwin had. Wallace requested Darwin's help in getting his theory published, never suspecting that Darwin had been sitting on essentially the same theory for years. Exactly what transpired next is perhaps not totally clear, but to prevent Darwin from losing his share of the priority credit for the theory, pieces from an earlier unpublished statement of the theory by Darwin were published jointly with Wallace's paper in August 1858. An abstract of Darwin's full theory and its supporting evidence was published in November 1859 as *The Origin of Species.*

The *Origin* is an impressive book, simply packed with observational data, obscure information, biological puzzles, surprising patterns in nature and results of some of Darwin's unusual experiments. (His experiments were sometimes astonishing—elsewhere, for example, he reports the results of testing a worm's hearing using, among other things, a bassoon.) And, of course, the *Origin* also contains a simple theory that makes neat sense out of nearly all of those obscure facts, puzzles and so forth. Darwin also devotes significant space to cataloging problems with the theory and to questions he doesn't know how to answer, as well as to discussion of what sorts of solutions might be possible for some of those problems. Unfortunately, most of Darwin's critics and many of his defenders have apparently never actually read the book. Those who have not cannot really appreciate the depth of Darwin's work—regardless of whether his theory is right or wrong.

In summary outline, Darwin's theory looked like this. Simple observation reveals that

(a) organisms typically produce more offspring than the environment can support.

The natural, nearly inevitable, "logical" result of (a) is that

(b) there will be competition among organisms of the same species for limited resources such as food, mates, nesting sites and the like.

Simple observation also reveals that

(c) offspring typically exhibit variations—differences both from parents and from each other—which can be inherited.

Furthermore

(d) sometimes such variations are entirely new, novel variations.

The natural, nearly inevitable, "logical" result of all this is

(e) any variations (novel or otherwise) that in that environment confer an *advantage* in the competition (variations that enhance *fitness*) will gradually spread throughout the breeding population.

The reason for (e) is that a variation that confers a competitive advantage will permit the individuals who possess it to leave, on average, more offspring than those who do not possess it. Over enough generations, those who lack the advantage and thus are continually on the short end of the competition for limited resources will gradually be bred out of existence. As (e) occurs repeatedly over time on an isolated population, novel variations will accumulate in that breeding population to the point that it will constitute a new species.

The competition involved is not necessarily bloody conflict. It may be very indirect or even slow and stately—a tree outgrowing and overshading another, preventing that tree from growing strong enough to produce any descendants at all. And representation in the next generation is the name of the evolutionary game.

### Early Religious Reaction

The first printing of *Origin* (1,250 copies) apparently sold out the first day, and reaction was not too long in coming. Response from the religious community was generally (but not unanimously) negative—often vehemently so. The overwhelming portion of the Christian community accepted a doctrine of the verbal inspiration of Scripture, and along with that a literalistic Genesis view of the origin of species. Darwin's theory apparently challenged that latter view.

His theory challenged other religious views as well. It was widely believed that science offered strong support for theism, especially in connection with arguments from design, such as those of William Paley. The idea was that science continually uncovered examples of absolutely exquisite adaptation in nature—adaptation that could be explained only as being the result of deliberate intelligent design. And design, of course, seemed to imply a designer. The designs that science explored seemed to exhibit immeasurable rationality, power and benevolence. On the basis of such empirical *scientific* data one could make a strong—perhaps even conclusive—case for the existence of the God of Scripture. One could, in short, construct significant theology from nature—"natural theology," it was called.

Thus many saw science as a powerful friend of theism. And suddenly, with Darwin, that friend had been revealed as a viper in our bosom. For if Darwin were right, all this exquisite adaptation that *looked* like design was really just the purely mechanical result of a materialistic natural selection operating blindly and deterministically on random, purposeless variations. Or if it really was design, it seemed to Darwin to be a callous and inefficient design. (Ironically, while at Cambridge Darwin had occupied quarters that had once been Paley's.) And lurking in the wings was the specter of human beings' getting reduced from the image of God to the happenstance offspring of the chance reproductive success of some primitive brute.

Nonetheless, by the early twentieth century many Christians had made their peace with evolution, although not with the Darwinian chance-driven, unguided version. But the fundamentalist movement would shortly initiate a counterattack.

### Early Philosophical Reaction

Not all objections to natural selection were religiously based. In *Origin,* Darwin had hinted that natural selection principles could extend to the origin of the human species. He subsequently developed that suggestion (in *Descent of Man,* 1871), as did one of his most prominent advocates, Thomas Huxley (1825-1895). But Wallace and (initially) Lyell wanted to insist that humans were in a separate category, and that natural selection could not account for our unique, human qualities. And in the context of insistent philosophical optimism in the progressiveness of the cosmos, Darwin's theory of change as being driven by utterly blind, uncaring chance struck rather a sour note. Nor did a universe in which evolutionary progress depended on wholesale death seem so benign. For natural selection to work, the vast majority of organisms ever born, hatched or sprouted had to die as ultimate failures. Purpose, direction, progress and sweet cosmic harmony apparently had just disappeared into a sort of blind mechanistic meatgrinder.

Of course, not everyone saw things in quite that light. Optimism and faith in progress—especially human social progress—did not die easily, and Darwin's views were grafted by some into already existing theories of social evolution (such as those of the Lamarckian Herbert Spencer [1820-1903], who coined the phrase "survival of the fittest") and extended into broader worldviews by others (such as Ernst Haeckel [1834-1919]). The former blends became known as "social Darwinism"—roughly the view that it is largely through evolutionary competition among humans that we have progressed socially beyond our primitive societal roots. In fact, according to some "social Darwinists" the continued workings of natural selection would eventually eliminate the "lower races" of humankind—a conclusion that Darwin accepted, albeit with some reluctance.

### Early Scientific Reaction

Not all of the objections Darwin faced rested on philosophical or theological bases. Despite the mass of data Darwin had compiled, genuine scientific questions still could be raised, a number of which Darwin anticipated and discussed in the *Origin* itself. For instance, not a lot of experimental evidence for the details of the process of natural selection was available. And the results of the process—the emergence of new species—had never been directly observed. There was substantial evidence that selection could produce variations within broad limits, but no direct evidence that it could cross those limits. Some argued that it could not. But Darwin, extrapolating beyond the direct evidence, argued that there were no such real limits in nature, and that our distinctions—between, for example, varieties and species—were arbitrary.

Second, the fossil record exhibited abrupt changes and discontinuities. Yet Darwin's theory seemed to say that speciations (and extinctions) were typically gradual. Transition fossils, which apparently ought to have been relatively common, were virtually nonexistent. Darwin had several responses to this. He argued, for instance, that the fossil record was sketchy and profoundly incomplete, that the geological conditions under which speciations were most likely to occur (when most transition forms would exist) were also conditions under which fossilization was least likely to occur. He also suggested that a new species might emerge from some isolated group in some restricted location, then spread out from there, outcompeting and replacing the old species elsewhere. In such cases any transition fossils would be confined to one small, unlikely to be discovered location—whereas everywhere else the new species would directly replace the old, with no transition forms ever having even lived there.

Other criticisms ran even deeper. Nineteenth-century physics calculations of the earth's age yielded results on the order of one hundred million years—vastly less than Darwin needed. He subsequently made various attempts to "speed up" natural selection to fit it into the span physicists were willing to grant, but the difficulty remained for several decades.

In 1867 Fleeming Jenkin (1833-1885) developed an equally serious objection concerning Darwin's view of heredity. Although Darwin accepted the doctrine of the heritability of acquired characteristics, he believed that the characteristics of offspring were a *blend* of the corresponding characteristics of their parents. But as Jenkin argued, such a mechanism of heredity would collapse natural selection. Variations first emerged in a single organism. When that organism mated with a normal member of its species, the variation inherited by the first generation of offspring would be diluted by half, by half again in the next generation and so forth. In short order, any favorable variation, instead of being selected, would be diluted down to essentially nothing.

In response to such objections Darwin focused increasingly on the Lamarckian principles that use and disuse of organs caused heritable alterations, on the doctrine that characteristics acquired during an organism's life were heritable and on other factors in addition to natural selection.

### Acceptance

But despite these and other questions, the result of the publication of *The Origin of Species* was the nearly immediate conversion of most of the scientific community to biological evolution—to some kind of descent with modification. Why that nearly immediate conversion to evolution? Major reasons were the simplicity, elegance, breadth and systematizing power of its explanations. Evolutionary theory, as Darwin developed it, brought together evidence from and provided explanations for various puzzles concerning the fossil record, natural history, embryology, vestigial organs, taxonomy, morphology, adaptation, distribution of species through geological time, distribution of species through geographical space, regional similarities between fossil and present species, differences between species in similar environments and so forth. (The theory's ability to explain various aspects of geographical distribution of species may have been what Darwin himself found most convincing.) Biological classification now became the *natural* classification of genealogy, and one could at last in principle apparently understand the significance of the unifying similarities and the distinguishing differences.

In addition, the explanations were not piecemeal but provided the unifying simplicity of system. Darwin had provided a rationally systematizing, organizing key. Biology could now, in a much fuller sense than before, coalesce into a discipline rather than be simply a collection of associated subdisciplines; and beyond that, biology itself was now brought together with geology and paleontology.

In the 1850s most scientists rejected evolution, the dominant view being fixity of species. But Darwin, providing the first real glimpse of possible details of a mechanism, collecting a huge body of relevant data and displaying the explanatory potential of evolution, gave the idea its first effective scientific attractiveness. By 1880 most biologists (except in France) accepted some form of evolution.

However, biologists still resisted Darwin's own proposed mechanism for evolution—natural selection—after the wide acceptance of evolution itself. Even such staunch supporters as Huxley had difficulty with it. And Darwin's attempt to solve some problems by expanding the role of Lamarckian-style factors in his own theory did not turn out very well either. In the 1880s August Weismann (1834-1914) demonstrated that neither use and disuse of organs nor characteristics acquired during an organism's life had any effect on heredity at all. After that, Darwin's natural selection mechanism had only very restricted influence for several decades.

However, roughly a third of the way into the twentieth century, developments in genetics provided a viable theory of heredity and an explanation of variation that not only meshed with Darwin's natural selection but also provided answers to some of the key questions about variations that Darwin had been unable to answer. The idea, roughly, was that heredity was controlled largely by discrete units—genes—with each parent contributing approximately half of the offspring's genetic makeup. Any given gene came as a whole unit from one parent or the other, and thus variations could be inherited complete—not diluted, as Darwin's own blending theory of heredity had threatened. Furthermore, since according to the new genetic theory inheritance had a molecular basis, changes in that molecular base—genetic mutations—could result in offspring with new characteristics. Here, then, was a possible source of the variations that Darwin's natural selection mechanism required. This "synthetic theory" of evolution—combining contemporary genetics and Darwinian natural selection—quickly rose to near absolute dominance in the scientific community.

# 4 DARWIN'S THEORY
## Popular Creationist Misunderstandings

**B**oth sides in the popular creation-evolution dispute, with some important exceptions, exhibit some serious and stubborn confusions about the views of the other side. That fact has had several unfortunate side effects. It has meant, for instance, that enormous creationist energy has been poured into attacking positions that no one actually holds and that have never been part of Darwinian theory. Anticreationists, concluding that their opponents do not understand the very theories that they are trying to attack (and perhaps not stating it quite so politely), often have not even bothered to respond. Creationists have then sometimes concluded from their opponents' silence that the attacks must have been utterly unanswerable and that the forces of evolution have thus been routed. In this chapter we will examine some of the most popular creationist arguments in the dispute and will see that they miss any known target.[1] (Anticreationist misconceptions about creationism will be discussed in chapter seven.)

### Confusing Darwin and Lamarck
As discussed in chapters three and four, there were historically a number of distinct threads of evolutionary thinking. In the Lamarckian picture, for example, life contained an innate drive toward continual upward progress, and in responding to that drive species continually evolved, attempting to scale some grand ladder of life. Evolution was built into life, and the mere

passage of time guaranteed change and ascent. The ascent that each ancestral strand of life experienced was completely linear, from single cell through graduated stages and on up. Organisms often acquired organs and abilities in response to need, and no thread of life ever fell to extinction.

As discussed in chapter three, Darwin did a fair bit of borrowing from Lamarck, accepting, for instance, the idea that traits acquired during an organism's lifetime could be passed on to the organism's descendants. That idea, however, was simply a fine-tuning device for Lamarck's system. Lamarck's core intuitions—such as innate upward drive—Darwin consistently rejected. Already in 1844 Darwin had written, "Heaven forfend me from Lamarck's nonsense of a 'tendency to progression.' "[2] Unfortunately, many creationists seem not to distinguish between Lamarck and Darwin, and consequently construct objections that, although perhaps problems for Lamarckian evolution, have no bearing on Darwin's views.[3] Several of the more prominent of such objections follow.

### Time Equals Evolution

*1. Resistance to evolutionary change.* As frequently noted, most fossil species seem to appear full-blown in the fossil record, persist relatively unchanged for a period, then disappear as suddenly as they arose. Quite a number of creationists note that the changelessness often persists for extremely long periods of time—sometimes hundreds of millions of years—and cite that lack of change as a problem for evolutionary theory. After all, if evolution is true, shouldn't the organism have evolved at least *some* during such a long stretch? Thus Gish, for instance, claims that such resistance to change over long stretches is "notoriously contradictory to what is expected on the basis of evolutionary theory." Other creationists echo the same theme.[4]

Such resistance to change would perhaps constitute a problem for Lamarck's conviction that nature had within it an inherent and constant drive toward evolutionary ascent; however, neither Darwin's theory nor current neo-Darwinian theories contain such a principle. According to Darwin's theory, if an organism is suitably adapted and successful in its environment, if the particular environment is stable, and if no significant selected mutations occur, there is no automatic reason to expect evolutionary change. (Indeed, Darwin discussed such cases in the *Origin*.)[5] Stability would be consistent with the theory. Time alone, then, does not induce change, and criticisms of this sort rest on a failure to distinguish the core of Darwin's theory from that of Lamarck.

*2. Living fossils.* A popular variant on this theme is the "living fossil" objection. This objection cites, for example, the discovery earlier in this century that the coelacanth (previously known only via thirty-million-year-old fossils) is alive and well and essentially identical to its ancient ancestors, then claims that such discoveries show that evolution cannot be right—otherwise the coelacanth certainly should have evolved in that much time.[6] Here we see the same misconstrual of Darwinian evolutionary theory. Indeed, Darwin himself was aware of living fossils.[7] Contrary to popular creationist claims, in Darwin's theory the passage of time does not make evolutionary change "inevitable."

### Evolution Is Linear

According to Lamarck's theory, evolutionary ascent was linear in the sense that on each evolutionary strand one form gave rise directly to the next on up the ladder. That picture has two significant consequences. First, if we pick any two types of organisms on any Lamarckian chain, either the first will be ancestral to the second, or the second will be ancestral to the first.[8] Second, intermediate forms will always occur between any two types of organisms that are on the same evolutionary strand but are not exactly next to each other on that strand.

Darwin's theory is not linear in that sense, and neither of the two above consequences is part of his theory. In fact, Darwin meant to *deny* the linear idea. The picture that he developed was of a tree (or a coral) with limbs branching from the trunk, other limbs branching from those limbs, more limbs branching from those and so on. One of the crucial concepts of his theory is divergence, with separate species splitting away from some common ancestor species, thus creating forks—not linear arrangements—in the paths of evolutionary development.

Consider this simple example. Suppose some family has for many generations had only one child—a son—in each generation. All those males, then, form a linear relation. No matter which two males we choose, either the first will be an ancestor to the second, or vice versa. The only relation any two males can have to each other is one of descent—father, grandfather, son, grandson and so on. They will form a single line of descent. Now compare that with a family that has many sons in each generation, each of those sons also having many sons. All of the males will still be related to each other, but many of the relationships will not be ancestral. There will be cousins, brothers, uncles, nephews and so forth. Cousins, for instance, will be related not because either is an ancestor of the other, but in that they share a *common* ancestor. Individual lines of descent within the broader picture—father to son to grandson, and so on—will still exist, but the overall picture will look more like a family tree. It is this latter, nonlinear picture that reflects Darwin's thinking about relationships among species.

Some influential creationists have missed this fundamental distinction between Darwin and Lamarck, and several of the following popular "refutations" of evolutionary theory presuppose and are relevant only to linear pictures—not to Darwin's theory or to other current evolutionary theories.

*1. Missing fossil intermediates.* According to this objection, evolutionary theory implies that if two types of organisms are related there had to have been forms intermediate between them. Some of these forms should at least occasionally turn up as fossils. For instance, if clams and snails are related, we should sometimes find fossil "snams"—organisms somewhere between the two related species. But no one has ever found fossil snams or clails—or dats or cogs, for that matter. Hence, evolutionary theory must be seriously wrong.[9]

This might be a telling objection to some linear evolutionary theories. But Darwin's theory gives no reason to expect snams or cogs. For two species to be related, in Darwin's theory, it is not necessary for either to be ancestral to the other but only that they have some common ancestor. But that they sprang from some common ancestor in the distant past does not at all imply the existence of some other species partway between the two species into which those two diverging lines ultimately developed.

That is not to say that specific missing fossil intermediates cannot or do not pose a difficulty for evolutionary theory. Even Darwin's view still has linear paths of descent within the larger family tree of species. Where two species share a common ancestor, separate lines of descent must still come from the common ancestor to each of the two species, and it is perfectly legitimate to expect fossil intermediates within each of those separate lines. The problem arises when from the mere fact that two species are related, one concludes that there should be intermediates between those particular two. That conclusion is legitimate only if the relationship is linear, and on Darwin's theory relationships often are not.

*2. Missing living intermediates.* A second related objection is as follows. If evolution is ongoing, and if it involves gradual change over time, then at the present moment we should see a packed continuum of species blending gradually into each other—there should be numerous living forms intermediate between other living forms. Indeed, according to Morris, evolution predicts a "continuum of organisms."[10] But no such things exist—there are no more living snams than fossil snams.[11] Some creationists conclude that evolution thus clearly does not fit the facts. (This misinterpretation also has a more subtle biochemical version that underlies several influential biomolecular criticisms of evolutionary theory.)[12]

This too is a question that Darwin discussed specifically in the *Origin* (chapter six). In fact, he admits that "this difficulty for a long time quite confounded me."[13] But he thought that his theory had the resources for handling it. Darwin's view was, roughly and incompletely, that new intermediate forms emerge only slowly, exist in relatively small numbers, and are typically, subsequently out-competed and displaced by their own descendants, becoming extinct. From that standpoint, one might thus expect gaps between species in the living world, as descendent species diverged ever farther from each other, the intermediate species linking each to their common ancestor being successively replaced. It thus is not quite correct to claim that a continuum of living species is a basic prediction of evolutionary theory. Darwin thought that he could explain within the bounds of his theory why exactly the opposite happened.

*3. Missing links: the monkey-human gap.* The principle that absence makes the heart grow fonder may help to explain the perennial popularity of missing links between monkeys and humans, even among some popular advocates of evolution. Many creationists take such absence to be their most endearing and important feature and cite it as a severe problem for evolutionary theory. It is, of course, perfectly true that if Darwin was correct some primates *were* ancestral to humans, and one would at least hope that an occasional fossil specimen would show up. But such a link would not be midway between *modern* monkeys, apes or whatever, and modern humans.[14] In Darwin's theory, modern monkeys and modern humans are only cousins, descended from some common, more primitive ancestor. Thus modern monkeys are not part of humanity's direct ancestry, and there is no reason to anticipate intermediates between the two. According to Darwin, intermediates would have to exist between that ancient common ancestor and modern monkeys, and between the ancient common ancestor and modern humans. Absence of *those* fossil intermediates could perhaps figure into a legitimate criticism of evolutionary theory, but that would be a *different* criticism. Unfortunately, some popular creationist writers do not distinguish between the two. Following are two such attempted objections.

*3.1. No humans currently emerging.* The question sometimes arises that if humans really came from monkeys, if monkeys really can turn into humans, why are monkeys not presently evolving into humans and emerging from the jungle? That question betrays more than one confusion, but the presently relevant problem is that it presupposes that according to evolutionary theory, monkeys of the sort we see today once evolved into human beings. This presupposition makes it apparently relevant to ask why, if the monkeys did it once, they cannot or do not do it again. But this presupposition is simply mistaken. According to Darwin's nonlinear evolutionary theory, modern primates are not our ancestors, but merely cousins descended from an ancestral line that split from ours thousands of generations ago.

*3.2. Missing ape traits.* Another, more subtle version of this same mistake is as follows. Present-day apes have a number of characteristics that human beings lack—for instance, modern apes have forty-eight chromosomes while humans have forty-six. After citing that difference, Taylor says: "This raises the questions of at what point in the transition from ape to man the two chromosomes became lost."[15] The claim that we lost them is appropriate only on the presupposition that the apes in question—modern apes, the only ones whose chromosomes we can count—are ancestral to modern humans. Darwin's theory, of course, contains no such linearity. Again, on his view, humans and apes are related not ancestrally but as cousins sharing a common ancestor somewhere in the dim past. On that picture, perhaps the common ancestor had forty-eight chromosomes, and apes kept all forty-eight while humans lost two. Or maybe the common ancestor had forty-six, which humans kept, while apes later added two. Or maybe it had forty-four, apes added four and humans added two. Or maybe it had fifty, apes lost two and humans lost four. Or maybe . . . The "two chromosomes became lost" claim seems to presuppose an interpretation of Darwin that is not completely accurate.

*4. "Lost" beneficial traits.* Natural selection is supposed to result in the preservation of beneficial variations and traits. Thus according to another objection, if evolution is true, no beneficial trait should ever be lost. But if none is ever lost, then humans should have every beneficial trait found in any species. Wysong, for example, points out that toads, lungfish, ticks, trees, turtles, silkworm moths, fleas, crotalid snakes, snails, bees and so forth all have traits that it would certainly be handy for us to have; but he notes that we lack those traits and asks, "Why did the human not retain such obviously beneficial characteristics in his evolution?"[16]

Here again, this objection illustrates quite a number of confusions. (For instance, the general claims about natural selection are misrepresentations, as we will see later.) But the main difficulty is that it presupposes a single line of descent that includes every species. Unless fleas, ticks and trees were our direct ancestors, there would not be the slightest reason to think that humans should have "retained" traits that they have. If Darwin is right, we and each of those species do share common ancestors, but it is perfectly possible that the cited traits developed within the different lines in question well after the line eventually leading to humans and that eventually leading to, say, fleas, separated. There is no particular reason to think that the traits in question were even there in the common ancestor to be retained. The objection, then, depends on misconstruing Darwinian evolution as linear.[17]

*5. Parent species and their descendants.* Another claim is that according to evolution, parent species would be replaced by the species they gave rise to, resulting in the extinction of the parent species. Thus parent species and daughter species would not simultaneously be alive and well for any significant length of time. But such cases have occurred, and they have "embarrassed" evolutionists, says Morris.[18]

But while that might cause unease for some types of theories, these situations pose no problem whatever to a branching, Darwinian theory. Branching lines of descent always come from some common ancestor. Normally, according to Darwin's theory, those lines diverge both from each other and from the common ancestor species. But nothing in the theory makes it *inevitable* that both will do so. A new species may simply bud off from the parent species, leaving that parent species unchanged. Darwin himself thought that the extinction of the parent species would be the normal result, but he claimed repeatedly only that this was a general tendency.[19] The other possibility was always open.

Other confusions have resulted from the failure to appreciate the difference between linear theories on the one hand and Darwinian and contemporary branching theories on the other. The above examples are, I think, the more common ones. But in general, objections based on mistaken presuppositions of evolutionary linearity will not ultimately achieve much in the creation-evolution debate.

### Evolution's Positive Arrow

Lamarckian evolution basically strove in one direction—upward. The steps
on the ladder were steps up, progressive steps. Change was typically betterment, often involving triumph over hampering limitations. Darwin's picture
was significantly different and did not have this basic positive flavor. Nonetheless, many popular creationists raise objections that presuppose exactly
the opposite.[20] Such objections obviously pose no real problem for evolutionary theory as Darwin developed it or as it is presently formulated. It
should be noted, however, that many popularizers of evolutionary theory
certainly talk as though they have fallen into the same misconstrual.

*1. Evolution as progress/betterment.* Misconstruals of Darwin in this
regard are more or less epidemic. Some creationists take it as virtually
axiomatic that evolutionary theory implies that species improve over time,
and that each descendent species is an improvement over its parent species.[21]
And creationists are certainly not alone in thinking that.[22] Nonetheless,
Darwin denied the idea of improvement, betterment or progress in a *value*
sense. Daughter species may be more adapted than their parent species, but
that does not make them better in any value sense, more advanced in some
objective sense, higher on some cosmic scale or anything of the sort. In fact,
adaptation may result in losses of abilities (evolving into a parasite often
involves this) or even in degeneration, in some intuitive sense. Furthermore,
adaptation is always adaptation to some environment, to some ecological
niche. There is no such thing as adaptation per se, irrespective of context.[23]
Two species, each of which is well adapted to its own environment, might
die more or less horribly in the environment of the other. In Darwin's terms,
neither of those species is "better" than the other. For Darwin there was no
overall value direction in which evolution was necessarily driven, and objections presupposing such are misconstruals of his views.

Misconstruals here can take subtle forms. Wysong, for instance, points
out that artificial selection frequently (perhaps always) produces domestic
varieties that would be less viable in the wild than the wild varieties from
which the domesticated ones were produced. Probably true. But he concludes that artificial breeding has thus not resulted in improvement of the
species, and he takes that as a difficulty for evolutionary theory.[24] What
Wysong has missed here is that improvement in Darwin's sense is not improvement in some overall, unconditional sense that would render a species
more viable in any circumstance, but is rather improvement with respect to
the species's prospects in the specific circumstance in question. The domestic

species—such as Wysong's example of sheep with legs too weak to jump fences—are well adapted to their domestic situation, and the weak-leg mutation is a part of that adaptation. Their particular environment is one in which sheep lacking that mutation are destroyed (by the breeder) before they are able to reproduce. The fact that they would last about ten minutes in some other environment (one with wolves and no protective fences) and are really badly adapted to that environment does not contradict any evolutionary expectation at all.

*2. Advantages and disadvantages.* It is sometimes assumed that according to evolutionary theory, every trait that passes the natural selection test must be advantageous. Thus evolution should not produce any trait that is neutral or downright disadvantageous. The fact that organisms do exhibit such traits is then advanced as disconfirmation of evolutionary theory.[25]

This objection also involves misconception. Darwin argued that pairs of traits were sometimes linked. (One of his examples was deafness and blue eyes in cats.) Where traits were linked, if one of the pair was *sufficiently* advantageous, it could be to the species's advantage to have that trait even at the cost of also having the accompanying neutral or disadvantageous trait. It might, in short, be more advantageous overall to have both together than to have neither. Thus, in cases of linkage, natural selection could result in species having traits that Darwin described as "independent of utility" or "without, as far as we can see, [being] of the slightest service to the species." In fact, Darwin thought that sexual selection could result in traits that were "an inconvenience and probably an injury."[26] Thus a species having neutral or disadvantageous traits, at least in the short run, is not an automatic difficulty for the theory.

*3. Traits-in-process.* A very popular related objection is that many traits are useful only when fully developed; when they are only partially formed during the various stages of evolutionary development they would in fact be seriously disadvantageous or even harmful. Thus, natural selection itself would select against such stages and would prevent such traits from ever developing, much less ever evolving to the point of being useful.[27] Wysong, for instance, paints a graphic picture of partially developed and uncontrollable arms tangling their possessors in brush and bushes, making them easy prey for predators and thereby eliminating the entire species before functioning arms can fully evolve.[28]

There are, of course, serious problems with such objections. As noted above, a developing trait might be genetically linked to some other trait advantageous enough to outweigh problems involving the partially developed trait, and it would thus not necessarily be selected against even though disadvantageous. Furthermore, from Darwin on, evolutionists have suggested the possibility that organs undergoing development might during the course of development serve functions other than those which the ultimately evolved organ will serve.[29] For instance, internal inflatable air chambers that function as swim bladders in some fish might develop air-exchange capacities and come to function as lungs. They thus would serve an advantageous function even during the period of development toward an alternative ultimate function, and consequently would not necessarily be selected against.[30] Further, in some cases advantages might be gained from even a partially developed trait, even if it served no other function. For instance, a possible early stage on the path toward development of an eye—a light-sensitive patch of skin—while itself not an eye and perhaps serving no other useful function, might still be useful to an organism preyed on by other organisms large enough to cast a shadow when approaching from above.[31]

But Wysong is probably right that natural selection would eliminate organisms that had developed arms but had not developed a means to control them. Any evolutionist would agree in a second. And no actual evolutionary theory implies otherwise.

*4. Evolution, needs and wants.* Lamarck claimed that evolution responded to particular needs of organisms, sometimes even supplying new organs when continued viability demanded it. That principle is not, however, part of present Darwinian theory. According to present theory, the acquiring of a new trait, ability or organ depends on whether or not relevant variations occur; but whether or not they in fact occur is totally independent of the species's needs or wants. Those who attempt to refute evolutionary theory by noting that an organism or species has not developed some characteristic that would be advantageous are simply misconstruing the theory.[32] Darwin's theory has no expectation of traits, abilities or organs automatically arising at need.

Popular evolutionary prose often fosters the same misinterpretation. For instance, Ricki Lewis, in a popular biology text, says that "eyes have evolved independently 40 times to meet the need for light-sensing organs."[33] Peter Douglas Ward, speaking of brachiopods, says, "To make themselves unappetizing to predators, the surviving brachiopods became poisonous to eat."[34] One could easily read these statements to imply that evolutionary processes were not only need-based but actually driven by intentions. Darwin would not have been amused.

5. *Natural selection as creative.* Another extremely popular objection involves limits to change observed in artificial breeding experiments. By careful selective breeding, distinct varieties of organisms can be produced, but such variation almost invariably seems to approach some boundary that no amount of further breeding can cross. For instance, starting from dogs one can produce new strains of dogs, but they are still dogs. If evolution were true, the objection goes, it should be possible to cross those boundaries, producing change indefinitely. Since it is not possible, evolution is clearly mistaken.[35]

Popular and plausible as that objection may seem, it does not work. Darwin himself insisted that evolutionary change beyond normal genetic boundaries depends on some change in inheritance resources (now identified as mutation). Selection alone can produce neither new species nor new characteristics. Unless new genetic variation arises, selection will execute the relatively unfit, but cannot produce anything new. Darwin's theory, then, typically demands both selection and new variation in order for something new to arise, and in the absence of such mutation the theory itself *predicts* that selection of any sort will be unable to cross the initial boundaries.[36]

The domestic breeding experiments do perhaps establish that selection *alone* is not creative—and that is precisely what Darwin thought. To cause a problem for Darwin here, one would have to produce situations in which selection was operating *and* sufficiently favorable genetic mutations arose but could not be fixed in the breeding population by that selection. I know of only one place where there is even an attempt to make such a case.[37]

### Uniformitarianism

Some of the most pervasive creationist criticisms involve the concept of *uniformitarianism.* The issue is particularly important to creationists. Old-earth geology rests directly on some form of uniformitarianism, and evolutionary theory demands vast stretches of time. Thus, if uniformitarianism can be successfully refuted, two major targets of young-earth creationists collapse at one blow.

### Lyellian Uniformitarianism

As discussed in chapter two, the initial idea of uniformitarianism was developed by James Hutton in the late eighteenth century, then gained influence through the work of Charles Lyell beginning in the 1830s. Lyellian uniformitarianism consisted, roughly, of two parts:

(a) the normative principle that geological explanations of the earth's history and structure should properly appeal only to presently observable processes operating at presently observable rates and intensities (or *actualism*);

and

(b) the claim that such processes, while allowing slow local geological changes nonetheless preserved a stable overall geological average state in the earth's surface taken as a whole (or *steady state*).

The steady state claim never fared well (in fact, Lyell himself had abandoned it by 1863), and geologists accepted instead the view that although global changes in the earth's surface were typically slow and gradual, there was indeed change over time—present geological conditions were not essentially the same as past geological conditions.[38] Despite the fact that geology rejected the steady state idea well over a century ago, some influential works still attribute such views to contemporary geology. For example, Wysong gives us the following definitions of uniformitarianism: "the past is exactly like the present" and "processes and *conditions* have always been as they are now" (my emphasis).[39]

Obviously, criticisms resting on the assumption that this is what contemporary science means by *uniformitarianism* will have no particular relevance.

### Classical Uniformitarianism

The conception of uniformitarianism that dominated geology until recent decades, which I will term "classical," consisted of the following components:

(a) actualism (as above)

plus

(b) claims of a real, but gradual, change over the course of earth's history. The overwhelming majority of creationists attribute this definition of uniformitarianism to contemporary geology. Typical, indeed nearly canonical, is Gish: "Present processes acting essentially at present rates over hundreds of millions of years are sufficient to account for all of geology" (see endnotes for several dozen additional examples).[40]

As it turns out, contemporary science has abandoned this definition. Unfortunately, in addition to failing to recognize that abandonment, many creationists who cite the definition have not understood its implications.

Geologists from Lyell on recognized that abrupt local geological occurren-ces—volcanoes, floods, earthquakes and the like—have acted rapidly and catastrophically, sometimes over wide (but generally not global) areas. That recognition was part of the actualism of the classical definition.[41] Obviously, organisms are drowned and buried rapidly in floods, are killed and buried in minutes by volcanic eruptions, and suffer similar fates in mudslides and earthquakes. Thus mere evidence of rapid death, burial and so forth is in itself not in the slightest contrary to classical uniformitarianism.

Although some popular creationists (such as Morris) have recognized that fact,[42] many have not. Many creationist attacks on uniformitarianism consist merely of citing evidence for some particular geological event being rapid or catastrophic. For instance, Morris (oddly enough) says that "the very exis-tence of fossils necessarily speaks of rapidity of formation," and "rapid and compact burial of the organism concerned . . . requires catastrophism."[43] (Note his claim that it requires catastroph*ism,* not mere catastroph*e.* He fails to distinguish the two on some other occasions as well.[44]) Wieland notes that fossils "show signs of rapid burial," shows a picture of a mother ichthyosaur "trapped in the process of giving birth" and seems to take the case to be thereby closed.[45] Wysong cites polystrate trees that could not have been buried slowly and concludes that they thus "pose . . . problems for an evolution-uniformity interpretation."[46]

Other examples are numerous.[47] But again, since classical uniformitarian-ism allowed floods, volcanoes, earthquakes, mudslides and other (presently observable) rapid processes that might produce the above effects, such crit-icisms are simply beside the point.

Morris, who is generally (but not consistently) clearer than are most creationists on what classical uniformitarianism actually means, sometimes argues that the problem for that view is one of *scale.* Classical uniformitar-ian views can, he believes, accommodate limited and local catastrophes of presently observed proportions, but they cannot account for the sheer mag-nitude of past vulcanism or the vastness of mass fossil graves. His position seems to be that accounting for such magnitude and vastness demands different processes from those seen at present, or enormously different rates and intensities from any seen at present, or both.[48] Indeed, it would demand even rapid or catastrophic *global* geological processes.

Morris may well be right here. In fact, several decades ago mainstream geologists began departing from classical uniformitarianism, adopting the view that rates and intensities of some processes had varied during geological history. (Despite some exceptions, such as worldwide ice-age changes, mainstream geologists until fairly recently were still generally suspicious of catastrophes on a global scale.) Interestingly enough, as early as the 1950s a few creationists—including Morris—noted and commented on such changes.[49]

Of course, once geology accepted the idea that rates and intensities of at least some geological processes need not be constant, attributing straight classical uniformitarianism to geology was no longer accurate, and criticisms based on that aspect of classical uniformitarianism were simply no longer relevant. Unfortunately, such attributions and criticisms continue to the present.

### Methodological Uniformitarianism

Despite geologists' traditional hesitations about theories involving global cataclysms, recent years have seen a virtual explosion of such theories within mainstream geology—theories concerning devastating meteor impacts, a rogue planet causing a twenty-six-million-year cycle of extinctions, and so forth. What exactly is going on?

What is going on is that the concept of uniformitarianism has shifted once again. The focus of uniformity has shifted from geological *processes* and *events* themselves ("substantive uniformitarianism") to the *laws* underlying such processes and events ("methodological uniformitarianism").[50] The normative stipulation now is that legitimate geological explanations are limited only by the boundaries of uniformly operating basic natural laws, plus extrapolations of or from them. But what difference could that make?

Consider this simple example. According to one present theory, the extinction of the dinosaurs was triggered by an asteroid's slamming into the earth and exploding huge quantities of dust and debris into the air, thus blocking sunlight and causing the ecosystem to crash. That was pretty clearly a catastrophic event of global proportions, well outside ordinary, everyday events regardless of scale. But neither that event nor its aftermath involved any occurrences outside ordinary, everyday natural law. The asteroid had formed according to normal formative processes, its path had been governed by ordinary laws of gravitation and motion, the explosion on impact was governed by laws of energy transformation, conversion and thermodynamics, and so forth. The impact and explosion products were distributed around the globe according to normal atmospheric laws, and they then blocked out the sunlight according to ordinary laws of optics. The consequences for plant and animal life stemmed from basic biological principles.

The results (if this theory is true) were utterly catastrophic and global, but not because any laws were suspended or broken, nor because new laws went into effect. In fact, it was precisely the continued, ordinary workings of the everyday laws that caused the catastrophe. Had any of those laws *not* worked, the global catastrophe might very well not have happened. The asteroid might never have formed. It might have missed the earth had gravity suddenly been suspended. Its impact might have had no effect had energy laws temporarily quit working. Plants and animals might have continued happily on despite the dust in the air and the absence of sunlight, had biological law not operated. Clearly, then, methodological uniformitarianism (continuity of and uniformity of law) is perfectly consistent with catastrophic, discontinuous events.

Similar sorts of considerations will show that continuity and uniformity of law is consistent not only with catastrophe and discontinuity but also with rapidity of rate, with alteration of rate, with different processes beginning or ceasing to operate and with those effects occurring on either local or global scale. What that means, ultimately, is that objections concerning scale of events, such as those mentioned earlier, do not automatically constitute problems for the sort of uniformity now employed in contemporary geology.

Morris and Morris claim not only that creationists have understood this latest shift in uniformitarianism but that creationists got it right long ago and mainstream geologists are beginning to catch on only now.[51] For various reasons I have some suspicions of those claims, but let's ignore them and try to get to the heart of the dispute.[52]

For Morris, the issue is not ultimately rapid process versus slow process, uniformity of law versus uniformity of rate and process, or anything of the sort. For Morris, any unlimited application of uniformity must assume the legitimacy of unlimited extrapolation of something or other from the present into the past—be it process, rate, intensity, law or whatever. Whatever it is, such unlimited extrapolation is reliable and legitimate only if there are no historical discontinuities in whatever it is that is being extrapolated.[53] Thus employing uniformitarianism as a basic principle presupposes absence of historical discontinuity. Not only do creationists see that presupposition as unscientifically arbitrary, but most argue that Scripture gives conclusive reason to believe that fundamental discontinuities—the flood, the Fall, the creation—have occurred. Those discontinuities are not merely internal to nature and are not driven by natural law like, say, asteroid impact discontinuities.[54] Here, then, is an underlying either-or. Either as a uniformitarian (of whatever kind) one assumes that there are no historical episodes when nature itself was disrupted, or as a (biblical) catastrophist one assumes that there were such episodes.[55]

Even some opponents of creationism may agree with this. Lewontin, for instance, says,

> Either the world of phenomena is a consequence of the regular operation of repeatable causes and their repeatable effects, operating roughly along the lines of known physical law, or else at every instant all physical regularities may be ruptured and a totally unforeseeable set of events may occur. One must take sides on the issue of whether the sun is sure to rise tomorrow. We cannot live simultaneously in a world of natural causation and of miracles, for if one miracle can occur, there is no limit.[56]

That is why proper catastrophism, as Morris and others see it, necessarily involves the non- or supernatural.[57] Indeed, that is why even the acceptance of global natural catastrophes by mainstream geologists does not constitute the right sort of catastrophism and is, in a deeper sense, still uniformitarian thinking.[58] That is why Morris and Morris can instantly identify Davis Young as a "uniformitarian die-hard" simply on the basis of Young's thinking that "some [geological] formations must have required long periods of time."[59] Extrapolation of *any* natural process to the long term presupposes a willingness to deny that that process was ever interrupted from beyond nature. And that, as Morris reads it, requires repudiation of the clear teaching of Genesis and is "the basic fallacy" of uniformitarianism.[60] In fact, uniformitarianism is seen by some creationists as a blanket philosophical policy of refusing even to consider the possibility of interruptions from beyond nature. As such, it appears to some creationists to be a derivative of, if not a form of, philosophical naturalism.[61]

That is not to say that creationists reject extrapolation of natural laws, processes and rates. Many creationists firmly insist that they are uniformitarian in that sense, but that such extrapolations are legitimate only *between* the interruptions to which nature has been subject.[62] For instance, according to many creationists, extrapolating present rates of decay of the earth's magnetic field and of stellar dust accumulation on the moon (and so forth) gives start-up dates for the processes in the recent past and does not require extrapolation past relevant interruptions (such as creation). Hence, those "uniformitarian" extrapolations are legitimate and indeed constitute evidence for a young earth. On the other hand, extrapolation of other processes (radioactive decay, transmission time of light from distant galaxies and so on) would yield huge ages, requiring extrapolation beyond those limiting interruptions (such as creation) and thus are not legitimate, do not constitute genuine evidence of great age and are to be explained in other ways (as part of a "fully functioning" creation).[63]

But how do we know which interruptions from beyond the natural we are to judge our extrapolations by? What constraints on our theorizing are there here? Morris's answer is *Scripture.* "The question eventually comes down to this: Do we, or do we not, really believe the Bible to be the Word of God?"[64] Uniformity holds sway except where God has told us otherwise. (As I will argue a bit later, there is nothing irrational or intellectually improper in giving that sort of answer.)

In trying to make the purely scientific case against either evolution or mainstream geology nothing is to be gained by attributing to contemporary science either Lyellian or classical uniformitarianism, representing contemporary science as rejecting rapid geological processes, representing it as rejecting the possibility of processes operating at different rates in the past than at present, or representing it as rejecting global historical geological catastrophes, then raising objections on the basis of those attributions. Contemporary geologists do not hold those views.

### Other Misconstruals

Popular creationist writings contain other misconstruals as well. Some argue, for instance, that advocates of evolution are guilty of double talk when they claim that some evolutions of species might be too fast to leave much fossil evidence, but too slow for human observation.[65] (There is no inconsistency—"fast" for evolution is anything under, say, one hundred thousand years. "Slow" for the human race might be anything over the five thousand years of recorded history. There is obviously some overlap here.) Some claim that evolution is inconsistent with extinction,[66] that it is irreconcilable with organisms having vestigial organs,[67] that it implies enlargement of organisms,[68] that it implies that in the same environment all species should develop the same traits,[69] that according to evolution any two species facing the same sort of environmental problem will develop the same evolutionary solution to the problem,[70] that according to evolution mutations should be primarily beneficial,[71] that evolution is merely the theory that all "organisms have, and had, parents,"[72] that it implies that there should be life on Mars[73] and that if mutation provides the material for evolutionary advance, then evolutionists are hypocrites for opposing toxic pollution and other sources of mutation.[74] Each of these claims is mistaken and most rest on a failure to understand in detail what evolutionary theory actually says.[75]

## Consequences

Such misconstruals are, again, seriously counterproductive, in both short term and long term. Short term, it simply stifles dialogue with opponents. On the one side, prominent popular creationists and their lay audiences sometimes exhibit a strong contempt for their opponents, suggesting that those on the opposite side of the issue must be really blind not to see how devastating the objections are.[76] Many anticreationists exhibit a contempt every bit as deep, based in part on the fact that some of the major arguments popular creationists advance so triumphantly are simply irrelevant to the real theory. One other effect is that since the most visible figures within the creationist movement have made the above misconstruals so prominent, the image of the entire creationist project has been tainted by them, and that has, I think, deprived serious and professionally competent creationists— of whom there is a small but increasing number—of any serious hearing.

Furthermore, regardless of whether evolutionary theory stands up to scrutiny, Christian lay audiences of all ages have been given an inaccurate picture both of evolutionary theory and of the ease with which it can be scientifically dismissed. That surely cannot be a very good long-term strategy.

# 5 TWENTIETH-CENTURY CREATIONISM
## The Historical Context

**A**s noted, much (though not all) of the Christian community had achieved peaceful coexistence with biological evolution within a few decades of 1859.[1] Evolution, it was widely held, was simply the means by which God had produced his creatures, just as various planetary laws were the means by which he produced night, day and seasons, just as various meteorological laws were the means by which he produced rain in season, and so forth. Taking evolution as God's means of producing species did presuppose an old earth having a history in the millions of years. But the old-earth issue had already been dealt with and was not considered particularly problematic within the Christian community. And the flood had ceased to be viewed as a major geological factor well before Darwin.

Reconciliation of old-earth views with Scripture was typically managed by taking the days of Genesis to be geological ages—the "day-age theory"—or by claiming the existence of a long gap between an initial creation referred to in Genesis 1:1 and a subsequent six-day creation recounted in Genesis 1:2 and following verses. According to advocates of the "ruin and restoration" version of gap theory, the earth had previously been populated with life (perhaps even people). But some catastrophe, sometimes associated with Satan's fall, had destroyed that world, leaving only geological structures and fossils. On this view, the six days of Genesis thus actually involved a re-creation of life on the geological ruins of that earlier world.

In any case, the vast geological ages demanded by Darwin's theory could apparently be reconciled with Scripture, and by the late nineteenth century even conservative Christians overwhelmingly accepted either the day-age theory or the gap theory concerning Genesis.[2] During the early years of the twentieth century there were virtually no visible Christian advocates of a young earth, of a geologically important flood (whatever its spiritual and historical importance might be) or of the necessity of taking Genesis as teaching any such doctrines. Nor did anyone entertain any serious doubts that the fossil record displayed some sort of progression.[3]

The stance of conservative Christians in the United States toward evolution was, however, a bit complicated, and was part of a larger collection of concerns. During the latter part of the nineteenth and on into the early twentieth century, conservative Christians had become increasingly alarmed as the Western world began apparently slipping from the grasp of Christianity. The German higher-criticism approach to Scripture, according to which the Bible was analyzed as if it were any other purely human text, was eroding the Bible's status as absolute divine truth. Friends and enemies alike saw the Darwinian movement as undercutting any claims to straightforward truth that Genesis might have. Culture in both Europe and the United States was becoming insistently secular as various traditional values and institutions gave way before new social and intellectual forces. And the advocates of both modernism and the "social gospel" in theology were deliberately and happily trimming the "faith of the fathers" to conform to those new forces.[4]

### The Rise of Fundamentalism

Conservative Christians responded in a number of ways. For instance, a group of influential conservative church leaders, many of whom were linked to the evangelist Dwight L. Moody, between 1910 and 1915 published a series of twelve pamphlets laying out and defending key conservative theological doctrines, such as the inerrancy of Scripture. The series was edited by A. C. Dixon (pastor of the Moody Church in Chicago), the evangelist Louis Meyer and R. A. Torrey (an enormously respected associate of Moody). Some consider this series, entitled The Fundamentals, to have been both the founding documents and the source of the name of the fundamentalist movement.[5] Those involved saw The Fundamentals as a reasoned attempt to reverse the erosion within both organized religion and society. Despite a huge free distribution, however, The Fundamentals did not itself immediately trigger the movement. But an organized movement did arise within a few years, the principal impetus coming from the World's Christian Fundamentals Association (WCFA), organized around 1919 primarily by William Bell Riley.[6]

Although critics widely accuse fundamentalism of being anti-intellectual, its beginning certainly does not fit that description. The authors of The Fundamentals were generally well educated—among them were a lawyer, professors (one from Princeton Seminary), a physician, a seminary president, an editor and a geologist. The author of the doctrinal statement of the WCFA was a college president (Wheaton College). Another key WCFA organizer, W. H. G. Thomas, had a Ph.D. from Oxford.[7] From its beginning fundamentalism has had a high view of education and has been involved in founding and operating schools and colleges, although not always of high quality by secular standards.

Fundamentalists have also from the beginning had a high view of reason. (Indeed, fundamentalists objected bitterly to Pentecostalism earlier in the twentieth century in part because Pentecostalism was seen as placing emotion above reason.[8]) In fact, traditionally they have not merely respected reason but have held that reason can firmly establish important Christian truths. In some sense twentieth-century fundamentalism is the primary intellectual heir of the nineteenth-century tradition of scientific natural theology. Despite contemporary myth to the contrary, fundamentalists have never been hostile to science as such. They have historically had a deep respect for science as they see it and have throughout their history been absolutely convinced that all results of *proper* science can be and should be integrated with what Scripture is taken to teach.[9] Where there were no serious perceived problems in reconciliation with Scripture, fundamentalists have always accepted the deliverance of mainstream science perfectly comfortably. In fact, some early fundamentalists believed that on some issues, Christians could learn from science how Scripture itself was to be interpreted.[10] The fundamentalist editor L. S. Keyser even once referred to "the sacred name" of science.[11]

Thus none of the early fundamentalist leadership rejected science's claims that the earth was vastly old, although they differed concerning the reconciliation of science with Scripture. For instance, Riley and the most prominent public defender of creation-style views in the 1920s, William Jennings Bryan, held day-age positions. (Riley said that "the testimony of geology"—science—made this interpretation of Scripture "certain."[12]) On the other hand, Dixon, Torrey, C. I. Scofield (of Scofield Reference Bible fame) and the most popular "scientific" opponent of evolution in the 1920s and 1930s, Harry Rimmer, all held gap theories.[13] Virtually none of the early fundamentalist leaders took the flood to be geologically significant, and many fundamentalists, including both Rimmer and the geologist G. F. Wright, one of the authors of The Fundamentals, believed that the Genesis flood was a purely localized event.[14]

As noted above, fundamentalists have always had a high regard for science *as they see it*. With some recent exceptions, fundamentalists' conception of science from the beginning of the movement has been fairly strictly Baconian—viewing science as essentially induction based solely on objective observational data and free of all speculation, hypothesizing, flights of theoretical fancy or philosophical agendas. This picture of science (about which more later) was tremendously popular historically and is the view still found in many dictionaries and in most popular creationist writing.[15]

Nearly any sweeping evolutionary theory failed to be legitimate science on this view, since any such theory involved hypothesizing theoretical processes operating in the deep, unobservable past. (And even were evolution in principle scientifically legitimate, recall that during this period there was widespread rejection of Darwin's specific natural selection mechanism even among professional biologists.) More serious, however, was the fact that many on both sides of the issue perceived Darwin's own theory as being simply incompatible with essential principles of Christianity and Scripture. And as strict biblical literalism became fundamentalist orthodoxy, evolution's apparent violations of specific Genesis statements would come increasingly to the fore in fundamentalists' criticisms.[16]

However, although many suspected that evolution and Scripture could not ultimately be put together properly, few were at this point interested in turning suspicion of evolution into a cause. Such theological heavyweights as Charles Hodge and B. B. Warfield did not object in principle to at least some form of evolution. Dixon, one of the editors of The Fundamentals, said that he would accept evolution if it were scientifically proven. Torrey, another editor, asserted that one could accept biological evolution and at the same time hold that Scripture was infallible. Howard Kelly, a Fundamentals author, was willing to accept evolution up to human beings. James Orr, another Fundamentals author, was willing to allow that at least to some extent, evolutionary processes might have been a means employed in

God's creating. G. F. Wright, yet another Fundamentals author, claimed in *The Origin and Antiquity of Man* (1912) that humans might be genetically connected to the higher primates. Even Bryan did not object privately to evolution up to human beings. Theistic evolution was apparently even taught in some Southern Baptist colleges.[17] (Other Fundamentals authors, however, made some pointed attacks on evolution.[18])

Overall, to the early fundamentalists the earth itself was ancient, and interpreting Genesis to allow for that was perfectly legitimate. The flood had probably been localized and in any case had not been geologically important in the sense of leaving profound marks on the earth and its geology. Evolution had a bit of a suspicious odor about it, but it was by no means anathema. The real enemies, at this point, were German higher criticism, the waning authority of Scripture, erosion of belief and the like.[19]

### Winds of Change

However, in the shattering aftermath of World War I, things began to change. Fundamentalists came to believe nearly universally that evolution was inherently, ineradicably materialistic and naturalistic. Perhaps even worse, it was driven ultimately by blind chance and was thus apparently irreconcilable with any sort of underlying divine purpose or guidance. In other words, fundamentalists perceived Darwin's theory not only as having a built-in philosophical agenda, contrary to the rules of good science, but as having a philosophical agenda that was violently contrary to Christianity.[20] Various antireligious Darwinists triumphantly insisted that evolution did indeed have antireligious and antiscriptural worldview consequences. Darwin himself had apparently conceded something in that direction in his rejection of the botanist Asa Gray's attempts at constructing a theistic evolution that could combine evolution and design. So it was neither accidental nor arbitrary that fundamentalist Christians would eventually settle on evolution as a deep enemy—they were being explicitly taught that by some of the advocates of evolution.[21]

Furthermore, after World War I fundamentalists and various other Christians increasingly came to see evolution as the cause of the bitter evils that had engulfed civilization. Evolution seemed to many to say that conflict was normal—even elevating. It seemed to say that survival was all that mattered—that is, that might (or anything else that enhanced one's personal or national chances of leaving offspring) made right. Evolution seemed to many to say that elimination of the weak to one's own advantage had the blessing of nature and life itself. Darwinism was widely held to have been one conscious motivating factor in Germany's behavior during World War I (and that was not necessarily sheer fantasy), and fundamentalists saw belief in evolution as underlying a wide assortment of social ills and as being responsible for a growing unbelief among the young.[22] In the view of some fundamentalists, even higher criticism, the earlier major target, could ultimately be laid at the doorstep of evolutionary thinking.

Evolution and Darwinism, then, lay deep among the roots of the ills besetting the early twentieth century. And fundamentalists now believed that unfortunately there were people bent on the destruction of the only hope of eternal salvation—Christianity—and who were to that end deliberately pushing evolution in churches, in the media and in the schools. Evolution *had* to be battled for the sake of the innocent, the young and civilization itself.[23] The gloves now came off.

The antievolution movement was spearheaded by one of the most prominent national politicians of the era, William Jennings Bryan. Convinced that the teaching of evolution underlay social, moral and spiritual erosion both in the United States and abroad, Bryan began a national antievolution campaign in 1921. One of the chief aims of the movement was to cleanse public schools of the teaching of evolution. The campaign struck a responsive chord, and in the early 1920s a number of Southern states outlawed the teaching of evolution in public schools. Even the U.S. Senate considered a partial radio censorship of evolution.[24]

Things came to a head in the 1925 Scopes trial in Dayton, Tennessee. That spring, Tennessee had banned the teaching of evolution in public classrooms, and John Scopes, a Dayton teacher, agreed to provide the American Civil Liberties Union (ACLU) with a test case. The ensuing trial, with Bryan leading the prosecution, was a three-ring (at least) media circus. Technically, the result was a win for the antievolution side, as Scopes was found guilty and fined one hundred dollars (later overturned). In terms of national public image and influence, it was a fundamentalist disaster. Scopes's defense was led by Clarence Darrow, considered by some to have been the best trial lawyer in the United States at that time. Bryan, before whom evolution and unbelief were not supposed to stand a chance, was perceived as having been simply clobbered—made to look uninformed (even about what his own opinions were), confused and simply unable to deal with the issues on the level of sophistication of his opponents.[25]

To the national audience, it looked as though fundamentalist pretensions to intellectual competence were utterly demolished, that the very best the fundamentalist antievolution movement could produce was not even in the same league as the other side. This picture of a fundamentalist fiasco in a barefoot Southern town—repackaged as self-righteous ignorance bent on intellectual repression—became the popular image of the movement for decades to come.

After the Scopes trial (and Bryan's death in Dayton a few days later), any serious respect and clout the fundamentalist movement and its antievolutionism had had in the national intellectual and political arena simply evaporated. Both were public laughingstocks—priceless and hilarious exhibits of what happens when backwoods yokels get a bit above themselves. The fundamentalist movement became virtually invisible at the national level and was repeatedly declared dead.[26]

That was not, however, quite true. Having been publicly humiliated in its attempt to reshape public institutions and directions on the national level, fundamentalists increasingly turned to construction of their own institutions—schools, colleges, publishing houses and other organizations—as well as to pursuit of antievolution concerns on the local level.[27]

After the embarrassment of 1925, and as the anti-intellectual image of fundamentalism became firmly fixed, the antievolution movement was increasingly plagued by a shortage of visible spokesmen with serious scientific credentials. Thus, given the high respect that fundamentalists accorded science—"properly" construed—any fearless defender of creationism who could make claims of genuine scientific expertise was destined to be a hero. The job was not long vacant. In fact, it was held simultaneously by two people: Harry Rimmer (1890-1952) and George McCready Price (1870-1963).

### Early Creationist Heroes

Rimmer had little actual scientific training, had no earned degrees at all and was in fact largely self-educated. That he was even self-educated is a testament to his perseverance, given the difficult circumstances of his early life. By the early 1920s Rimmer (at that point a traveling Presbyterian minister working with young people) had become interested in the evolution issue, had taken a geology correspondence course and had begun lecturing against evolution. He had also, in 1921, built a home laboratory and had founded (indeed, more or less *was*) the Research Science Bureau.[28]

Rimmer was a quite effective lecturer. He had, during an earlier year of medical training, picked up an impressive vocabulary, and he now also seemed to have the prestige of genuine science—the Research Science Bureau—behind him. And before long, having been awarded honorary degrees by Wheaton and one other college, he was *Dr.* Harry Rimmer. His reassuring message, seemingly authoritatively scientifically based, was that despite the battering that creationists had taken, it was, in his own words, "all right for Christians to go on reading and believing the Bible." Perhaps even better, Rimmer confirmed for antievolutionists what many of them suspected—that despite all their pomp and degrees, it was the mainstream evolutionary scientists who were the real jokes, who had bought possibly the silliest, most unscientific, obviously false theory ever hatched. While mocking Scripture, the evolutionist Jonahs had themselves swallowed a whale.[29]

With those credentials and that message, Rimmer became perhaps the most popular creationist lecturer of the 1920s and 1930s. In fact, Rimmer's advocacy of gap theory was partially responsible for its becoming the dominant fundamentalist reading of Genesis during that period and on into the second half of this century.

Another creationist thread was emerging, however—one that would ultimately displace gap theory as the most visible creationist view. Its rise was connected with the career of the other early-twentieth-century creationist hero, George McCready Price, whose views grew out of Seventh-day Adventist (SDA) theology.

Seventh-day Adventism had been established by Ellen G. White (1827-1915), who claimed to have a "spirit of prophecy." Her followers took her pronouncements to be divinely inspired and ranked them with Scripture. Among her pronouncements were that the Genesis days were ordinary days (that was linked to the SDA's policy of worshiping on the seventh day—Saturday), that the flood had been global and that it and other events associated with it were responsible for the major geological strata, fossils and so forth.[30]

During one of his stints as a schoolteacher, Price, at that point around thirty years old, first seriously confronted evolution. Having very little formal scientific education, he began a process of self-education and concluded that if the geologists were correct that the earth was vastly old, that the various strata had been laid down over millions of years and that fossils appeared in the geological strata in some sort of progressive order, then evolution just might be right after all. Price came near to accepting evolution but ultimately became convinced that White and her claim that the flood accounted for the earth's geology and its fossils were in fact right—indeed inspired. That meant that most of the earth's surface geology had been formed in a year or less and that strata and other geological features thus did not reveal anything at all about long periods of time. It also meant that any alleged geological order among fossils (which Price rejected in any case) had no significance with respect to historical development—evolution—at all. The organisms had all lived and died within a year of each other.[31]

At one stroke, then, White's flood geology simultaneously deprived evolution of the vast stretches of time it required and robbed it of some of its most popular evidence—the alleged progression in the fossil record. If White's flood geology could be given a scientific foundation, or if the standard geological theories could be scientifically shown to collapse, then evolution was demonstrably dead.

Price came to these conclusions around the turn of the century and spent the next several decades advocating flood geology and attacking mainstream geology. While his confidence in flood geology came in significant part from White's writings, the core of his scientific case was the existence of geological formations in which strata (and fossils) are out of their supposed proper order—fossils generally thought to be older are above fossils generally thought to be younger. Such reversals obviously require some special explanation from the mainstream geological establishment. Actually, several explanations are possible. One involves the idea of overthrusts, where one section of the earth's crust is pushed up onto and slides over another section. When that occurs, the older (bottom) strata of the section on top sit directly on top of the younger (upper) strata of the section underneath. Price argued that such explanations were nothing more than unsupported artificial dodges intended only to enable conventional geology to evade or distort data that would otherwise totally discredit it.[32]

If there was any order to fossils—which, again, Price was not about to admit—it was simply the result of different kinds of organisms' tendency to sink in the flood waters after different intervals, or perhaps of different kinds of organisms' different abilities to stay ahead (temporarily) of the rising flood waters. Price eventually concluded, and claimed as his greatest discovery, that any fossils could occur in the rocks in any order. Geologists who tried to date strata in terms of the fossils contained were engaged not only in circular reasoning (since they also, Price claimed, dated the fossils in terms of their strata), but in circular reasoning based on a woefully false premise.[33]

Having settled on flood geology and rejected both mainstream uniformitarian geology and evolution by the early years of the twentieth century, Prince engaged in both extensive investigation of geological literature (as opposed to direct investigation of the rocks) and extensive writing (more than two dozen books) over the next several decades. His most influential work was *The New Geology,* first published in 1923. In it Price outlined a "new catastrophism" involving only a single catastrophe—the Genesis flood.[34]

Although most of Price's early converts were Seventh-day Adventists, his work did command respect within the fundamentalist movement, where it was received as welcome further confirmation that *real* science (Price explicitly endorsed Baconianism, about which more later) both unmasked the poverty of evolution and conformed to Scripture.[35]

There were a number of attempts at organizing creationist science societies—such as the Religion and Science Association (1935) and the Deluge Geology Society (1938). Most were relatively short-lived, breaking down over personal, theological and geological disputes. Flood geologists, gap theorists and day-agers often could not get along. And Seventh-day Adventists, who constituted the bulk of the flood geologists, were often viewed with suspicion, or even alarm, by mainstream fundamentalists, in particular over the SDA elevation of White's writings to the same level as inspired Scripture.[36]

A generational and educational divergence was brewing as well. Younger conservative Christians entering scientific careers were increasingly better educated and tended to feel the force of scientific cases for an old earth, fossil progression, changes in species over time and so forth. In many cases that was accompanied by an increasing professional embarrassment over the public image of ignorance and incompetence that fundamentalists and creationists had given to Christian scientists. In an effort to free Christians in science from that image and to free science from its popular image as an enemy of religion, a group of evangelical Christian scientists founded the American Scientific Affiliation (ASA) in 1941. Most of the group had Ph.D.s in scientific disciplines, and most were college teachers.[37]

By the late 1940s, the ASA had dismissed both Rimmer's and Price's work as simply not scientifically competent, or anywhere close to it. By the mid-1950s, nearly all of the membership of the ASA accepted mainstream old-earth geology, and by the end of the 1950s an overwhelming portion accepted theistic evolution—the idea that evolution was one of God's means of creating.[38]

### Return of Flood Geology

The drift was not absolutely unanimous in that direction, however, as a young engineer destined to become flood geology's most influential spokesman of the century, Henry M. Morris (b. 1918), had joined the ASA in 1948. Despite having only a B.S. degree, Morris became an instructor in civil engineering at Rice in 1942. While there, he began to experience some unease over Genesis, geology and evolution. Believing that God would not have failed to speak on such crucial issues, Morris engaged in extensive Bible study and became convinced that Scripture inarguably taught that the earth had been created in six literal days in the relatively recent past. What to make of the earth's geology was still a puzzle, until, learning of Price through a reference in a Rimmer book, Morris read Price's *The New Geology* in 1943. He became almost instantly converted to Price's flood geology, and in 1943 he joined the Deluge Geology Society and began the first of his own creation science books. (An earlier book, *That You Might Believe,* was primarily an evangelistic apologetics book. Throughout his career Morris has linked creation science and evangelism, in the unshakable belief that any compromise of the Genesis message is often the top of a slippery slope leading from old-earth theories to theistic evolution to liberalism to humanism to atheism.[39])

Although Morris's original confidence concerning young-earth flood geology was grounded in his interpretation of Scripture, he believed that true science would yield exactly the same sort of results and began work in 1947 on what was intended to be the "definitive volume on recent creation and Biblical geology." Other activities took priority, and the volume was still unfinished in 1957 when Morris—by then with a Ph.D. in hydrology and head of the civil engineering program at Virginia Tech—was approached by John Whitcomb, a theologian and Old Testament scholar at Grace Theological Seminary in Indiana, about the possibility of collaborating on a book detailing both biblical and scientific cases for Genesis flood geology.

Morris agreed, and the result was *The Genesis Flood,* first published in 1961. The book initially received almost no attention outside fundamentalist and creationist circles—where it was an absolute smash hit. (And remains so. In 1995 it was in its thirty-fifth printing.) It was very quickly so successful that flood geology and creationism became virtually synonymous, despite flood geology's never having previously achieved strong popularity outside the "theologically suspect" SDA movement.[40]

Several things contributed to its popularity. First, Whitcomb and Morris were very up-front about the order of precedence of Scripture and theory. A straightforward reading of Scripture set the framework, the boundaries and the agenda for any scientific theorizing. Many conservative Christians saw that as both a reassuring and a refreshing change. To many such Christians, it seemed that evangelical scientists had for several decades been explaining to them why, on the basis of arcane scientific theories, Genesis could not possibly mean what it seemed on the face of it to say. Whitcomb and Morris, like Rimmer earlier, were encouraging Christians to read it and believe, and to ignore all the games about "symbolic interpretations" and so forth.

Second, the book seemed to be honestly scientific (equations, technical terminology, multitudinous references to scientific books and journals), and contrary to the popular image of fundamentalists and creationists, that was a strong factor in its favor. The important feature here was that it seemed to be open, candid science. The facts were treated apparently objectively and fair-mindedly, and the results were nearly invariably what one would expect if Scripture were straightforwardly true. The fit was marvelous—even astonishing. Naturalistic evolutionists, because of their agenda of unbelief, had to twist the facts of nature. Theistic evolutionists, because of their pathetic longing for secular respect, had to twist the facts of Scripture. But let Scripture and nature speak straightforwardly, and they meshed beautifully. In rejecting the old-earth fantasies of the geologists and the evolutionary fallacies of the biologists, creationists thus had the authority of Scripture and the prestige of true science behind them. David had slain the giant again.[41]

*The Genesis Flood* sparked a resurgence of flood geology and was a key catalyst in a wave of new creationist science organizations—most immediately the Creation Research Society (CRS), the Bible-Science Association and others. (In 1958 the SDA had already founded its own creationist think tank—the Geoscience Research Institute—which has probably done the best actual science within the creationist movement.) Beginning as an informal "team of ten," eight of whom had earned science doctorates (although none were in geology), the Creation Research Society was organized in 1963 around formal affirmations of scriptural inerrancy, a creation week, a global flood, special creation of Adam and Eve, and the doctrine that acceptance of Christ is necessary for salvation. Although it was not explicit in its doctrinal statement, the CRS is also committed to a young earth. Morris was influential in the CRS from the beginning and in fact served as its second president.[42]

A second Morris organization, the Institute for Creation Research, was founded in 1972 for the purpose of producing creationist educational materials. The ICR grew out of a split within an earlier organization and until 1980 had ties to Christian Heritage College. The ICR is probably the most visible contemporary creationist organization. It publishes extensively and produces creationist radio programs. Most of the popular creationist figures—Morris, Duane Gish, Gary Parker, Ken Ham—either are or have been part of the ICR staff.[43]

The movement made another bid for broader influence with legislation in Arkansas and Louisiana in the early 1980s, mandating equal time in public-school classrooms for creation science—purely empirical evidences for young-earth, flood geology theories and for nonevolutionary biology theories. But such attempts have not survived legal challenges based on the claim that creation science is not science but is in fact thinly veiled religion and thus has no place in the public classroom—at least not in any real science class. The creationist movement is thus at present in the rather odd position of having actually won the allegiance of a significant portion of the American public but of being unable to translate that support into the one arena that has long been a key target—public-school classrooms.[44]

Those attempts also triggered sustained anticreationist activity, both from some private organizations and from most national scientific organizations.[45] Creationist activities and views have been perceived as extremely dangerous. Patterson claims that creationist success in the schools "would mean the extinction of science and a return to the Dark Ages," while seventy-two Nobel Prize winners signed a statement claiming, among other things, that such success might eventually jeopardize "our capacity to cope with problems of food production, health care, and even national defense."[46]

In the following chapter we will take a closer look at the creationist views themselves.

# 6 CREATIONIST THEORY
## A Brief Introduction

The Genesis Flood *occupies much the same position in the popular* creationist movement as Darwin's *Origin of Species* occupies in various evolutionist circles—and there may be as few people on either side who have actually read it. But although the movement is still in some sense defined by Whitcomb and Morris's book, creationist positions have developed and changed over the thirty-odd years since its original publication. To explain present creationist positions, I will begin with an overview of *The Genesis Flood,* then look briefly at two subsequent works—Morris's 1974 *Scientific Creationism* and Morris and Gary Parker's 1987 (revised) *What Is Creation Science?*

### 1961: *The Genesis Flood*
According to Whitcomb and Morris, there are only two basic pictures of reality—one oriented toward God, seeing all things as ultimately dependent on him, and one oriented toward nature and humans, seeing all things as independent of any deity, as products of purely natural processes. Very broadly speaking, the first is a philosophical creationism picture, the second is a philosophical evolutionism picture.[1] Underlying the evolutionary view is the belief that nature and natural causal sequences drive and govern everything. Obviously on this view there can be no discontinuities, no breaches of the natural order, no intrusions of the supernatural into history.

On a creation-oriented view, however, such breaches of natural causal order are certainly possible, and even to be expected. Indeed, if the world's and our own very existence is dependent on divine activity, then at least the initial creation lies outside any purely natural causal process.[2]

According to Whitcomb and Morris, the basic choice between the two outlooks is beyond the range of science—it is ultimately a philosophical or spiritual matter. But which picture one chooses will obviously have significant consequences for one's science, and will have spiritual consequences as well. On the basis of a prior acceptance of Scripture as divinely inspired, straightforward and true, Whitcomb and Morris adopted the broad creationist stance. From that perspective, a science that arbitrarily assumes at the outset that there are no discontinuities—an evolutionary, uniformitarian picture of the origin and history of the cosmos—will pretty clearly get at least some things muddled. Indeed, its inaccurate governing presupposition will guarantee an unavoidably skewed picture of nature, its origin and history. So uniformitarian, evolutionary science will be associated with both scientific and spiritual problems, and that will have consequences for society and culture as well.[3]

Once one has adopted the broad creationist picture, one confronts such questions as, How many discontinuities in the natural causal order are there? Where and what are they? What consequences have they had for the remaining causal order? Whitcomb and Morris thus take it as their initial task to discover what God has told us in Scripture concerning his creation and subsequent activities. Many of those activities will constitute discontinuities in natural processes. Since ordinary science would, of course, break down exactly at points of divine intervention, divine revelation is the only possible means of discovering such facts and the only possible grounds for correctly understanding both the interventions and their subsequent scientific consequences.[4] Whitcomb and Morris's second task, once they have determined what God has revealed concerning initial creation and subsequent earth history, will be to show that legitimate scientific data (with which creationists profess to have no quarrel) can be "oriented" within that biblical framework and around those discontinuities, and that the resulting system will be a more systematic, more plausible, more honest system than can be produced within a uniformitarian, evolutionary framework.[5]

Here, then, is the picture they claim to find in Scripture. In the beginning, God both created the basic materials of the cosmos and a primitive, largely undifferentiated, completely water-covered earth. That initial creative act was in the relatively recent past, no more than about ten thousand years ago. Since that creation was out of nothing, and since the present First Law of Thermodynamics prohibits either creation or destruction of energy, principles other than those presently observable were obviously in operation. Thus present processes do not provide any sort of key to this part of the past. Construing uniformitarianism in geology as the principle that present processes *are* the key to understanding the past, Whitcomb and Morris conclude that uniformitarian geology is already derailed before it even begins.[6]

During the first creative day (a day of twenty-four hours) the earth was bathed in light—energy—which triggered all sorts of physical and chemical activity in the surface material of the earth. Powerful geological activity probably occurred, with some of the earth's "basement rock" being moved, deformed, metamorphosized and so forth, and with quantities of water being trapped in and under the earth's crust.

On the second day, part of the earth's water covering was elevated and transformed into water vapor that formed a completely enveloping canopy around the earth, giving rise to a global greenhouse effect and a uniform and placid global climate.[7] The intense geological activity of the first day probably continued, with the remaining surface water experiencing intense agitation and profoundly affecting the earth's surface materials. As various forces separated lighter from heavier materials, areas underlying heavier materials began to sink, and that sinking triggered corresponding uplifting (possibly involving vulcanism) of areas of lighter materials. Water, responding to gravity, flowed into depressed areas, which thus became ocean basins, with the uplifted lighter areas forming new continents. Once such land masses appeared above the water, they were, that same day, clothed in vegetation—grasses, herbs and trees. Whitcomb and Morris note that no natural mechanism for the sudden appearance of such growth is available, and they attribute it to divine miraculous intervention.[8]

Plants, soil and subsequent organisms were created complete as part of a fully functioning, stable system. The inevitable consequence of creating a dynamic, complete and fully functioning system is that at least some things in it will necessarily have the appearance of age. For instance, in an ecologically varied forest, at least some trees would have to be created as mature despite being only minutes or hours old. Whitcomb and Morris suggest that the same principle might apply to radioactive substances, meaning that such materials might well have been created complete with decay products, which would completely invalidate radiometric dating (such as carbon dating). Such radiometric dating frequently has been cited as demonstrating that young-earth theories must be mistaken, but if the initial creation was complete and fully functional as Whitcomb and Morris understand those themes, such demonstrations are useless.[9]

Within the week, sea creatures, birds, land animals and humans were created, and existed in perfect harmony with each other and the earth. Unfortunately, that situation did not last. Humans disobeyed God's command and fell. The Fall had huge consequences—death entered the world, the ground was cursed and began producing weeds and thorns, some creatures were altered (serpents lost their legs and became repugnant to humans), the relationship between humans and animals was altered for the worse, some animals became carnivorous and acquired appropriate teeth, claws and other specialized organs appropriate to carnivores, and the entire creation became subject to the bondage of decay associated with the Second Law of Thermodynamics. Whitcomb and Morris read that law as the principle that all things tend toward disorder, decay and dissolution.[10]

Clearly, these were not just natural changes and occurrences, and thus any uniformitarian approach would be helpless to account for them. One might argue that the world could not have functioned without the Second Law, but if it is true that the world *as presently governed* requires such a law, that only reinforces the point that the Fall represents a genuine discontinuity in the history of the earth—in short, that a uniformitarian approach is sterile in the light of the picture given to us by Scripture.

Obviously, according to Whitcomb and Morris, all strata bearing fossil animals date from after the Fall, since there was no death prior to that point. However, despite the advent of death and the other above-mentioned changes, there was little significant geological activity after the Fall and before the flood. This was due in part to the absence of rain before the flood and the absence of violent air movement (because of climatic effects of the vapor canopy). There was thus little erosion, sedimentation and so forth, and by this time there was little remaining crustal movement, such as earthquakes, volcanoes or other tectonic activity.[11]

The vapor canopy continued to serve a number of crucial functions. Again, the resultant greenhouse effect moderated the global climate, but it also shielded the earth's surface from cosmic rays. Such shielding contributed to longevity (hence the great ages of the patriarchs), protected organisms from mutations and genetic degradation (hence the relative harmlessness of marriage to near relatives) and prevented fermentation and other similar processes.[12]

But eventually the vapor canopy was destabilized—possibly by either interstellar or volcanic dust triggering condensation. At that point the canopy collapsed, or, as Scripture puts it, the windows of heaven opened. Simultaneously, the water trapped in and under the crust, having been subjected to intense heat and pressure, exploded out of its pockets, shattering the crust at various points. That shattering gave rise to further violent crustal activity—volcanic and other—which Scripture describes as the breaking up of the fountains of the great deep. The devastation was global. Much, perhaps most, of the prior surface biology and geology was scoured away by the subsequent deluge and tsunamis. This incredibly destructive activity continued for perhaps up to five months.[13]

Despite the raging destruction, the results were not completely chaotic. Bottom-dwelling marine organisms were killed first by the forces involved in the underlying tectonic breakup and were the most likely to be buried and eventually fossilized. Shallower-living organisms were at next risk as walls of sediment being ripped from continental surfaces slammed into the shallows. Some land creatures could temporarily escape destruction—at least until the flood waters and tsunamis overwhelmed even the highest ground. In general, the order of destruction and burial, and subsequent fossilization, was governed by three principles. First was ecological zonation: the lower one's habitat (from sea bottom to mountaintop), the sooner one was likely to be killed and buried. Second was mobility: the greater one's ability to escape to higher ground, the longer one could stave off the inevitable. Third was hydrological sorting: the denser and less buoyant and the more streamlined and less subject to currents one was, the sooner one was likely to sink and be buried.[14] Thus although there were thought to be numerous exceptions (which evolutionists tried to finesse by such ad hoc mechanisms as geological overthrusting), the fossil record had a rough quasi-order from simple and smooth to complex and differentiated—precisely the order, according to Whitcomb and Morris, that one would expect from a global cataclysmic flood. In fact, the alleged tendency of "prehistoric" animals to evolve to huge size over time is probably explained by the greater ability of the larger individuals temporarily to escape the rising waters, which led to their being buried in higher strata. Conditions were ideal for fossilization: quick death, rapid burial and no scavengers.[15]

Several months later the waters receded, in part by reevaporation, in part by a new round of geological activity pushing some land above the water. However, the ratio of land surface to water surface never reached the pre-flood level. Sediment rapidly hardened into stone, and the huge mats of vegetation that had been stripped from the land and buried began their rapid transformation into coal.[16]

With the canopy gone, or at least depleted, global temperature variations, air movement, seasons and other meteorological phenomena became vastly more pronounced. In fact, with the end of the canopy greenhouse effect, the world's only period of glaciation (there was at most one) may have occurred. Once a new atmospheric equilibrium was established in terms of all the new postflood conditions, the present global climate emerged and stabilized. Geologically the earth's crust may still be readjusting to the flood and to postflood changes. Plants spread over the new continents, and animals began a rapid dispersal from Mt. Ararat. With the canopy and its protection gone, both humans and animal species probably experienced some genetic degeneration at this point. (It is *kinds,* not species, that are fixed. In fact, following the flood the number of land species actually may have increased.) Removal of the canopy and the consequent increase in cosmic rays reaching the earth's surface may have also temporarily accelerated rates of radioactive decay. But as vegetation re-covered the earth, oxygen production increased, and the resultant ozone layer began to provide partial protection once again.[17]

This picture, Whitcomb and Morris contend, explains the existence of huge fossil beds, the prevalence of sedimentary stone in most places on the earth's surface, quick-frozen mammoth remains in Siberia and Alaska, the rough order of fossils, evidence of huge ancient lakes, raised river terraces, distribution of oil fields and other gross features of the geological record. It would also explain the quantity of atmospheric helium, the level of sea salinity and other such physicochemical data. In their view, such things can be accounted for only by unimaginably powerful and widespread catastrophes. They cannot be explained in terms of slow, gradual, uniform, ongoing geological processes—especially since, Whitcomb and Morris argue, none of the relevant processes seem to be operating now. There are no known places where coal and oil are now being formed, where fossils are in process of formation, where continent-sized glaciers or lava fields are being formed, where thousand-square-mile overthrusts are being produced. Present, uniform processes, then, simply do not provide the catastrophic resources that even uniformitarian geology must—inconsistently—appeal to for its own alleged explanations. Creationist catastrophist flood geology thus does a better job of creating systematic and logically consistent explanations of the raw data than does any sort of evolutionary uniformitarianism.[18]

Although creationists since the early 1970s have consistently referred to their position as "creation science" or "scientific creationism," Whitcomb and Morris did not seem terribly concerned during the 1960s about whether their views fit some technical definition of science. In fact, *The Genesis Flood* generally reads as though they thought their views did not. They defined *science* simply as "knowledge"—such knowledge, however, including only what could be proved by the scientific method. That method, they insisted repeatedly, could properly deal only with present processes and presently reproducible experimental results. That meant that historical geological investigation of the prehuman past (or the unrecorded past) could not count as science.[19]

In addition, they considered unprovable assumptions and presuppositions to be philosophy rather than science. But both approaches to the past, creationist and uniformitarian, were based on deep assumptions—assumptions that not only were unprovable but were chosen on moral, even spiritual grounds. Both dealt with prehuman history, and both dealt with unreproducible phenomena. Thus, said Whitcomb and Morris, "neither procedure is scientific." It was not merely that historical geology happened to fail to be science; it *necessarily* failed to be science. In fact, given its unreproducibility, the only possible means of learning about the earth's history was revelation. Knowledge of the prehuman past was possible, but such knowledge demanded a prior acceptance of the claims of revelation.[20]

But Whitcomb and Morris attempted to make their system as much science as such a topic permitted. Although taking account of the miraculous and of divine intervention, they did not just say "Miracle!" or "Well, God did it somehow" or "Must have been some unique unknowable process here." Within the constraints they saw Scripture as setting, they tried to provide natural explanations appealing to recognized natural processes. Recall, for instance, the appeal to various possible natural triggers of the condensation of the vapor canopy. Scripture does, on their view, identify some breaches of natural causal order. But having once located those breaches, they attempted to explain what parts of them they could and to trace out what consequences they could in terms of known laws and processes of nature.[21]

In any case, the ultimate issue wasn't whether it was strict science or not, or which outlook provided the neatest interpretation of the data. The ultimate issue was a spiritual one. Scripture portrays the flood as a divine judgment. So denying the flood was not just a geological matter, it was buying into an implicit denial of God's activity in human affairs and an implicit rejection of ultimate human accountability. Similarly, evolution was not simply a biological matter. What Darwin did was to plug one of the most gaping holes in the broad atheistic uniformitarian scheme of reality—the diversity of life and the origin of humans. In giving it the prestige and apparent authority of science, Darwin made that scheme much more powerfully attractive. And that made unbelief that much easier and more comfortable. So as Whitcomb and Morris saw it in 1961, maybe *The Genesis Flood* wasn't absolutely pure science. But if it was not science, that was because it was even more important than mere science could be.[22]

### 1974: Scientific Creationism

This somewhat unconcerned position of the mid-1960s began to alter by the early 1970s. Creationists had once again set their sights on public-school classrooms. One of the organizations that had formed in the aftermath of *The Genesis Flood*—the ICR—had been organized primarily to produce creationist education materials. Its first major effort, Morris's 1974 *Scientific Creationism,* was consequently published in two editions—a "general edition" for specifically Christian audiences and a "public school edition" designed to be acceptable in the public-school classroom.[23] Some significant shifts were involved. In *The Genesis Flood* Whitcomb and Morris had said that "the basic argument of this volume is based on the presupposition that the Scriptures are true" and that "our conclusions must unavoidably be colored by our Biblical presuppositions and this we plainly acknowledge." Indeed, they had suggested that to take their approach one "must also *first* be convinced" (my emphasis) that the early chapters of Genesis were "genuine divinely-given testimony concerning terrestrial and human origins."[24] And as a result of the unreproducibility of the past and the inescapable role of presuppositions in thinking about the past, studies of prehistorical events and processes had been denied full scientific status. But now not only was this creationism *scientific* creationism, as the title indicated, but it could stand completely independently of Scripture. (That contrasted with *biblical* creationism, which did rest explicitly on Scripture.) As Morris put it, "*Scientific Creationism* (General Edition) is essentially identical with the public school edition, except for the addition of a comprehensive chapter which places the scientific evidence in its proper Biblical and theological context."25 So Scripture was now apparently a scientifically dispensable addendum. The gain, though, was that a creationist picture could be advanced as legitimate science purely on science's own terms.

Further, whereas in *The Genesis Flood* the creationist framework was assumed for spiritual and philosophical reasons and the task was merely to show that the data could be "oriented" within that framework, now the data were taken as independent scientific *evidence* for creation.26 In *The Genesis Flood* Whitcomb and Morris had claimed that they needed only to show that it was "reasonable and possible" to construe the data in a biblically creationist direction.27 The task Morris now faced in *Scientific Creationism,* however, was the more demanding one of constructing positive empirical argumentation for creationist conclusions independently of Scripture. Although he does not explicitly appeal to Scripture (prior to the last chapter), it is evident that the structure of the guiding theory is the one developed in *The Genesis Flood* on an explicitly Scripture-driven basis.

However, the arguments that result from trying to turn the previous mere consistency of data into independently supporting evidences often seem fairly tenuous.28 For instance, the derivations of the "waters above" (vapor canopy) and the "fountains of the deep below" are quite strained, and a Tower of Babel explanation (minus the actual tower) of the diversity of languages is asserted with hardly even a pretense of argumentation, except for the unsupported assertion that "there really seems no way to explain the different languages except in terms" of divine action. "Tradition," Morris says, locates this occurrence "near Babylon." And although Morris does not appeal explicitly to Scripture, he appeals to "historical tradition" in locating the flood survivors near Mt. Ararat.29

Morris presents a variety of arguments and evidences against both an old earth and biological evolution. The arguments and evidences include claims that evolution faces problems involving the well-established Second Law of Thermodynamics, arguments that the staggering complexity of living systems having arisen by random chance is essentially mathematically impossible, the stubborn persistence of gaps and jumps in the fossil record, the apparently astonishing continued well-being of "living fossils," proposed evidences of contemporaneous existence of humans and dinosaurs, arguments involving space dust, ocean chemicals, human population growth, harmfulness of mutations, purported decay of the earth's magnetic field, flaws in radiometric dating and others.[30] Morris continued to keep his distance from Price's earlier claim that there was basically no order in the fossil record, although Morris did insist that the order was merely a general order to which there were important exceptions and that in any case the fossil progression did not indicate ancestral development. And by the time of *Scientific Creationism,* Morris had settled on a correlation between the standard geological periods and the various phases of the flood.[31]

Morris also seemed to have temporarily changed his position concerning the Second Law of Thermodynamics. In *The Genesis Flood* he and Whitcomb presented the Second Law, or at least the processes operating according to that law, as part of the "bondage of decay" resulting from the Fall. But in *Scientific Creationism* Morris claimed that one of the triumphs of the creationist picture is that "the creation model . . . *predicts* [Morris's emphasis] this decay law," since "directional changes in an initially perfect system are bound to be in the direction of imperfection."[32]

In *Scientific Creationism* Morris also continued development of the "two model" approach, which had been hinted at but not very clearly laid out in *The Genesis Flood.* The two-model idea has often been misconstrued as primarily involving two competing scientific theories—a broadly Darwinian (or neo-Darwinian) theory of biological evolution and an empirically based young-earth special creation theory. However, the two models are not scientific theories but are two broad styles of construing the world, with associated styles of theorizing—in effect, worldviews.[33] Unfortunately, many popular creationists use the term *evolution* to refer both to the larger philosophical worldview model and to the more restricted biological theory. That has created confusion among their opponents as well as among their own sympathizers (more later). But as at least some creationists see it, the two sorts of evolution are deeply connected, as follows.

Worldviews can be divided into two very broad basic types. According to the first (evolution), material reality is self-existent, self-developed and self-governing from within itself. According to the second (creation), material reality exists and is governed from outside itself. Secular science has arbitrarily adopted as a philosophical policy to accept as scientifically legitimate only those scientific theories and principles that would fit into worldviews within the first category. The formal statement of that policy is a broad doctrine of uniformitarianism, according to which (as creationists read it) every scientific theory must simply assume that nothing beyond the natural is relevant to the rational scientific explanation of anything. Secular science, then, has chosen to confine itself to theories that are compatible with the philosophical naturalism of the first category of worldviews. Biological evolutionary theories and historical geological theories are the sorts of science that those naturalistic worldviews demand. And since they are deliberately structured in conformity to the uniformitarian demands of such worldviews, they too have philosophical naturalism inherently built into them. Acceptance of such theories, then, involves acceptance (perhaps unwittingly) of that built-in naturalism as well. Thus acceptance of old-earth theories—which ultimately rest on a uniformitarian rejection in principle of the very possibility of divine intervention in the earth's history—really ultimately amounts to at least practical acceptance of philosophical naturalism and the whole philosophical evolutionary worldview.

So when Morris claims that the geological ages and evolution are synonymous,[34] what he actually means is that since old-earth views rest on an a priori rejection of the possibility of divine activity in geological history, in accepting that view one is thereby accepting the idea that the cosmos is self-existent and self-governed—that is, one is accepting the philosophical underpinnings of a naturalistic evolutionary worldview.

Creationists furthermore frequently argue that if the scientific playing field were leveled—if the scientific theories of biological evolution and old-earth geology were not preferentially protected behind the motherly philosophical skirts of uniformitarianism and actually had to face data on the data's own terms—they could not empirically survive that unprotected confrontation.[35] (And beyond the merely empirical, creationists of course accept what they see as clear scriptural grounds for believing that on at least three historical occasions God interrupted and permanently altered the natural governance of the cosmos. Thus any picture generated under this broad uniformitarianism inevitably is either incomplete or else partially inaccurate.)

Again, the creationist use of *evolution* in the two different senses—uniformitarian, naturalistic, cosmic developmental worldview versus Darwinian biological theory—has created confusion and misinterpretation. Creationists do use terms like *philosophy of evolution* and *evolution in the broad sense* to refer to the worldview, but they also use less clear terms like *total evolution* and even completely ambiguous terms like *evolutionary system,* often without specifically indicating what such terms are supposed to mean. Critics frequently have taken all such terms to refer to the biological theory—with consequent serious misconstrual, as will become evident later.

Although neither of the two models is, according to Morris, purely scientific in that neither can be confirmed or falsified scientifically, both do generate predictions in terms of which one can compare and evaluate the models, and that comparison and evaluation can be done *scientifically*.[36] The evolution model, says Morris, would predict that there would be continual changes in natural law, stars, galaxies, geological processes and in the biological realm. Species would blend into each other, mutations would be beneficial, and complexity would always be on the increase. The creation model, on the other hand, would predict stability of natural law, of stars and of galaxies. Species would be distinct, mutations would be harmful, and stability or even degeneration would be the only pattern over time. The data, argues Morris, clearly favor the creation model.[37]

### 1987 (Revised): *What Is Creation Science?*

Despite achieving a wide creationist popularity, the creationist empirical arguments of the 1970s—as presented not only by Morris in 1974 but by other creationist writers as well—were both strained and vague, and frequently rested on broad generalities that often exhibited an ignoring of technical details and data. Trying to deal with technical details and painfully precise data is what in fact often makes science such a tricky and difficult business. And creationists were frequently slow in recognizing that whereas casual fitting of loose and general data to vague theory is often relatively easy, getting the niggling details to work is the real key to science and is generally where the wheels fall off.[38]

But by the early 1980s, things in at least some creationist circles were beginning to change. The arguments in Morris and Parker's *What Is Creation Science?* were more clearly "scientific" than those of *Scientific Creationism* and had much less of the appearance of makeshift attempts to mirror Scripture without mentioning Scripture, with whatever materials came to hand. The arguments were more sophisticated, at least attempting to come to grips with technical scientific detail. There were more specifically biological arguments against evolution (compared to the previous overwhelming focus on geology), and the arguments exhibited a deeper familiarity with technical biological detail than previously.

For instance, one of Parker's arguments (surrounded by some technical detail) went roughly as follows. Amino acids perhaps can be formed by naturally occurring means, but their "natural" chemical modes of interaction are not those required for life—indeed, they are typically destructive of life processes. Amino acids interact in life-essential ways only when their interactions are driven against the grain (so to speak) of normal chemical processes by biologically structured processes and contexts. But if that is so, then obviously life—biology—could not have been generated by and hence have emerged out of purely chemical and physical processes. Hence, life could not have emerged unaided out of any purely natural, material, non-biological background.[39]

Whether the argument ultimately stands up or not, and whether Parker's reasons for thinking amino acids behave as stated ultimately hold up or not, this is certainly a far cry from most earlier popular creationist efforts. Parker went on to present other arguments involving, for example, homologies, mutations, distribution patterns of organisms having hemoglobin, convergent evolution, evolution of complex systems apparently requiring precise multiple simultaneous independent development, and other matters involving at least some technical biological details.[40]

The move in a more thoroughly empirical direction and the attempt to gain access to public-school classrooms presented creationists with a rather fine line to tread. In order for the issues to have the deep significance creationists attributed to them, they had to be inextricably linked to religious, spiritual matters. In order to be legitimate candidates for public-school science class discussions they had to be purely scientific as well, and thus, on popular public definitions of science, had to be detachable from spiritual, religious or philosophical matters.

Morris and Parker attempted to stay on that fine line by arguing that while both models are worldviews and are thus beyond science when taken as wholes, each incorporates scientific features and implications that can be compared and evaluated apart from any deeper philosophical or religious matrix in which they may be embedded. Thus

> each model is essentially a complete worldview, a philosophy of life, of origin and destiny. Neither can be either confirmed or falsified by the scientific method, since neither can be tested or observed experimentally, and therefore they must both be accepted on faith. Nevertheless, each is also a scientific model, since each seeks to explain within its framework all the real data of science and history.[41]

And the relevant scientific issues and implications "can be discussed completely on the basis of scientific data, without reference to their philosophical implications, and thus . . . can appropriately be discussed and evaluated in public schools solely in terms of their respective ability to explain data."[42]

The distinction between scientific creationism and biblical creationism was now firmly in place, and in contrast to the insistence (in *The Genesis Flood*) that one could not get things right without a prior acceptance of Scripture as revelation, there was now a flat, almost outraged denial that Genesis played any role in the scientific case being made for creation.[43]

### The Present

The creationist movement has not remained static over recent years. Some changes—like the emergent distinction between biblical and scientific creationism just discussed—have not directly affected the content of creationist views. But those views have experienced change too. Some of the changes are fairly widespread within the movement, and some are associated with an important division emerging within the movement.

Microevolution—evolution within kinds, perhaps even involving the emergence of new variant species by means of natural selection—is now nearly universally accepted among creationists. The very early creationist denial of any pattern at all in the fossil record has given way to an admission that there is a general, overall order (with some prominent exceptions)— but an order that is not indicative of ancestral descent. In addition, some creationists have begun to abandon earlier denials of overthrusting in some key geological instances. Many have given up on claims of mixed dinosaur and human fossil footprints. Various traditional creationist objections to evolution (based on biochemistry, on entropy and the like) have become a bit more sophisticated.

Some of the scientifically least-defensible objections to uniformitarianism (such as those based on alleged changes in the velocity of light) have begun to meet serious opposition within the creationist community itself. Various creationists have begun trying to do creationism on a thoroughly rigorous scientific basis, and some of the results (such as those connected with stacked petrified forests, lake sedimentation patterns and processes) have been scientifically interesting.

So in recent years, at least to some degree, the movement has begun to turn a corner away from some aspects of its past. The move is not necessarily away from a picture something roughly like that depicted in *The Genesis Flood,* but away from easy, sometimes uncritical defenses of that picture, and away from easy, sometimes inaccurate criticisms of evolutionary theory. Unfortunately, some of the popular and most visible segments of the movement have not always been very involved in that transition. And, also unfortunately, large numbers of well-intentioned lay Christians have been convinced by popular creationist writers and lecturers that one can in an evening master some obvious commonsense facts that expose the utter silliness of evolution—facts that despite their complete obviousness even to people with no science background at all have allegedly somehow totally eluded those with Ph.D.s in geology and biology.[44] But there is barely beginning to emerge a new generation of creationists with legitimate and relevant credentials who are undertaking to actually do some of the painstaking, detailed drudgery that underlies any genuinely live scientific program.

This emergence has begun to produce a separation in the creationist movement—an upper and lower tier, so to speak. I think that what ultimately separates the two tiers is different levels of respect for accuracy and completeness of detail, and different levels of awareness that a theory's looking good in vague and general form is an enormously unreliable predictor of whether in the long run the theory will be disemboweled by recalcitrant technical details. That appreciation is something that typically comes only with a legitimate scientific education, which some of the creationist popularizers and many in their audiences lack.[45]

Here is a simple example of how vagueness versus precision makes significant differences. Suppose a theory says that if we add chemical A to chemical B, the mixture will become hot. If we mix them, and the mixture heats up to anywhere between, say, 150 and 300 degrees, that heating can be cited as confirming evidence for the theory. Suppose now that we make the theory a bit more specific: if we add A to B the mixture will generate a 175-degree temperature. With this new, more specific theory, nearly every temperature between 150 and 300, except for a few right around 175 degrees, now constitutes a *problem* for the theory, rather than confirmation. The point is that it is relatively easy to fit a wide range of data to a vague theory, whereas increasingly precise theories make the data-theory fit increasingly difficult.

Even if the theory is precise, if our data are imprecise the same sorts of situations arise. If the theory predicts 175-degree heating, but we test the heat only by sticking a finger into the mixture, a fairly wide range of temperatures will seem like confirmation. Once we put a thermometer into the mixture, however, most of the temperatures that passed as confirmation with the finger test will now be exposed as actually disconfirming the theory. The point is that while data-theory fit is relatively easy if either is vague, increasingly precise data and increasingly precise theories make the data-theory fit increasingly difficult.

Popular creationist theories are often in the "it'll get hot" category, and popular creationist confirmations are frequently in the "it feels hot to my finger" category. And popular creationists frequently fail to proceed to the tougher tasks of producing precision and dealing with irritating details. Here is a simple example. The presentations of one of the most popular creationist lecturers in the United States contain a frequently repeated phrase—the fossil record is one of "billions of dead things buried in rocks laid down by water all over the earth." He claims, without argument and without any further detail concerning precisely what either the rocks or the burials should look like, that this is exactly what one would expect from the flood. He leaves the impression, in effect, that geologists and evolutionists are blind for not seeing that this is compelling evidence for a global flood.[46]

If one wants more specific explanations, creationists typically appeal to ecological zonation, hydrological sorting and mobility. Of course, those principles themselves are thoroughly imprecise and address only the most general of the fossil record features. (Incidentally, so far as I know, creationists have never pointed to a single instance of a modern flood that sorted the animals it killed.)

Here is simply one example of one detail that popular creationists, to my knowledge, have never so much as mentioned, but for which ecological zonation and hydrological sorting are utterly irrelevant. An *encephalization ratio* is a measure of the ratio of brain size to body size. It has nothing whatever to do with overall size, shape, streamlining or anything of the sort. Yet many lines in the fossil record exhibit a progression in encephalization ratio.[47] Talk of "billions of dead things buried in rocks" is simply too over-generalized to be of much scientific relevance here. And recall that the global flood idea was in trouble with geologists—many of whom were also clergymen and had no antireligious agenda—long before Darwin, natural selection and so forth. Perhaps those geologists should not have abandoned the flood explanation. But the troubles involved *details* of the geological record. None of those geologists had somehow just missed the general fact that there were "billions of dead things buried in rocks laid down by water all over the earth."

(The same thing could be said for some popular evolutionist arguments. For instance, some evolutionists explain the stubborn persistence of fossil gaps in terms of inherent imperfections in the fossil record. That record is no doubt imperfect. By some estimates we have fossils of less than 1 percent of all species that have ever lived. But the problem with the proposed blanket explanation is that it turns out that there is a specific pattern to the imperfection, a pattern that one would not expect on a straightforward Darwinian view.[48])

The newly emerging upper tier of the creationist movement, however, seems to have little patience with the vague popularized treatments and is, again, undertaking to do the meticulous detail work that a genuinely scientific creationism requires. As yet, this upper tier is not associated with any particular organization. Some work representative of this emerging group has been published by older-line creationist periodicals, and some of the individuals involved still have some links to older creationist organizations. But those organizations as a whole are still well within the lower tier. (The Geoscience Research Institute, which over many years has done much of the really legitimate creationist-related science, remains curiously invisible outside Seventh-day Adventist circles.) Also firmly within the lower tier are virtually all of the popular creationist writers and speakers, although a very few might be classified as borderline cases.

Although it is a bit too early to tell much, some shape is beginning to emerge. A loose coalition is forming around a few key books—*The Mystery of Life's Origins* and *The Creation Hypothesis,* for instance. (Some other works, such as Johnson's *Darwin on Trial* and Denton's *Evolution: A Theory in Crisis,* have served as catalysts.) Most of this group's present work seems to fall into three areas: (1) constructing a competent philosophy of science defense for the legitimacy in science of the hypothesis that life embodies design and structure not well accountable by purely natural means; (2) exploring detailed technical—and perhaps ultimately intractable—problems with attempts to explain relevant data, structures and events (like the origin of life) by purely natural means; and (3) attempting to construct rigorous, legitimately scientific positive cases for creationist positions (such as design theory) in various areas of conflict with mainstream theory.

It is, again, a bit early to tell where all this may come out. But those in the emerging upper tier are starting out with serious credentials (Ph.D.s from Cambridge, Harvard, the University of Chicago and Berkeley, for instance) in relevant areas (such as philosophy of science, paleontology, chemistry, mathematics) and with a recognition that shortcuts will not do. Future work produced—whether right or wrong—is not likely to be either uninformed or more polemical than substantive.[49]

Having in the preceding two chapters seen the basic framework of creationist views, we now turn to look at how various of those views have been misconstrued or overlooked by many critics of creationism.

# 7 CREATIONIST THEORY
## Popular Evolutionist Misunderstandings

**A**s we saw in chapter four, creationist criticisms of evolutionary theory are often irrelevant simply because they are based on misunderstandings of that theory. But creationists are not alone here. Arguments raised against creationism also often rest on misconstruals of the targeted positions, and such arguments are often likewise irrelevant. In this chapter we will examine a variety of such misconstruals.

Actually, the confusion in some sources sympathetic to evolution extends even to evolutionary theory itself and sometimes includes some of the same misconstruals of evolutionary theory found in creationist writings. Such misconstruals range from the obvious (linearity, progressiveness, directionality) to the relatively more obscure (that greater similarity always indicates more recent divergence).[1] That is not, however, particularly surprising, since many proevolution writers (editors, "humanists" and even such science popularizers as Isaac Asimov and Carl Sagan) are not biologists. Indeed, even high-school biology texts have sometimes been written by professional authors rather than by professional scientists. However, we shall not pursue that further.

### Microevolution and Macroevolution
Evolution is sometimes defined as a change in gene frequency within a breeding population. Nice examples of such changes are numerous, perhaps

the most famous involving the peppered moth. This moth comes in two color schemes—a darker and a lighter. In the industrial heartland of nineteenth-century England, the darker sort was substantially more common. The explanation was that it blended into the sooty environment much less obtrusively than the lighter sort, which was much more at risk of being picked off and eaten by birds. However, with the coming of environmental legislation, industrial pollution was significantly reduced, the tree trunks on which the moths roosted became less sooty and lighter, and suddenly the darker version began to stand out while the lighter version began to blend in much more nicely. Birds adjusted their sights accordingly, and within a relatively short time the lighter version, now having a better chance of escaping being eaten long enough to reproduce more effectively, became predominant. A shift in gene frequency within the peppered moth population, from darker genes predominating to lighter genes predominating—in short, evolution—had occurred before our very eyes.

This sort of shift is often termed *microevolution* and is distinguished from *macroevolution,* which involves more major shifts from one kind to another or across higher taxonomic categories. Some evolutionists object to the distinction, claiming that all evolution is microevolution and that macroevolution is typically not qualitatively different, but merely involves an accumulation over time of a quantity of microevolution. However, the distinction does occur quite frequently in both creationist and evolutionist writings and is, I think, ultimately harmless, so I will adopt it for convenience.

The creationist position (and it can be found in creationist writings from the 1940s to the present) is that microevolution is undeniable.[2] Furthermore, natural selection is often taken to be the mechanism driving microevolution.[3] However, creationists disagee on the specifics. Some take natural selection operating on mutation (perhaps divinely ordered) to be one possible mechanism.[4] Others take natural selection operating on precreated resources within the existing gene pool to be the mechanism.[5] (On this view, the peppered moth population, for example, might have been originally created with genes both for lightness and for darkness, and natural selection simply picks between those already existing genetic resources as circumstances warrant.) Some earlier creationists cited some sort of hybridization.[6]

But while they embrace microevolution, creationists staunchly reject any macroevolution. Microchanges may accumulate over time, but there are boundaries beyond which they cannot go.[7] Thus, on the creationist view, microevolution cannot give rise to macroevolution, and the two are not merely quantitatively different. In fact, on the creationist view macroevolution—by whatever means—simply never happens.

### Kinds

That raises the question of exactly where creationists place the uncrossable boundaries. The basic creationist answer is that microevolution can never cross the boundaries of *kinds* (the more technical term is *baramin*).[8] Kinds are considered to be fundamental units of the original creation. Very roughly, a kind consists of all the organisms that are descended from some originally created organism (or pair of organisms), roughly similar to some versions of the contemporary *clade* concept.[9] There is no absolutely settled creationist position concerning how—or even if—the "kind" classification relates to standard taxonomic categories such as genus, family and so forth. Some have suggested family; others have suggested that it might be genus in some cases, family in others or even species in some special cases.[10]

Unfortunately, although the intuition is relatively clear, the most authoritative definition among popular creationists is the following: "A kind may be defined as a generally interfertile group of organisms that possesses variant genes for a common set of traits, but that does not interbreed with other groups of organisms under normal circumstances."[11] Under this definition a kind is generally at least as narrow as a species, which is precisely the opposite of the usual creationist claims.

Regardless of what such definitions might imply, creationists agree nearly unanimously that there is no simple correspondence between kinds and species. That has a number of consequences, first for anticreationist representations of what creationism is and second for some of the arguments advanced against creationism.

*1. Evolution.* If evolution is defined simply as shifts in gene frequency within a population, then most creationists accept evolution.[12] Creationists are, again, perfectly happy to admit—even insist—on microevolutionary shifts. What they object to is not such shifts (evolution, on this definition) but only what seems to them to be unwarranted extrapolation of microevolution to macroevolution—of extrapolation from changes within defined groups to changes across such groups.

*2. Direct creation of all species.* It is frequently claimed that according to creationists, all species were directly created by special acts of God.[13] Contemporary creationists do not hold that view, and some creationists had already abandoned it roughly half a century ago. Since creationists accept microevolutionary development within the boundaries of created kinds, and since kinds at least in some cases include multiple species, some creationists accept the view that descendants of some originally created organisms radiated out into different species, although all such species would still be within the same kind as the original parent organisms. Indeed, given the latitude of the *kind* concept, and given that creationists limit microevolution only to within the boundaries of kinds, microevolution can in principle have a very wide range. Morris sometimes allows common ancestry to extend even above the level of species, and according to Dean Kenyon it is possible that "new species, genera, and occasionally even families, may have arisen by natural means."[14]

*3. Original presence of all species.* A related misconstrual is that according to creationists, all species—including all current species—were present on the originally created earth.[15] Creationists are not committed to that position. As indicated above, adaptive radiation and speciation subsequent to the original creation are consistent with the views of many contemporary creationists. On that view, some species present now might not have been present at the creation, although all kinds present now would have been. But again, kinds in many cases do not correspond to species.

*4. Fixity of species.* Perhaps the most common misconstrual related to the above is the claim that creationists hold that species are fixed and unvarying, and have been so since the creation. For instance, according to Theodosius Dobzhansky, "[creationists] fancy that all existing species were generated by supernatural fiat a few thousand years ago, pretty much as we find them today."[16] That, again, is simply not the case. (In fact, this quote embodies both the present misconstrual and the previous one.) Creationists do sometimes differ on the mechanisms involved in species changes (whether mutation or simply sorting and isolation from among precreated genetic resources), but among both major creationists and major creationist groups there is essentially unanimity that species were not all simply frozen at the creation. In fact, most major creationists hold other key doctrines that preclude such fixity, as will be seen shortly.

### Related Anticreationist Arguments

A number of the evidences for evolutionary theory involve evidences for speciation, such as the famous fossil horse series, the adaptive radiation of fruit flies in Hawaii and, earlier, Darwin's finches, mockingbirds and turtles in the Galápagos Islands. These are perfectly legitimate evidences, but evidence does not simply announce to us what it is evidence for. Particular data are given the specific evidential status they have in part by underlying assumptions within a broader interpretive system, and if those underlying assumptions are rejected there is no guarantee that the data will still have the same evidential status. In a different system the same evidence may seem to support some different theory, or it may even cease to be considered evidence at all.

Here is a simple example. In the early days of Copernicus's theory that the earth spins on its axis, opponents of that theory noted that birds did not get blown west at several hundred miles per hour whenever they released their grip on a tree branch. Given the physics those opponents accepted, if the earth was spinning the birds should have been blown away; so they took the fact that they were not as overwhelming evidence for their own theory that the earth was not spinning. Of course, we cheerfully accept the fact that birds do not get blown west, but we no longer take that fact as evidence for the earth being stationary, in large part because we have adopted a different background system of physics. The point is that what something is or is not evidence for is in part a function of the broader conceptual system, or conceptual grid, into which it is being placed.

That has some consequences for the present case. It is perfectly rational and scientifically legitimate for evolutionists to take cases of microevolution and related speciation as indirect supporting evidence for macroevolutionary theory. However, that does not in the slightest make it automatically illegitimate for creationists to deny that microevolutionary data supports macroevolutionary theory. It only properly constitutes such support if extrapolation from the micro case to the macro case is legitimate, and that is precisely what creationist presuppositions call into question.

If creationists denied microevolution, then the above evidences (not to mention the peppered moths) would indeed constitute serious problems for them. But creationists accept it. What they reject is the extrapolation. Thus, to refute creationism on this point takes more than merely pointing to the data of peppered moths, fossil horse sequences and Darwin's finches.[17] There is simply no disagreement there. It requires making a case for the legitimacy, indeed the necessity, of the extrapolation. Making such a case may be perfectly easy—but it must be made before mere citation of the data can have compelling weight.

## Thermodynamics

Perhaps the most prevalent of the misconstruals of creationism involves the Second Law of Thermodynamics. There are several ways of stating the Second Law, but for present purposes the following intuitive characterizations will be adequate. In a system that neither loses nor gains energy from outside of itself (a closed system), although the total amount of energy within the system remains constant, the proportion of that energy which is no longer usable within the system (measured as entropy) tends to increase over time. An equivalent formulation is that in a closed system there is over time a spontaneous tendency toward erosion of a specified type of order within the system.[18]

Creationists nearly unanimously claim that this Second Law poses a nasty problem for evolution. Unfortunately, exactly what creationists have in mind here is widely misunderstood. Creationists are at least partly at fault for that confusion. One reason is that as noted earlier (chapter six), most popular creationists use the term *evolution* ambiguously—sometimes to refer to the cosmic evolutionary worldview (or model) and sometimes to refer to the Darwinian biological theory. Although a coherent position can be extracted from some of the major creationists (such as Morris, Gish, Wysong and Kofahl), this ambiguity has rendered some parts of their writings monumentally unclear. One has to read extremely carefully in order to see which *evolution* is being referred to, and some critics of creationism either have simply not noticed the ambiguity or perhaps have misjudged which meaning specific creationists have had in mind in specific passages. And critics are not the only people who have sometimes been bamboozled. Other creationists who take their cues from those above have also sometimes missed some of the key distinctions and have advanced exactly the original misconstrued arguments that critics have wrongly attributed to major creationists.

In a word or two, we have a four-alarm mess here. But let's see if we can clear up at least some of it.

First, when claiming that the Second Law flatly precludes evolution, major creationists almost invariably have in mind evolution in the overall cosmic, "evolution model" sense.[19] The clues to that meaning are the almost invariable use (especially in Morris's writings) of phrases like *philosophy of evolution* or *cosmic* or *universal* or *on a cosmic scale*. The universe as a whole system is taken to be a closed system (classically), and according to the creationist definition of *evolution model,* that model is unavoidably committed to an internally generated overall increase in cosmic order, since on that view reality is supposed to be self-developed and self-governing. What Morris and others mean to be claiming is that any such view according to which the entire cosmos is itself in a process of increasing overall order is in violation of the Second Law.[20]

Critics of creationism almost without exception take this initial creationist claim to be about purely biological evolution on the earth and respond that the Second Law applies only to closed systems, whereas the earth, receiving energy from the sun, is thermodynamically open.[21] But since the system actually in question here is the entire universe, which is the "prime example" of a closed system, the response that the Second Law only applies to closed systems is beside the point creationists mean to be making in this case. That is not to say that the creationist argument is ultimately correct here, but only that if it is defective the problem is not the one initially proposed.

When discussion turns to evolution in the more restricted sense—biological evolution on the earth—then obviously it *is* highly relevant to point out that the earth is not a closed system and that thus the Second Law by itself does not directly preclude evolution. But Morris, Gish, Wysong and others admit that, and have for decades, although not always in a terribly clear manner. How does that admission emerge?

Morris, for instance, claims in numerous of his writings that a system being open is not alone enough to cause a reversal of disorder or a decrease in entropy. There are, Morris claims, some additional requirements that must be met before that can happen. For instance, the flow of energy coming into the system must be adequate, and there must be some already-existing "code" and "conversion mechanism" by which the incoming energy can be harnessed, turned into some form that is useful and usable in the system, and then properly directed and productively incorporated into the system experiencing increasing order. These additional requirements are not requirements of the Second Law itself but are requirements that Morris thinks we have good empirical grounds for accepting. Simply throwing raw energy into a system generally does not produce increased order but destroys some of the order already there. So the view is that special conditions—codes, conversion mechanisms and the like—are needed before growths in order can occur even in open systems.[22]

That raises the question, How do these codes and conversion mechanisms themselves arise? Some creationists may hold that the Second Law itself

flatly precludes such codes and mechanisms arising naturally. Others take
the odds against the codes and mechanisms being generated naturally to be
massively overwhelming. But Morris says that the natural development of
such codes and mechanisms may, for all he knows, be possible, although
it is unlikely. So although the Second Law does impose some conditions,
and although other empirical experience seems to impose some additional
constraints, at least in principle, according to Morris, all of those conditions
and constraints can perhaps be met:

> It is conceivable, although extremely unlikely, that evolutionists may
> eventually formulate a plausible code and mechanism to explain how
> both entropy and evolution could co-exist.[23]
>
> This objection does not preclude the possibility of evolution.[24]
>
> It may of course be possible to harmonize evolution and entropy.[25]
>
> This of course does not preclude temporary increases of order in spe-
> cific open systems.[26]

Morris says similar things elsewhere—from at least 1966 on.[27]

So what, then, is the problem? A major one, according to Morris, concerns the required codes and mechanisms:

> No one yet has any evidence that any such things exist at all.[28]
>
> Neither of these has yet been discovered.[29]
>
> So far, evolutionists have no answer.[30]
>
> [The special conditions are] not available to evolution as far as all
> evidence goes.[31]

Notice the invariable qualifications: "yet," "so far" and so on.

And what that all means, according to Morris, is that "the necessary 'law'
of evolution, if it exists, still remains to be discovered and evolutionists must
in the meantime continue to exercise faith in their model in spite of entropy."[32]

Those last five quotes, incidentally, come from four different books written from 1972 to 1986, hardly an obscure brief departure from Morris's
usual views. And this same sort of view is found in Gish, Wysong, Pearcey,
Bird, and Kofahl and Segraves, from 1976 to the present.[33]

Unfortunately, Morris typically summed up this whole series of points by
suggesting—as in that last quotation—that the root of the whole problem
was entropy and the Second Law, and further, unfortunately, announced
that until evolutionists construct plausible theoretical conditions, creationists are "warranted" in using terms like *impossible*.[34] But that the Second
Law by itself precludes biological evolution is not (again unfortunately) a

completely accurate representation of what he meant. The situation has not been helped by the fact that other creationists, perhaps confusing the logic of the situation, have rehearsed Morris's or Gish's presentation of the above position, then still flatly claimed a "direct contradiction" or that the Second Law itself showed biological evolution to be "impossible."[35] Combining the creationists' inaccurate summations of their own position concerning biological evolution with their ambiguous use of the term *evolution* to mean either the philosophical model or the biological theory despite their different views concerning the Second Law in those two contexts, it is perhaps not surprising that Morris should find that among "leading evolutionist professors, . . . most of them do not seem to understand the problem."[36]

But critics are not completely without fault in all of this, and quite a number of critics apparently have not read Morris and others with sufficient care. A very typical misconstrual comes from John W. Patterson, who overlooks Morris's key distinction, consequently mistakes Morris's position, then uses that mistaken position as grounds for making some rather nasty accusations about the character of creationists. In one key discussion, Patterson presents two quotations from Morris's *The Troubled Waters of Evolution,* as follows:

> Evolutionists have fostered the strange belief that everything is involved in a process of progress, from chaotic particles billions of years ago all the way up to complex people today. The fact is, the most certain laws of science state that the real processes of nature do not make things go uphill, but downhill. Evolution is impossible! [p. 110]
>
> There is . . . firm evidence that evolution never could take place. *The law of increasing entropy* is an impenetrable barrier which no evolutionary mechanism yet suggested has ever been able to overcome. Evolution and entropy are opposing and mutually exclusive concepts. If the entropy principle is really a universal law, then evolution must be impossible. [p. 111][37]

Patterson then introduces the idea of open systems, accuses creationists of "deceit" and proceeds with the discussion.

But Morris has been misread here both times. In the first quote, the reference to *everything* being involved in progress, beginning with "particles billions of years ago," is Morris's signal that he is talking about the global evolution model—not merely local processes, as Patterson takes it to mean. In the second quotation, Morris *is* referring to "biological processes and phenomena." But notice that he explicitly refers to firm evidence here—this is not simply a derivation from the Second Law. The Second Law does present some problems—problems that no mechanism *"yet suggested"* (my emphasis) can overcome. All this is exactly in line with Morris's position on the Second Law and biological evolution sketched above. And even more telling, less than a dozen pages earlier in the very book Patterson is quoting from, Morris had flatly stated: "It may of course be possible to harmonize evolution and entropy by imposing special conditions on the systems affected."[38] Those conditions are the "code" and "mechanisms" mentioned earlier. Morris had again argued that mere openness of a system was not a sufficient condition for decrease in entropy, and then noted that "so far, evolutionists have no answer to such questions."[39]

If I am reading all of this correctly, in the first quotation Morris had applied the Second Law to the entire cosmic system—which Patterson himself described as the "prime example" of an isolated system, and "the only kind to which Clausius's Laws apply."[40] In the second quotation Morris is referring to the open biological system but is claiming that there are some additional empirical constraints beyond mere openness of system necessary to generate reversals of entropy, and that no evolutionist has "yet suggested" a plausible way of dealing with those constraints. Patterson misreads Morris both times, points to the possibilities of open systems—which Morris had admitted a dozen pages back—and accuses creationists of "deceit" and of "distort[ing] the subject to their own advantage." Elsewhere he raises the suspicions of creationists "knowingly telling 'whoppers' " here in keeping with their "long tradition of 'whopper'-telling and obfuscation" and notes that for creationists mere ignorance of thermodynamics would be a "marked improvement."[41] (Many critics, not understanding that the "open system" response does not damage Morris's actual position, take Morris's refusal to alter his position in light of that response as further evidence that creationists never change their views.)

Perhaps the most puzzling misconstrual on this topic is that of Delos McKown, who claims that the creationist objection here is that "there never has been and is not now enough energy to power evolution."[42] I do not know of a single creationist who has ever presented that objection, and McKown provides no references. In fact, some major creationists state explicitly—and repeatedly—that quantity of inflowing energy is not the problem at all.[43]

None of this is to say that Morris's uses of the Second Law are without problems. (And his views may be changing away from the foregoing picture.[44]) But if there are difficulties, misconstruals such as the above will not locate them.

### The Universe as Fully Functioning

The principle that the universe was created fully functioning has an extremely long history. As discussed briefly in chapter six, contemporary creationists accept the idea and conclude from it that at least some appearance of age is absolutely unavoidable in a fully functioning universe, even were it in fact created only moments ago.[45] Any humans would have the appearance of some age or other, and if such humans were expected to care for the creation, harvest food for themselves and so forth, the apparent age would have to be at least beyond infancy. Similarly, if the world were created as ecologically fully formed, plants would unavoidably have to have the appearance of varying ages. And if God wished to present the new humans with a dazzling stellar night sky involving a wide variety of objects at genuinely stellar distances, he would have to either sit and wait millions of years for the light to arrive at the earth or else create light in transit—again, giving the appearance of age.[46]

Creationists differ concerning how far one should take this idea. Some appear to think that appeal to apparent age should be kept to the absolute minimum required by considerations like those in the previous paragraph—only to those instances where the very existence of a fully functioning young creation makes it inevitable.[47] Others are willing to employ it on occasion as an optional explanatory device. For instance, as noted earlier Whitcomb and Morris suggest that radioactive materials may have been created complete with apparent daughter decay products, as if those materials had already been decaying over some long stretch of time.[48] Were that the case, radiometric dating would typically indicate ages much greater than was actually the case.

*1. Missing the principle.* Critics of creationism, however, frequently miss this component of creationist views. Sometimes the miss is egregious, sometimes more subtle. Here is an example of the first sort from Dawkins:

> [The young-earth claim] is incompatible, not only with orthodox biology and geology, but with the physical theory of radioactivity and with cosmology (heavenly bodies more than 6,000 light years away shouldn't be visible if nothing older than 6,000 years exists, the Milky Way shouldn't be detectable, nor should any of the 100,000 million other galaxies whose existence modern cosmology acknowledges).[49]

A more subtle version comes from Frank Sonleitner. Speaking of similarities and variations across organisms in cytochrome c, Sonleitner says: "Thus, if all these forms were created a short time ago by an intelligent, rational creator, cytochrome c should have an *identical structure* in all these forms!"[50] There are several underlying presumptions here, but one of them is that any variation in cytochrome c had to begin from square one at the creation. Looser versions of the "fully functioning" view at least allow the possibility of some variations being embedded within the initial creation.

Now, one might not like that concept, but one does not have the right to simply ignore it and construct criticisms that depend on ignoring it.[51] One might consider the concept in some way inappropriate or argue that it is not legitimately scientific—on grounds of nontestability or of improper supernaturalism, for instance. Perhaps so. But that is a different matter, and that case must be made. But one cannot do as, for example, Humphries does, admitting that it is logically impossible to tell the difference between an old earth and a young earth with the appearance of age, then five sentences later suggesting that science "shows clearly that [the earth] is very old," concluding that young-earth views thus "cannot be correct."[52]

*2. Deceit.* Nearly every anticreationist objects (many almost bitterly) to the apparent-age implications of the creationist doctrine of full functionality, claiming that it threatens to make God into a deliberate deceiver.[53]

But we need to be a bit careful here. Exactly why would apparent age be deceit? Rocks and fossils do not come with an age stamped on them. The age we assign to them is a result of application of theory, interpretation of various features and so forth.[54] Suppose that we are wrong and that fossils and so forth really are young. Why should we hold God morally responsible for *our* having made some mistaken theoretical interpretations? Or do we presume that our theories are so good that we are correctly interpreting what the rocks and fossils actually say—so that if they do not mean what we think they say about their age, then their Creator is responsible for their prevarication? Either way looks a bit intellectually shaky.

Suppose, furthermore, that creationists are right—as I think they are— that instantaneous creation of a large-scale, fully functioning universe could not help but exhibit apparent age in at least some respects. In that case, how might a Creator prevent scientific creatures of that universe from being misled? One obvious way would be simply to tell them (even indirectly) how old things really were. And that, claim creationists, is exactly what God has done in Scripture.[55] One might not like that claim, or might argue that we cannot appeal to such claims on scientific matters, but, again, one cannot lodge the moral objection of deceit while ignoring the full creationist position here.

As a simple example, take the case of Eve on a creationist reading of Genesis. Eve presumably had the appearance neither of a fertilized egg nor of a newborn (though her true age was essentially zero), but of some more advanced age. But that would hardly seem to imply that God was engaged in some sort of deceit toward Adam here. Given that Adam called her "woman" because "she had been taken out of man" (despite his having slept through the operation), he evidently was informed in some way of what had happened. In that sort of case, the mere existence of apparent age did not imply deceit.

Thus to make the case linking apparent age and deceit stick here, anti-creationists have a bit more work to do. Perhaps that work can be done. But that is a different issue.

(There is one further oddity about this issue. Numerous theistic evolutionists make this same "deceit" claim. Yet many of them do not charge God with deceit over the fact that our moral and spiritual interpretations of the world are routinely drastically wrong. Why should it be a more obvious ground for a deceit charge that our human scientific theories might be wrong than that our human moral and spiritual theories might be wrong— especially since the latter are for the Christian ultimately more important?)

### Effects of the Flood and the Fall

According to creationists, both the Fall and the flood involved major, global changes in geology and biology. Critics of creationism frequently ignore those aspects of creationist positions, constructing criticisms that are often consequently irrelevant. Some examples follow.

*1. Flood waters.* Some of the criticisms here are simple misrepresentation. For instance, Harris constructs an imaginary classroom dialogue in which it is supposed that if there really are "waters above," astronauts and their spacecraft would no doubt puncture the celestial dome and create the flood all over again.[56] Creationists, of course, claim that the canopy, having collapsed in connection with the flood, is no longer there. The criticism is thus irrelevant. (And what creationist believes in a dome, anyway?)

A fairly common criticism of creationist flood geology involves noting that Genesis 7:19 indicates that the waters covered "all the high mountains," citing creationist literal interpretation, then calculating how much water would be required to cover the entire planet to a depth twenty-two feet higher than Mt. Everest. The answer, which is staggering, then becomes grounds for further objections—such as that if the extra water was in a vapor canopy, the atmospheric pressure required to hold it up would have been crushing, and the energy released by the fall of that water would have effectively incinerated the earth.[57]

Criticisms of that general type may well be legitimate, but not in their present form. Nearly all creationists believe that the geomorphology of the earth is vastly different now from the way it was prior to the flood. According to creationists, the flood involved massive tectonic activity (the breaking up of the fountains of the deep, Gen 7:11) and was followed by a period of intense mountain building (the waters fled, the mountains rose, and the valleys sank down, Ps 104:6-9). Thus present mountains and past mountains were not the same, and, in fact, many creationists argue that the earth displayed much less variation in altitude then than now. Thus problems based on calculating the amount of water necessary to cover present peaks will not automatically show any internal difficulty for creationist theories.[58]

*2. The ark.* Conditions on the ark form the basis for another group of objections to creationism.[59] Sometimes the misconstruals are relatively insignificant (Diamond has Noah in the ark for only forty days and nights, and Scott overlooks the presence of Noah's three daughters-in-law on the ark[60]), but others are serious enough to undercut the criticisms involved. For instance, given the number of species in the world, ark crowding is a perennially favored problem. However, creationists were long aware of the potential difficulty here and have a number of standard responses. One involves attempts to show that once the detailed calculations concerning volume, number of species, species size and needs and so forth are actually done, the problem disappears.[61] Another, which goes back at least half a century, is based on the now-standard creationist acceptance of microevolution within kinds. The idea is that the ark needed to carry only adequate representation of the various *kinds,* which could after the flood give rise by microevolution and speciation to the full present range of species within the respective kinds.[62]

However, that creationist view is often overlooked. For instance, Kitcher cites the slowness of some Australian marsupials, arguing that they could not have traveled from Ararat to Australia quickly enough after the flood.[63] Fezer wants to know what the anteaters ate immediately after coming off the ark.[64] But creationists are not necessarily committed to either anteaters' or slow marsupials' being on the ark. Given that for creationists only kinds must be represented, and that some species within kinds arose later by microevolution, one cannot simply arbitrarily pick a species (or genus or perhaps even family), assume that creationism includes that species (genus, family) as being on the ark, and generate a problem based on those assumptions.[65]

This objection comes in varied forms. For instance, every human parasite and disease organism, some objectors claim, must have been on the ark (making things rather unpleasant for Noah and family).[66] Quite a number of responses are possible here, but the one used above can be advanced here also. Only the basic kinds need have been represented, with full speciation coming later. In fact, just as bees are all of a kind but only some sting, parasite species might be of kinds that also have benign variants, those being the ones on the ark. And who said that the post-Fall ark was a pleasure cruise anyway? The animals were the guests; humans were the deck hands.

There might, of course, be other difficulties with this sort of solution (such as the high rate of postflood speciation necessary—although that is less of a problem with some organisms[67]), and if such are legitimate difficulties, they should be pressed. But again, that is a different criticism. One cannot simply ignore the creationists' proposed solution when constructing the initial criticisms.

*3. The Fall and death.* According to creationists, one major episode in earth history was the Fall. The Fall triggered some major changes: suffering, carnivory, degeneration, harmful mutations and death. According to at least some creationists, the traits required for carnivory and other such antisocial behavior resulted from post-Fall mutation.[68] For such theories, criticisms that creationist claims about God's goodness conflict with the idea of God's having deliberately created such traits and creatures misses the mark, as do claims that on creationist views every biological structure must have some created purpose.

The creationist view that death entered the world only at the Fall has consequences as well. For instance, there could be no animal fossils predating the Fall (although things like fossil trackways would presumably still be possible), much less dating to the creation. And according to most creationist views, there should be few fossils prior to the flood. Despite that, one still finds statements like the following in such otherwise reputable sources as *The American Biology Teacher:*

The creationist hypothesis implies that all living things should be traceable through a series of unchanged fossil ancestors back to the creation date. No new forms should appear after the date of creation, nor should any present day organisms exhibit significant differences from their fossil ancestors.[69]

Here in two sentences we have fixity of species, denial of speciation, all species present initially, death from the creation and fossilization from the creation all attributed to creationism, which explicitly denies every one of them.

*4. Design flaws.* One extremely popular objection to creationism is that organisms often exhibit what initially appear to be design flaws, or at least designs that appear to be less than optimal. (Indeed, such objections go back to Darwin.) Surely, the objection continues, a perfect designer would not produce imperfectly designed organisms.[70] (Evolution, it is argued, accounts nicely for such apparent design flaws. Natural selection can work only with available materials and often has to jury-rig some existing trait into a different function—for example, a wrist bone was the only available resource for constructing the panda's "thumb." The "thumb" works, but an omnipotent, omniscient designer starting from scratch and with no limitations would have done better than a stopgap makeover of a wrist bone.)

This point does carry some weight. But creationists do have a response here, and whether or not the response ultimately works, one cannot simply ignore it. The response is that design imperfections are not part of the original creation plan but are design degradations stemming from the Fall.[71] The mechanism may well be mutation and natural selection—and if so, design imperfections are evidence for microevolution. But creationists accept microevolution. Thus at least some of these apparent design flaws can be incorporated straightforwardly into creationist views, with creationists having neither to deny the suboptimality (which can be done in some cases) nor to give up their basic design claims. Of course, one could perhaps argue that this proposed explanation will not work for some cases. Perhaps so, but that requires an additional case.

## Other Misconstruals

The above examples represent the major popular anticreationist misconstruals of creationist positions, although there are others. One critic claims that creationism predicts both that some species will have different genetic codes and that "protein structure will depend upon conditions of life."[72] Although those ideas are consistent with creationism, they simply do not follow from any known creationist doctrine. Others assert that creationists have "no consistent explanation for fossil stratification"—without even mentioning creationist explanations involving ecological zonation and so forth. Such explanations may not work, but one cannot simply ignore them without comment if the issue is whether or not creationists have an explanation.[73] Another critic cites *Scientific Creationism* as "an authoritative statement of creation-science doctrine" and charges that creationists argue that "disproof of evolution is proof of creation"—despite the fact that the first chapter of the cited work says that "neither can be proved" and that "there is no observational fact imaginable" that cannot be reconciled in one way or another with both models.[74] Others confuse Cuvier and Agassiz, and confuse the views of one or the other of them with those of contemporary creationists.[75] Still others confuse the present creationist mature-creation idea with the nineteenth-century views of Phillip Gosse, even though there are significant differences.[76] (Many of them get Gosse incorrect as well.) Others claim that creationists appeal to miracles to explain "all phenomena."[77] Still others accuse creationists of "denying the existence of fossils."[78] Oddest of all, perhaps, is the *HarperCollins Dictionary of Biology*'s definition of special creation: "a theory of evolution that postulates the formation *de novo* by an all-powerful creator" (p. 498). Obviously, criticisms that rest on misconstruals generally establish nothing whatever.

Of course, none of this implies that creationism is right, consistent or anything of the sort. It may have all sorts of radically severe and totally destructive difficulties. But one cannot show that this is the case independently of doing the actual homework of getting the view straight to begin with.

# 8 PHILOSOPHY OF SCIENCE
## The Twentieth-Century Background

**A** *number of significant issues in the creation-evolution dispute hinge* on exactly what science is or is not. For instance, various creationists maintain that evolution is not science, basing that conclusion on a particular definition of science. Opponents of creationism (and various federal courts) frequently charge that creation science is not genuine science but is thinly disguised religion. That conclusion, too, is based on a particular conception of what science is and is not. Questions concerning proper definitions and conceptions of science, how it works, why it works, what it can and cannot in principle tell us and so forth are the proper domain of philosophy of science.

The proper definition of science was not discovered carved in stone somewhere or in the bottom of a test tube. It has, indeed, taken a number of centuries for humans to learn what is now known about how to investigate nature. Scientists have had to learn by trial and error what sorts of questions can be addressed to nature, how to put those questions into nature's language and how to read nature's answers to those questions. In part, humans have had to (slowly) learn from nature itself how to investigate nature. The historical scientific process has involved not merely discoveries about nature but also discoveries about how to investigate nature.

As one would thus expect, conceptions of science and scientific method have sometimes changed historically, just as scientific theories themselves have changed over time. And, in fact, those changes frequently have been linked. Things that have been learned concerning the what and how of nature have sometimes had consequences for the what and how of investigating nature. And changes—sometimes philosophically driven—in theories about the what and how of proper scientific investigation have had effects on which theories about nature have been accepted.

In this chapter we will briefly survey changes in conceptions and definitions of science, focusing primarily on this century. As we will see later, standard dictionaries (which are, of course, written by fallible humans and are far from inspired) and many of the more vocal figures on both sides of the creation-evolution dispute seem to be unaware of the results of several decades of recent research into the nature of science, its history and of scientific method.

### The Traditional Framework

Many of us were raised with a fairly high view of science—or at least a high view of science as it was supposed to be done. We were presented with a picture of the scientist as passionately committed to discovering truth, but as pursuing that truth in an utterly dispassionate manner strictly according to the dictates of scientific method. Why was method so important?

As long ago as the fourteenth century it had become clear (or at least seemingly clear) that humans had various tendencies that were not to be trusted. Our emotions, hunches, religious prejudices, traditions, philosophies and perhaps even reason simply were not always reliable guides when it came to grasping the inner workings of the cosmos. These unreliable, scientifically counterproductive human tendencies had somehow to be kept from contaminating science and preventing it from getting at truth. By the sixteenth and seventeenth centuries, many thinkers believed that the most effective way of doing that was in terms of precise and rigid rules of procedure—rules rigorous enough to guarantee that any of these underhanded and subversive human tendencies were excluded from the scientific process. These rules of procedure, designed in part to screen human subjectivity out of science, came to be known as "the scientific method." The necessity of such a method appeared to many to be a major implication of the sharp contrast between what seemed to be the sterile scientific muddles of the medievals and the explosive scientific advances of the seventeenth century (by Galileo, Kepler and, later, especially Newton).[1]

Of course, volumes could be and have been said about "the scientific method"—whether or not there is or ever was such a thing, whether it did or even could work as advertised, whether there was some single method ("the" method), what it was supposed to look like in precise technical detail and so forth. But the core aim, arising largely in the sixteenth and seventeenth centuries, was to formulate a means by which the pursuit of truth about nature could be freed from human limitations and fallibility. Such a means, were it available, would be nearly transcendent in its capabilities, and from at least the eighteenth century on some regarded science in more or less transcendent terms.[2]

But what exactly was this method, and what principles provided its foundations?[3] First, science was supposed to be thoroughly *objective*. It was supposed to function totally free of human speculation, choice, politics, preference, emotion, bias and preconception. Over time, many demanded increasingly insistently that philosophy, metaphysics and in particular religion not be allowed to gain any sort of foothold or influence within the processes of science. The more mechanical the procedures of science could be made, the better.

Second, science was supposed to be *empirical*—grounded on empirical data and empirical data alone. Empirical data seemed to be ideally suited to serve as the foundation of an objective science, because, at least supposedly, observation was purely neutral, purely objective, reproducible and shared, in the sense of being the same for all similarly situated observers. The physical senses seemed to be simply neutral faculties for registering, without comment or editorial, various aspects of nature. The senses presented to us what was out there, whether we liked it or not and whether it destroyed our favorite theory or not. And the senses presented the same data in the same circumstances to every normal person. They thus provided the same objective messages direct from nature to everyone. If science was based on empirical data, then we all had a common set of touchstones dictated by nature, and if we insisted that our theories grow out of and conform to those nature-dictated data, then nature itself—and not we humans—had the final say concerning our theories. And having our theories about nature controlled by nature was the ultimate in objectivity.

Third, science was supposed to be utterly *rational*. Even if we began from empirical data dictated by nature, we could still go wrong in our theorizing from that data unless we were extremely careful in how we got from those data to the theories that were the end product of the scientific enterprise. Thus the processes of theory construction, theory evaluation, theory testing and theory acceptance had to be protected from the infection of human subjectivity, bias, blindness, distortion and dishonesty. The way to do that, it was thought, was to demand that all scientific processes be rigorously logical, mathematical and rational so that there were no cracks through which human subjectivity could force an entry. If one began with absolutely objective nature-dictated data, then proceeded by absolutely rigorous logical processes from that point, one could be confident that the end products—theories—were also free of any distorting human taint. They would be the indirect objective dictates of nature herself. Thus no conclusions, no theories, were to be accepted unless they were the logically implied, rigorously confirmed, empirically proven outcome of the scientific method. Such results would be impervious to any assault. Here at last would be truth that could be trusted, free of human self-deception—a place to stand.

This sort of view was attractive because it promised a means of surmounting human limitations. And to many it had a further attraction as well—one clearly visible as early as the eighteenth century. The exclusion—in the name of objectivity, rationality and truth—of any legitimate role in science for anything nonempirical, such as metaphysical or philosophical principles, also ruled out any legitimate role for religion, theology or Scripture. The implication was that genuine science need not, should not and indeed could not take any notice of religion and Scripture when going about its lawful business.

### Inductivism: Bacon and Early-Twentieth-Century Positivism

Although various parts of the above picture of science have roots going back even as far as the Greeks, the most influential early statement of such a view came from Francis Bacon in 1620.[4] According to Bacon, one had to begin by assembling a substantial collection of empirical data, gained both from ordinary observation and from experimentation. The collected data had to be organized and classified in specified ways. Bacon then outlined a process of *induction,* which involved a variety of procedures designed in effect to strip off nature's complications and lay bare the basic, simple governing principles of the physical realm. When this inductive process had been completed from an adequate empirical base, those fundamental governing principles were supposed to emerge in a nearly mechanical fashion. Follow the proper cookbook rules, and nature revealed her secrets.[5]

And this picture seemed to work in many cases. For instance, gas law equations correlating temperature, pressure and volume apparently could be derived simply through the collection of lots of experimental measurements, observation of the patterns of relationships between various particular temperatures, pressures and volumes, then construction of general equations through a simple logical extension of those patterns.

This picture of proper science became powerfully influential and provided some of the components of early-twentieth-century positivism. The underlying ideal, here again, was that science was thoroughly empirical and nonspeculative and that it proceeded systematically, methodically, according to specified rules, with every move rationally justified in terms of an inductive logic. Philosophical, metaphysical or theological principles, hypotheses, flights of fancy—indeed, anything not ultimately empirical—were to play absolutely no role in the processes of science. This in fact is the picture of science one typically finds in dictionaries, in older science texts and in some contemporary writing.

Unfortunately, it has some rather severe, indeed fatal problems.[6] Although there are a number of major technical problems with the view, we will consider only one here. While it may be possible, with some relatively simple assumptions, to extend patterns found in specific collections of empirical data into generalizations concerning that sort of empirical data, there is simply no known rigorous logical procedure by which *theoretical* principles can be inferred from empirical data. Specific data collected from experimental observations may exhibit patterns that would rationally justify one in drawing the general conclusion that at specific temperatures, gas pressure is always correlated in a particular way to volume. (Even here, however, in drawing the general conclusion that this relationship holds even for samples of gas not tested, one is relying on several assumptions—particularly the uniform operation of laws of nature.) But there is no known logical procedure by which one can rigorously infer directly from empirical data the theory that gases are composed of unobservably small bits of matter with complicated properties and behaviors. In general, genuine scientific theories involving unobservable, theoretical entities and processes cannot be logically inferred from empirical data alone. More specifically, there is no formal logical procedure by which the theory *explaining* some collection of empirical data can be inferred from those data themselves.

That presented a serious difficulty for Baconian "inductivist" views, because well before the twentieth century, science had taken a definite theoretical direction. Science now dealt with atoms, fields, genes, entropy, the prehuman past—all sorts of nonobservable things. Indeed, according to contemporary physics some theoretical entities (such as unbound quarks) are *in principle* unobservable. If there was no rigorously logical way to generate such theories purely from empirical data, then either such theories were not legitimate parts of science, or this view that science properly included only what could be rigorously logically generated from empirical data was itself simply mistaken.

Various scientists and philosophers tried various responses to this dilemma. The physicist Ernst Mach, for instance, concluded that theories about invisibly small atoms were metaphysical, not scientific, and thus had no place in genuine science. Others argued that theories that seemed to refer to unobservable things like atoms really did not imply their existence at all or were perhaps just misleading forms of speech.[7]

But it seemed to many people, including many positivists, that theories involving unobservable theoretical objects and processes had become so crucial to science and to scientific explanations that they had to be admitted as legitimate.

### Hypothetico-Deductivism

Scientific theories, then, dealt with unobservable objects and processes and could not be derived by formal logic from empirical data alone. How then could they be incorporated into science in a way that did not sacrifice the empirical, objective and rational character that science was supposed to have? Making it all worse was the realization that not only did theories not arise from data by any straight logic but in fact they were *creative inventions* of human scientists. And who knew what sorts of wild, unruly things went into the human inventive process? Genuine science apparently could not operate without theories. In fact, theories were in some respects the centerpieces of science. Yet these theories originated from processes seemingly completely unsusceptible to rigorous rules—from creativity. How could science take the products of such human creative processes into its very heart and survive as objective, rational and empirical?

The answer that various positivists adopted came to be known as the hypothetico-deductive method of confirmation.[8] According to this view, a theory did not gain its legitimacy from its *origin* as a logical implication of empirical data but rather from the accuracy of its empirical, logical *consequences*. The way it worked was roughly as follows. A scientist trying to explain some collection of data could propose any old theory he or she might wish, for any reason or for no reason. Source and origin made no difference whatever. The scientist would then test the theory by logically or mathematically deriving from the theory various empirical or experimental predictions. For instance, a prediction might stipulate that if the theory was right, specified sorts of experiments should yield specified sorts of results. The scientist would then perform the experiment(s) and observe whether or not the empirical predictions of the theory were correct. If they were, then the theory was considered to have been confirmed to at least some degree by the data. If the theory's predictions were mistaken, then the theory would be in trouble. So the scientist would propose a hypothesis (a provisional theory), then deduce empirical consequences from the theory—hence the name *hypothetico-deductive.*

For example, when Newton proposed his laws of motion, Edmund Halley derived from them the prediction that a previously observed comet should again be visible at a specified time. When the comet (since named for him) showed up on schedule as predicted, that successful prediction was taken as confirming Newton's theories. Or in the twentieth century, Einstein's theory of relativity generated a prediction that light should bend when traveling through an intense gravitational field. That prediction turned out to be correct and was accepted as confirming Einstein's theory. On the other hand, the astronomer Kepler worked for years developing a mathematical theory concerning the motion of Mars. Unfortunately, at one point the theory predicted a position for Mars that was off by a small fraction of one degree of arc. On the principle that if the theory predicted any empirical data that (although extremely close) were not exactly accurate, then the theory itself must be wrong, Kepler junked years of his own work and began again.

The hypothetico-deductive method had several attractions. First of all, it allowed full legitimacy to theories in science. Such key parts of scientific understanding as atomic theory did not have to be rejected as metaphysics, as Mach had thought. And despite the presence of human creativity in the invention of theories, science retained its basic character. It was still empirical in that the predictions in terms of which a theory was judged were empirical predictions. It was still rational in that the predictions were generated logically or mathematically, and when a theory was rejected it was on the basis of neutral, shared empirical data that were logically inconsistent with the theory and its predictions. And it was still objective in that nature had the last word on the fate of a theory, in terms of whether the theory's predictions did or did not turn out to be true of nature.

The human creative process was still involved in theory formation, but any wild or unobjective factors in that process were now quarantined by the hypothetico-deductive method. Nothing depended on how or why the theory was originally proposed. So when Copernicus proposed his theory of the solar system in part because of his deep adherence to Neo-Platonic philosophy, or when Kekule's theory of benzine rings arose from a flash of insight connected to a daydream he had before the fire, that did not disqualify the theory from consideration. It simply made no difference. The only thing that counted was how nature, via neutral, objective, empirical data, treated the theory—either confirming it or contradicting it.

Unfortunately, the hypothetico-deductive view ultimately was not completely satisfactory either.[9] For instance, since any theory has an unlimited number of empirical consequences, it is impossible to test all of those consequences. This means that in principle it is always possible that next week, next year or next century some new data will come to light that will contradict the theory's predictions. The upshot is that no theory can ever, even in principle, be proven conclusively to be true. There is always the chance that at some point in the future it will have to be abandoned. Thus the theoretical results of science are always unavoidably tentative. So although a theory may be very well confirmed, it never can be conclusively confirmed.

We intuitively feel that some theories are better confirmed than others. If that is right, that would mean that confirmation comes in degrees. Historically, many people have thought that part of being rational was ensuring that the strength of one's belief in a theory matched the degree of confirmation of the theory. That would mean, of course, that we would need some sort of logic system that could tell us the degree to which a given collection of empirical data confirms a given theory. Various people did extensive work trying to develop such a logic, but simply were unable to do so. It may well be that there can be no such logic. So scientific theories could not be logically *proven* in terms of their predictions and consequences, and there seemed to be no rigorous way of even deciding to what degree these unprovable but scientifically essential theories were confirmed.

But the worst was yet to come. As it turns out, any given collection of empirical data is always consistent with and can be explained by any number of distinct, alternative theories.[10] (This point was noted at least as early as the thirteenth century.) Some of the alternative theories may be simple and some dreadfully complex, but multiple alternatives are always possible. This is true no matter how large a set of data one has. We may be able to think of only one theory consistent with all the relevant data (or maybe no one can think of any), but that has to do only with our abilities—not with the logic of the situation.

As a simple analogy, think of a theory as a line passing through dots on a graph, the dots representing bits of data. No matter how many dots one puts on the graph, there will always be an unlimited number of lines that will pass through them all. Some of the lines may be elegant and smooth and some may look like spaghetti, but that is a different matter. Similarly, an unlimited number of theories will be consistent with any collection of data, no matter how large.

The history of science contains a number of nice examples here. For instance, right after Copernicus proposed his theory of the solar system, the astronomer Tycho Brahe proposed an alternate theory that, it could be shown mathematically, was observationally indistinguishable from Copernicus's. Every bit of data predicted by Copernicus's system would be predicted by Brahe's, and vice versa.

Of course, in the graph case we may prefer one sort of line to others, and in the scientific case we may prefer one sort of theory to the others, but that is of no relevance to the truth or falsehood of the theory unless we have some philosophical grounds for thinking that nature's preferences and ours are similar.

This fact—that no matter how much data one has there are always multiple possible alternative theories—is often expressed by saying that empirical data *underdetermine* theories. That implies that empirical data alone can never uniquely confirm just one single theory from among empirically equivalent alternatives. Data alone can never provide us with any grounds for choosing one theory over alternative theories that are consistent with all of the same data.

This means that if we do choose one of the theories and claim that it is really true, our choice must depend at least partially on nonempirical factors, whether philosophical, theological, societal, personal or whatever. Often such choices rest on considerations of *simplicity* or *elegance* or even *mathematical beauty* (although just exactly what those terms mean in the scientific context is disputed, to say the least). For instance, Copernicus's system was favored over the earlier Ptolemaic system in part because of a complicated collection of properties usually described as *simplicity*. But of course, the claim that nature prefers the simple over the complex among empirically indistinguishable theories is itself a philosophical claim—and one that not everyone thinks is true.

Again, given the underdetermination of theory by empirical data, if we wish to pick out one theory and claim that it is true, that claim must rest in part on factors beyond mere empirical data. We thus have a choice. Either we give up any hope that science can justify our claim that we know various theories to be actually true, or else we give up the view that science is completely empirically driven. In either case, we must give up the old claim that science presents us with objective proof of its theories. In light of that, what could be salvaged of the traditional shiny image of science?

### Falsificationism

So scientific theories cannot be rigorously proven to be true by experimental results or other empirical data. Indeed, given that any possible set of data, no matter how extensive, is consistent with an unlimited number of alternative theories, it is difficult to see how empirical data alone could even provide grounds for thinking that a particular theory was *probable*. Perhaps science had to give up any dreams in that direction.

But it appeared that science could at least expose the inadequacy of mistaken theories. Theories whose empirical predictions turned out to be wrong were evidently thereby empirically *falsified*. Science could still progress in the sense of discovering and giving up theories that were falsified by the data. Indeed, in the view of Karl Popper, for example, nothing was truly scientific unless it was at least in principle capable of being falsified either directly or indirectly by empirical data. Thus in order to be properly considered a part of science, a claim had to be honestly at risk from potential empirical data. There had to be some way at least in principle of allowing nature not only to confront the claim but to contradict the claim empirically. So science retained some of its traditional character in that the little that could still in principle be confidently said about specific theories—that they were false—was rationally dictated by nature via empirical data.[11]

As it turns out, though, popular falsificationist doctrines have some serious difficulties. (Popular falsificationist views almost always invoke Popper's name but do not accurately reflect his views, as we will see.) A major problem, and to many a surprising one, is that it is impossible to *conclusively* falsify any scientific theory by means of empirical data. Not being able to prove theories true was a nasty blow to the old view of science as objectively and empirically rigorous. Not being able to prove theories false was little short of disastrous.

Why can scientific theories not be empirically proven to be false? The immediate reason is this: theories by themselves do not generate empirical predictions and thus cannot even be tested directly. The predictions of a theory are typically of this sort of logical form: in a specified situation with specified starting conditions, values measured with specified instruments operating in specified ways will be of specified magnitudes. For instance, some atomic particle theory might tell us that if we begin with a certain type of particle in a particular state, kick it through a linear accelerator, then capture it with some sort of particle detector, the detector will measure a particular value of a specified property of that particle. Now, in order for the theory's prediction to be tested in that experimental situation, there must be some basis for believing

(a) that the derivation of that prediction involving the theory is logically or mathematically correct;

(b) that there really is a particle there;

(c) that the particle is of the requisite sort;

(d) that the particle is in the assumed initial state;

(e) that the accelerator is operating as designed;

(f) that all of the theories (particle, electronic, engineering and so on) involved in our views about what happens inside an accelerator are correct;

(g) that the detector is operating as designed;

(h) that all of the theories (engineering and so on) involved in our views about what happens inside the detector are correct;

(i) that our reading of the apparatus's measurements is accurate; plus

(j) some other things that we will skip.

Now, suppose we run the experiment and things do not come out according to prediction. What has gone wrong? It might well be that the theory being tested is wrong. But it might be that something on the above list has gone wrong. And notice that (b), (c), (d), (f) and (h) depend heavily on various scientific theories. But scientific theories, recall, are never proven, so no matter how confident we are about the theories that our experiments and predictions depend on, there is always at least an outside possibility that one of them is mistaken and we just do not know it yet. So even if a prediction turns out to be flatly contrary to nature, that does not yet demonstrate conclusively that it is the theory being tested that is mistaken.

This does not mean that it is just a free-for-all. In derivations of predictions, scientists try to employ only other theories for which they have rational (though nonconclusive) reasons for considering true. Thus, if the predictions turn out to be mistaken, we will have rational (though nonconclusive) reasons for thinking that the problem probably lies with the theory being tested.

The fact that theories can be evaluated empirically only in terms of their empirical predictions and that deriving such predictions invariably requires employment of other theories, principles and assumptions guarantees the logical possibility that problems concerning the predictions may have their source somewhere other than in the theory itself. And that logical possibility removes the prospect of rigorous empirical proof of the falsehood of even the most woeful theory. Thus the view that the scientific method can at least conclusively eliminate mistaken theories and the view that being legitimately scientific requires being in principle conclusively falsifiable are both simply inadequate. The history of science is in fact packed with cases where predictions have gone wrong but where scientists, rather than giving up the theory in question, have challenged one of the other assumptions involved in the derivation of that prediction. (I will detail some examples later.) Rigorous falsificationism, then, fares no better under intense scrutiny than did the earlier views.

Notice that what had been happening was a gradual weakening of the high status accorded to science, its methods and its results. Science might still be the best we could do, but it no longer was seen as producing certainty or unshakable proof, either of truth or of falsehood. But at least whatever it did produce was still free of any taint of human subjectivity and immune to social, philosophical, political, religious or ideological influences, was it not? Science might no longer be epistemologically omnipotent—capable of unerringly leading us into all truth and knowledge—as various people had thought, but it was at least still epistemologically *pure.*

Or was it? Falsificationist views are almost universally associated with Popper, but almost all popular writers who appeal to him drastically misunderstand crucial and consequential aspects of his position. For instance, if being legitimately scientific required being scientifically at risk (falsifiable), then, as Popper himself pointed out, to be part of science even simple observational, empirical data statements had to be at risk as well. It had to be a genuinely open possibility that observational, empirical data could legitimately be repudiated, ignored or deliberately tossed out by scientists in the light of other scientific considerations. The positivists had argued that theories and hypotheses had to be evaluated in the light of empirical data. But if the data themselves had to be falsifiable in principle, in terms of what did one evaluate them?

Popper's position here was that scientists accept certain data by convention or by communal choice. So on a strict Popperian falsificationist view, what had previously been cited as the ultimate objective bedrock of science—empirical data—now became itself subject to human choice. The twin claims that only what can be falsified is scientific and that empirical data are scientific thus have unsettling implications. Nearly all the popular pushers of "Popperian" falsification have missed Popper here.[12]

So there were hints buried in Popper that empirical data are not the rock solid, secure foundations once thought. In fact, Popper himself rejected the picture of science as built on immovable, rocklike empirical foundations. The picture he preferred was that of a building erected on piles driven deep into a swamp. The piles never reach absolutely solid bedrock, but if there are enough piles driven deep enough into the swamp, the structure built on top will be stable enough for any reasonable purpose.[13] All of this, of course, was flatly contrary to the basic outlines of the traditional conceptions of science.

In fact, by the late 1950s and early 1960s, positivism, inductivism, hypothetico-deductivism, falsificationism and other traditionally flavored philosophies of science were increasingly rejected. Various key principles shared by these views did not seem to be working out right, and each of them faced nasty technical difficulties unique to themselves. But the culminating blow came from a slightly different direction, initially stated most influentially by Thomas Kuhn in his 1962 *Structure of Scientific Revolutions.*[14]

### Kuhn and Postempiricism

While nearing the end of doctoral work in theoretical physics, Kuhn became interested in some issues involving the history of science. As he probed more deeply into that history, it seemed increasingly clear to him that neither science nor scientists historically behaved in ways the above views of science might lead one to expect. For instance, scientists did not simply grind blindly and mechanically through data trying to get theories to emerge (inductivism), nor did they spend the bulk of their time trying to confirm proposed theories (hypothetico-deductivism), nor did they spend much of their time trying to show theories to be mistaken (falsificationism).

Worse yet, when confronted with empirical data that seemed to undercut accepted theory, they sometimes did not even notice the problem; and when they did, they frequently shrugged and continued to accept the theory anyway. For instance, Ptolemaic astronomy continued on in the face of known problems with empirical data for about fifteen hundred years. In one of his major works, Newton derived from his theory a value for one aspect of the moon's orbit, noted in passing that the value was about fifty percent off the actually empirically observed value, and continued happily on. Einstein, once asked what he would do if an upcoming experiment contradicted his theory's prediction, reportedly replied that if the experiment contradicted his theory then nature was wrong, because the theory was right. At the present moment, it has been known for decades that the two probably most respected theories in physics—general relativity and quantum mechanics—are mathematically inconsistent with each other. But no one is unduly alarmed and proposing abandoning either one. And the striking thing about this sort of behavior is that it was pervasive throughout science—these were not isolated aberrations. What on earth was going on here?

Kuhn concluded that communities of scientists work within the context of *paradigms*. In general terms, a paradigm is a normative conceptual framework within which scientific work is conducted and evaluated. More specifically, it is a meld of (primarily) four constituents: symbolic generalizations, metaphysical commitments, values and exemplars. For example, the Newtonian paradigm involved a number of Newton's equations (the symbolic generalizations), the presupposition that everything was composed of invisibly small bits of matter governed by absolutely deterministic natural laws (a metaphysical commitment), and an insistence that accuracy of prediction, measurability of results, observability of subject matter and so forth were marks of good science (values). (Newton himself did not accept all of these.) In various examples of Newton's work, one could see specifically how all those components worked together to define one's science (these examples being the paradigm's exemplars). A paradigm, then, contained not only conceptual categories, theoretical postulates and interpretations but also presuppositions concerning the world that those postulates were supposed to fit, how they ought to fit that world, proper procedures for trying to construct such fits and criteria for judging when such attempts were or were not successful.[15]

Most of the time, Kuhn argued, the scientific community worked within the boundaries of a generally accepted paradigm, and that paradigm defined what counted as a legitimate scientific problem and what sorts of proposed solutions to such problems were to be considered scientific. Since the paradigms involved thus defined what science was, there was little interest in trying either to confirm or to test the paradigm. It was simply assumed to be correct, and any apparent problems were considered to be just that— merely apparent and generally unimportant. During these periods of "normal science," scientists were interested primarily in extending the paradigm into new areas, in trying to figure out how to construct solutions acceptable within the paradigm's boundaries to scientific puzzles that still remained unsolved and in trying to clear up ambiguities within the paradigm itself.[16]

Occasionally, however, a paradigm would get into serious difficulty—for instance, there would be too many problems that apparently could not be solved in the terms that the paradigm allowed, or significant quantities of data contrary to the paradigm would accumulate to the point that they could no longer be casually ignored. When that happened, the scientific discipline involved in the problem would enter a crisis state, push the panic button and put serious energy into trying to solve the difficulties. Sometimes that worked, and solutions to the problems were found. Sometimes solutions would not emerge, but no one could suggest any alternative paradigms that could do any better. But sometimes when no solution was forthcoming in terms of the old paradigm, some promising alternative paradigm would be proposed, and the discipline would be converted to the new paradigm. This shift from old to new paradigm was what Kuhn termed a *revolution*.[17]

This may all appear quite commonsense and harmless, but that appearance is a bit deceptive. Paradigms, on Kuhn's view, not only shaped scientific problems, solutions, decisions and procedures but even partially shaped the scientists' very perceptions and observations. What one *saw* was to some extent a function of the paradigms one accepted. This powerful influence of paradigms had a number of important consequences. If different people operating with different paradigms to some extent experienced different perceptions, then observation could no longer function as a shared, neutral bedrock for science. And if paradigms involved metaphysical principles and values, and if those played a role in theory construction, theory evaluation and theory choice (as Kuhn argued), then even if two scientists in different paradigms could share all the same observational data, they might be unable to agree on the proper explanation or interpretation of that data. Worse yet, according to Kuhn, one's paradigm was interwoven even with what one understood various terms, including scientific terms, to mean. Thus two people immersed in different paradigms might not even be able to fully comprehend each other's theories and arguments. But since paradigms defined science, immersion in a paradigm was a prerequisite for even being a scientist.[18]

Most important, Kuhn argued that our human paradigms make some partial contribution to the world that we experience. Since the world of our experience is the only world to which we have any access, that would mean that scientists operating with different paradigms are in some sense working within different worlds. There would thus be no single world that all of us experience and to which we could all appeal as an objective, neutral arbiter of our scientific disputes (even if we could understand each other well enough to define our disputes properly).[19]

Kuhn did think that there were limits to how much effect paradigms could have in these various areas. But still, his view implied that there was no complete and independent world "out there" for science to investigate, no complete set of absolutely objective empirical data for scientists to appeal to in such investigation, no universally accepted neutral scientific method to pursue. And if scientific *Truth* was supposed to be about some objective world outside of us, then there would be no such truth. Indeed, Kuhn argued that *Truth* had no relevance to science at all.[20]

So whereas one of the underlying aims of inductivism and related views was to ruthlessly keep humans and humanness from infecting and infesting the purity of true science, Kuhn, or at least his more enthusiastic followers, planted humans so firmly in the middle of things that humanly chosen paradigms even partially constitute the very worlds that science investigates. A substantial number of those people who claim to be Kuhnians and who talk some sort of "paradigm" lingo have simply missed these consequences.

The general philosophy of science community, after a brief, albeit rocky honeymoon with Kuhn, pulled back a bit from several of Kuhn's positions. For instance, the key concept of a paradigm proved to be uncomfortably fuzzy on closer technical examination. Some argued that Kuhn's view of the history of science (which underlay several of his views) was not completely accurate. Challenges arose over the degree to which paradigms (and mindsets generally) affected perception and meaning. Serious objections emerged concerning Kuhn's claims of how paradigms partially constituted worlds. And claims that the concept of truth played no important role in science came under serious criticism as well. By the late 1960s and early

1970s, philosophy of science was clearly steering away from any sort of straight Kuhnianism.[21]

But Kuhn's work pointed to some crucial lessons that have been incorporated into more contemporary philosophy of science. Kuhn's work was first published several decades ago, but his influence and legacy are still substantial. Contemporary philosophy of science, including the lessons learned from Kuhn, is the subject of the next chapter. But briefly, what Kuhn did was to advance the idea that the involvement of things beyond merely the empirical is both inevitable and legitimate in science. We humans cannot even in principle avoid having various of our broad metaphysical and value convictions play some role in our science. Our senses and our reason are not simply detachable from deeper streams that flow within us, so we cannot construct a "pure" science employing only those detached faculties. This at least suggests the possibility that even political themes, religious themes or other things that deeply shape our being might have some inescapable, perhaps even legitimate role to play in our science and scientific theorizing.

# 9 THE NATURE OF SCIENCE
## A Contemporary Perspective

**D**espite *the contentions of Kuhn (and others) that Truth plays no* essential role in science, the majority of scientists and philosophers of science today accept some type of *realism*. Realism is, roughly, the view that there are genuine truths concerning nature, that those truths are independent of human beings, that human scientific theories can at least in principle be true, that many of our actual scientific theories are in fact true or roughly true, and that in some cases we can know (or at least be rationally justified in believing) that specific of our theories are true (such as that there really are atoms, DNA strands and so on). Most people intuitively accept realism, and most science texts assume some form of realism.

But as discussed in the previous chapter, since theories are inescapably underdetermined by empirical data, if we are going to select some proposed theories and claim that they are true, then that selection cannot be made on a purely empirical basis. At least some nonempirical considerations will have to play some role in that selection.

### Basic Components

Science, then, involves three basic types of components. Those three are data, theories, and the nonempirical, partially philosophical principles and factors that I will call *shaping principles*. One of the crucial lessons about science that have been learned in the twentieth century is that science could not even in principle function without this third sort of component. Another is that the source and character of various components of science are vastly different from what was traditionally thought. Let us briefly examine each of these components.

### Theories

As a rough-and-ready approximation, theories come in two broad types. The first group is generally referred to as *empirical* or *phenomenological* theories (or sometimes as empirical regularities or phenomenological laws). These involve postulated regularities within the empirical, observable realm, with no reference to underlying causes or explanatory mechanisms. Such regularities include, for instance, the uniform relationships among empirically determined features of gases (temperature, volume and pressure), which are encapsulated in Boyle's Law and Charles's Law. The second broad type is called *explanatory* theories. These involve postulated objects, events and properties which are typically not directly observable and which underlie specific empirical regularities or sets of natural events and constitute mechanisms that provide an explanation of those regularities or events. For instance, one can explain the empirically observed gas behavior described by Charles's and Boyle's laws in terms of events, properties and objects that are not directly observable—motions and specific interactions of gas molecules. Thus the explanatory theory that there are gas molecules and that they have certain properties and behave and interact in specified ways tells us why, or provides an explanation of, the empirical regularity that at a constant temperature the volume of a gas will decrease if the pressure is increased.

The distinction between these two types of theory is not completely precise. Experimental regularities can play an explanatory role in some contexts, and explanatory theories can be involved in explanations not only of empirical matters but also of other, less fundamental explanatory theories. But although not completely precise, the distinction is accurate enough to be adequate for present purposes.

The term *theory* as used in the scientific context has nothing to do with whether or not it has been tested, confirmed, refuted, accepted by scientists or rejected by scientists, or whether it is held only tentatively and provisionally by scientists or anything of that sort. It has to do only with its structure and how it functions within various scientific processes and contexts. Newton's theory of gravitation is exactly that—a theory. But when mountain climbing you would be well advised not to act as though it were merely idle, provisional speculation.

As discussed in the previous chapter, theories—especially explanatory theories—cannot be generated by purely logical or purely mechanical means from empirical data. They are a result of creativity and invention. As also discussed in the last chapter, theories cannot be either conclusively proven or conclusively disproven solely on the basis of empirical data. Indeed, scientists frequently continue to hold theories firmly even in the face of apparently contrary evidence.

And as we will see, the structure and character of specific theories, the concepts that they employ, their evaluation, and criteria governing their acceptability or unacceptability and their acceptance or rejection are all linked not only to data but also to the shaping principles one accepts. And those shaping principles do not emerge just out of empirical data either.

### Data

The previous chapter discussed two challenges that have been raised to the traditional conception of empirical data. First, Popper was driven to the conclusion that the judgment of whether or not something constitutes legitimate empirical data is not forced on us by nature but is in part a result of human choice. If so, empirical data will not be as purely objective as once thought. Second, Kuhn argued that the paradigms one accepted affected one's very perception. If so, empirical data are not as neutral, independent and dictated by nature as once thought.

Although there are problems with both Popper's and Kuhn's particular doctrines concerning empirical data, our experiences, even sensory experiences, do have some surprising overtones to them. For centuries perception and observation were thought to be purely passive processes—an external, independent nature simply imprinted various information on our minds via the senses, and the observer had no role in the process other than being the passive recipient. As it turns out, that apparently is not the case. There is more of the observer involved than just mechanically operating sensory faculties, and that involvement, although perhaps preconscious, is an active involvement. In many cases of perception, we unconsciously "fill in" various aspects of our own experience, generally without realizing it, and the shape that this filling takes is molded in part by our expectations, our intellectual commitments, our theoretical predispositions and even our general sort of mindset. Perception apparently is not just one's senses sending nonnegotiable reports to one's brain.

Human perception seems to some degree to be active, and science does not seem to be immune to that aspect of the human condition. Here are a few brief examples. In the 1880s Thomas Huxley—Darwin's bulldog, as he was known—worked on a newly discovered entity sort of halfway between dead matter and living organism known as *Bathybius haeckelii.* Huxley and others believed that there had to be such an organism, and its discovery was no particular surprise. Indeed, it was considered a triumph of a general evolutionary paradigm. There were numerous observational confirmations concerning this quasi-organism. Its existence was not even controversial in some circles. But other scientists with the same equipment and techniques, but without Huxley's mindset, could see nothing like an organism at all and indeed categorized it as purely mineral—which, as a matter of fact, scientists now do also.[1] Somehow, background mindset had filtered into what was and was not taken to be observed.

Or again, in the late nineteenth century, proponents of two different sides in a dispute concerning heredity fairly uniformly reported different observed behavior of chromosomes during meiosis.[2] And in physics Rene Blondlot and his collaborators made elaborate observations and reports concerning his newly discovered N-rays. In fact, there were more than one hundred independent observational confirmations from other scientists. The only problem is that there are no such rays, and some other physicists could not see anything even when adherents of N-rays pointed alleged effects out to them.[3] A more familiar case is the famous history of the canals of Mars. Elaborate, detailed maps were produced of the canals—of which there are none. And earlier, in biology, there was the homunculus—and detailed observational reports complete with drawings of the little people encapsulated within the human sperm cell.

What about these scientists? Were they all incompetent? Were they frauds? No. They were simply actively involved in their own observings, as all humans are. They were unconsciously, and perhaps unavoidably, filling in their perceptions. I do not mean here that they were saying, "Well, the part I can't clearly see must look like this." They were not just connecting the dots. They may very well have been accurately reporting the content of their conscious perceptual experiences. But that experience had been filled in before they had conscious access to it. I do not wish to overstate the case here, but that seems to be the way human beings sometimes and to some extent unavoidably operate. And that preconscious "filling in" is sometimes molded by theoretical expectations or shaping principles to which one is already committed.

That being the case, some data may already have an *internal theoretical orientation,* and those data can then sometimes, to some extent, empirically reinforce that very orientation. This does not mean that by adopting any old mindset, or by convincing oneself of any old bizarre theory, one can actually experience the world as conforming to one's chosen fantasy. But it does mean that to the extent that this theoretical orientation of data happens, data will not be the wholly neutral, objectifying force traditionally thought.

### Shaping Principles

What might some of these extraempirical factors be? Some will be familiar and unsurprising. For instance, to do any science one must assume that natural laws and processes operate in a consistent manner—that a chemical reaction that occurs in the lab on Tuesday will also happen if it is run again on Thursday and will occur exactly the same way if done under identical conditions next year on Pluto. If nature were not consistent in this way, experiments done today in a lab would tell us absolutely nothing about the workings of nature on the next block next week. This consistency is usually referred to as the *uniformity of nature.* We must also assume that the external world is real, that the senses are in general reliable, that our concepts and thought processes are appropriate for investigating and comprehending the world we are in, and so forth.

But beyond that, one cannot do any substantive science without beliefs about what characteristics make an explanation a good scientifically acceptable explanation, about exactly what the relationship between theory and data ought to be, about what sorts of conceptual frameworks are and are not legitimate in science, about what kinds of theories are or are not legitimate, about what sorts of considerations it is proper to introduce into science, and so forth. And scientists in different periods have had different answers to those questions—the accepted answers have changed over time.

Indeed, in many cases scientific advances have been associated with, if not dependent on, changes in the answers to those questions. For instance, what is popularly referred to as the Scientific Revolution had connections to several such changes. Earlier attempts to understand nature often involved seeing nature as a huge, interconnected organism, the parts of which were interdependent with and adjusted to other parts in much the way that the various parts of a living organism were. That picture was supposed to guide the shape of one's theorizing. It was replaced by a picture of nature as a giant, complex machine, the parts of which were purely mechanical and interacted with each other in the rigidly mechanical way that the cogs of a machine interacted with each other. On that picture, theories were supposed to postulate purely material structures that, when interacting in purely mechanical ways, would result in the data observed.

Some scientists claimed that matter could only be scientifically construed as the absolutely passive recipient of impulses and forces. Others argued that matter might have some powers of action inherent in it. Some scientists argued that the only forces admissible into true science were those involving actual contact and impact of bits of matter. Others believed that it was scientifically legitimate to attribute to matter the ability to cause effects at a distance, with no intervening contact—a view that the first group derided as "occult." (Many thought that gravity and magnetism fell into this category.) Some scientists believed that matter was ultimately lumpy—composed of tiny, indivisible particles. Others stoutly maintained that matter was ultimately continuous, with no lumps, no smallest particles. As we saw in chapter two, in the early days of geology, theories were widely considered to be good scientific theories only if they conformed to Scripture. Early in the twentieth century scientists insisted that natural laws were deterministic. That view was abandoned with the advent of quantum mechanics.

These are just a few simple examples, but it can be seen that the answers one accepted to these questions would affect what kinds of theories were even considered, what kinds of data were seen as real data, what kinds of explanations were considered legitimately scientific and what sorts of theories and explanations were to be ruthlessly barred from science as being mere mystical nonsense. And since all of these principles involved *philosophical* positions concerning the nature of data, of proper theory, of acceptable explanation and of legitimate interpretation of data, disputes concerning them could not be settled "scientifically" by direct appeal to empirical data, observation or experimental results. Part of what was at issue was what principles should govern precisely those processes—in what terms one was supposed to interpret data, and in exactly what manner one was supposed to construe experimental results, and exactly what principles were properly supposed to govern attempts to rest theoretical implications on observational data.

But if these principles do not arise from data, where do they come from?

Since humans are integral beings, theorizing, evaluating and so forth involve multiple aspects of one's self. In some cases, they involve even deep worldview commitments. This broader self-involvement in one's "scientific" activities is neither completely avoidable nor regrettable. It is simply the way human persons work, and science, being a human pursuit, reflects this integral character as well. The political, social, philosophical, even psychological characteristics of various periods and people have served as sources of various shaping principles. Such principles are often unstated, and in some cases scientists are not even aware that they are employing them. The principles are simply buried deeply in the structure of what scientists of a period "feel" is or is not reasonable, sensible or plausible, and they operate on that level.

Here are just a few quick examples. As noted in chapter three, some historians think that the structure of Darwin's theory, or at the least its quick attractiveness, depended in part on various nineteenth-century British political and economic doctrines. As also noted earlier, Copernicus's theory of the solar system had the character it did in part due to Copernicus's staunch adherence to certain principles of Neo-Platonic philosophy. Nineteenth-century field theories in physics exhibited some striking affinities to key doctrines of the nineteenth-century Romantic movement. It has even been argued that quantum mechanics, with its emphasis on uncertainty, randomness, incomprehensibility (in a certain sense) and lack of causality, owed its basic character to the depressed mood in post-World War I Germany, where it originated.[4] And some scientists—including Einstein—rejected the dominant interpretation of quantum mechanics for largely philosophical reasons. Some contemporary theories (including one concerning alleged distribution patterns of primitive tools) have been rejected basically on grounds of political correctness.[5] And one of the original developers of the theory that the moon's material was exploded out of the earth's surface by a cosmic collision reported that the theory was initially resisted out of fear that catastrophists would claim that the theory provided evidence for their views.[6] Even nationalism seems to get into the act here. One of the surprising features of the history of science is the number of times that theory acceptance or rejection followed national boundaries.[7] And historically, even theological themes played key roles at times—and not just in fringe science. (More about that later.)

Now, some may not like all of that and may argue that allowing such factors to affect one's theory construction, theory evaluation and so forth constitutes a horrible mistake. Fair enough. But as we have seen, nonempirical factors of some sort are essential to the functioning of science. And no one knows any clearly correct way of separating scientifically acceptable nonempirical factors from scientifically unacceptable nonempirical factors. Many attempts to make such distinctions are historically and philosophically uninformed and ultimately depend on either some simple and clearly mistaken definition of science, like those discussed in the previous chapter, or the U.S. Constitution, which is hardly authoritative in matters of philosophy of science.

Given the variety of worldviews and the variety of alternative possible shaping principles, it is not surprising that the character of what was accepted as genuine science has changed several times historically. There simply does not seem to have been any such thing as *the* scientific method. There have been deep changes concerning such key nonempirical, philosophical issues as what sorts of theories are or are not acceptable; the permissibility or impermissibility of theoretical hypotheses; the extent and type of admissible teleological considerations; the type and scope of causal principles required; the criteria of what does or does not constitute an explanation; the external constraints (if any) to which theories can be properly subjected; the type of logic (if any) to which science should be required to conform; and so forth.

### Interactions

Does all this mean that anything goes, that one can simply stipulate that a favorite nonempirical doctrine is part of one's science and proceed merrily on one's way? No. It turns out that the three basic types of components in science—theories, data and shaping principles—interact with each other, and those interactions do impose some checks and limits. And nature has something to say here as well.

Doing science does not involve merely taking those three basic types of components and gluing them together. They interact with each other, affect each other, in some ways even transform each other. Here are some simple examples of such interaction. If our senses tell us anything, it is that the earth is stable and stationary. We do not feel it move (except in California), nor do we see it move. Yet for various (perhaps very good) reasons, we have accepted the theory that it does move, and consequently we simply ignore the claims of our senses on this issue. (We think we can explain why our senses insist that the earth is not moving, but that is a different matter.) Here we reject alleged direct empirical data on the basis of a theory we accept.

In the nineteenth century an otherwise apparently competent observer, a physician, reported cases of hair continuing to grow on the heads of corpses in coffins until the coffins burst under the pressure. We now reject such alleged data reports out of hand on the basis of certain biological theories we accept. Here again, theory is used in judging purported data. Mathematical precision has not always been considered an important characteristic of theories, but once it became important, many qualitative theories were considered to be less satisfactory than those same theories had been previously. Here the status of specific theories changed because of a shift in a shaping principle (with no change in the data).

Science is a complicated, historically shifting interplay among nature, theories, data and a host of often-unstated nonempirical principles that shape our thinking, evaluating, theorizing and even perceiving. Since the parts are so interwoven, changes in one part frequently have consequences for the content and contours of other parts. Parts do change over time— theories are replaced, shaping principles alter, and so forth. And sometimes entire systems involving all three components are overturned and replaced by others.

### Tenacity

Of course, with multiple components involved, whenever things are not going smoothly a number of ways of trying to adjust the system are possible. And oddly enough, it is often *data* that seem to get the short end of the stick, at least in the short run. Scientists historically have demonstrated a fairly fierce loyalty to theories and shaping principles, often in the face of apparently contrary data. Recall the examples in the previous chapter involving Newton, Einstein and others. In a brief account of twentieth-century quantum mechanics, a Nobel Prize-winning physicist, speaking of two physicists after whom an equation is named, said, "[Their] only contribution . . . in this respect was that they were sufficiently bold not to be perturbed by the lack of agreement of the equation with observations."[8] So defending their equation even in the face of contrary data was considered a contribution to science. And in fact, that is right.

This *tenacity* of scientists in the face of apparently contrary data is part of the reason science has developed as far as it has. Our theories are not perfect. In fact, it is so common for scientists to be aware of data apparently contrary to their theories, even at the very time that those theories are being proposed, that one historian/philosopher of science has declared that every theory is *born* refuted. Recall from the previous chapter the case of Newton pointing out such data while he was in the very act of presenting his theories.

Given that every theory faces known problematic data from the moment it is proposed, if scientists threw out every theory that was beset by empirical problems, there would be no theories and hence no science. So the tenacity of scientists, their refusal to give up a theory merely because the empirical data seem to contradict it, is part of what makes science work. Thus to demand that a theory be given up merely because one can cite some, or even a lot of, apparently contrary data is to mistake how science works.

Of course at some point, after the theory has been given enough of a chance and when the problems with the theory have become serious enough, the rational response probably is to junk the theory if there is an alternative that is workable enough. Fair enough. But the problem here is that no one knows how to define *enough* in these contexts, and scientists can disagree rationally on that point—some thinking that it is time to give up the theory, others thinking that perhaps the theory can solve its problems if given just a bit more time. And intuitions about when the situation does or does not warrant abandonment of a theory are among the things governed by shaping principles. This will be another of the sorts of cases where judgments concerning the legitimacy of accepting a theory will depend on the character of the interactions between the theory, data and shaping principles.

### Systems Analysis

So our perceptions, theorizing and evaluations of theories all seem to have an inescapable human tinge to them. And given the significant interflow among those various components, human tinges in any one of the areas have at least the potential to seep into the other areas as well. Thus we cannot eliminate humanness from science (as inductivists wanted to do), nor can we quarantine that humanness in one small corner of science (as hypothetico-deductivists wanted to do). Science is done by humans, and it cannot escape what is inescapably human. Our science is limited to humanly available concepts, humanly available data, humanly available patterns of reasoning, humanly shaped notions of understanding and explanation, and humanly structured pictures of what the world must be like. How could it be otherwise? Science seems to have a serious and incurable case of the humans.

But that again does not mean that anything goes. At some point our science has to confront nature in some way, and despite some flexibility, nature just will not stand for some things. But we do not just approach nature with our theories, nor do we just confront theories with data. We rather do something much more closely akin to trying to fit upon reality (or our experience of reality) a global, conceptual grid in which the three components are integrated together. The conceptual grid almost never completely fits. But since it constitutes an interwoven system, we often cannot simply perform a quick cut-and-paste repair job on some small area without altering things elsewhere. And if relations between nature and the conceptual grid get strained enough (there's that undefinable term again), the whole data/theory/shaping principle mix may become so unwieldy as to constitute as a whole a rationally anomalous system, and the system may simply capsize, taking its shaping principles, theories and alleged data down with it.

If that is right, then the way one is to judge large-scale scientific conceptions—including their metaphysical, philosophical, shaping principles—involves evaluation of how they fare *as systems* when trotted out to confront nature. Of course that confrontation is not a direct, simple process, since how one sees and assesses the confrontation will itself be flavored by one's shaping principles. Although the process is not viciously circular, there are no rules concerning exactly how that assessment should go or concerning when continued allegiance to the system is just plain irrational. But I suspect that we are all created with some very basic, deep conceptual outlines of rationality among our cognitive faculties and that there are thus some common, shared, broad constraints.

This is linked to a point made earlier—that not only must nature take a hand in the development and evaluation of our scientific theories (that is what is meant by calling science *empirical*) but in our process of trying to fit our conceptual grids onto nature, nature can also teach us some things about how to do science—about our shaping principles. That is why the history of science is in part a history of our learning what we can ask nature, how to ask it and how to read the answers. Numerous changes in conceptions and methodologies of science historically have been exploratory responses to nature's treatment of earlier grids when those grids were brought into the scientific trenches.

One important implication of seeing science this way is that although the effects are quite indirect, if philosophical positions, value judgments and even theological doctrines are deeply embedded in science as shaping principles, then they too are subject to some degree of empirical risk and empirical correction as nature responds to the systems of which those principles are components.

Some philosophers (and others) have gone directly from the inescapable inclusion of nonempirical factors within the scientific matrix to the thorough subjectivity of science.[9] But one must not get carried away by pessimism here. If nature does impose constraints on our conceptual grids, and if nature can impose corrective nudges on our systems (including their nonempirical shaping principles), and if we are created with some deep conceptual constraints within us, there may at least be limits to how far off the wall we can get. So even if there is some fuzziness, even if proof is out of the question, we need not necessarily fall into irrationality, and we certainly need not be stuck in the slough of subjectivity. Realism of some sort is not out of the question.

**Explanatory Power and Other Clues**
But if the production of truth within science is not automatic, purely mechanical or via some direct logical route, how are we to recognize it should we meet it? What are the earmarks of theoretical truth? In theoretical matters, those earmarks are largely indirect and circumstantial, highly fallible and not particularly empirical. They are, in fact, tied up with shaping principles. In general, theories are considered to be more likely on the track of truth if they are (among other things) empirically adequate (cover the relevant data in some acceptable manner), are self-consistent, are consistent with other acceptable scientific theories, are consistent with important and rationally defensible nonscientific principles, have a good past track record, have proven to be resilient enough and conceptually rich enough to overcome apparent difficulties consistently, and have been fruitful—having given rise to unexpected understandings and having inspired innovative investigations and developments. Some would add that theoretical beauty or simplicity is another signpost toward truth, although that is a bit controversial.[10]

Another key, one that is frequently misconstrued, is *explanatory power*. Data do not come with labels revealing to us what underlying mechanism is responsible for producing them. Thus they do not in some direct fashion tell us what they are evidence for. (Thinking that the proper theory for explaining some body of data could be identified for us by those very data themselves was one of the more serious mistakes the inductivists made.) But if one can construct a theory that can explain the data, or within which the data can be smoothly interpreted, the fact that the theory has that explanatory power does constitute support for the theory. The data for which the theory provides a sensible explanation, or the parts of the empirical world that the conceptual grid fits, do constitute evidence for the theory.

For instance, the theory that a gas is composed of individual, freely moving molecules functions very nicely in explanation of empirical gas laws (such as Boyle's and Charles's). And the fact that the empirical data of gas behavior, when interpreted according to the concepts of the theory, are consistent with the principles of the theory provides some reason for thinking that there is something right about the theory. The theory may, of course, turn out to be wrong—that is part of what is meant by admitting that even though scientific theories are often rational to believe, they are never proven. And giving the proposed theory a say in the interpretation of the data does not somehow immunize the theory from empirical challenge from that very data. If the theory is wrong enough, the data served up by the world, even when interpreted according to the mandates of that theory itself, will still violate the theory's dictates.

Explanatory power is particularly important in areas where repeatability and direct experimentation are especially difficult—such as astronomy, historical geology, paleontology and historical biology. In these areas and in other theoretical areas as well, explanatory power can provide positive support for theories dealing with the unobserved and unobservable.

Despite all of the difficulties, then, there are some features that can be taken as indicators that we are on the right track. But we must not get completely carried away by optimism. After the twists, turns, false starts and revolutions found in the history of science, it would be pretty amazing if we were the ones in the right time out of all history who were here when the truth finally arrived. And whether or not we can sensibly claim that our theories are true may depend in part on whether or not we have rational reasons for accepting the shaping principles on which those theories partially depend.

### Some Present Applications

Given our present concern with creation-evolution issues, three philosophical characteristics specifically of evolutionary theories and explanations are worth noting. First, Darwin was aware of the crucial role that explanatory power had to play in any theory of the unobservable past. In chapter thirteen of the *Origin,* for instance, he appealed to explanatory power over thirty times but appealed to consistency of the data with his theory, predictions of the theory and so forth only five times combined. Similar patterns are found in chapters ten, eleven and twelve.

Second, the case for evolution as Darwin developed it was a cumulative case. As Darwin saw it, each type of evidence presented had some weight of its own, but the convergence of all of the independent sorts of cases toward the same theory and the ability of that theory to explain and to accommodate all of those seemingly independent cases produced a cumulatively compelling case.

Consider this analogy. If you have one piece of circumstantial evidence against an accused burglar, you do not have much of a case. But if you have twenty pieces of circumstantial evidence, none of which is in any way dependent on any of the others, and they all converge on the same suspect, you start thinking that you are onto something. In fact, you might think that the cumulative weight of the case is even greater than the sum of the weights of the individual parts. That was the nature of the evolutionary case as Darwin saw it.

Third, evolutionary explanations frequently—even typically—do not purport to reveal exactly how some particular evolutionary development or species transition came about in actual fact. They rather tend to outline some way in which the development or transition *could* have come about. They are, in Darwin's terms, "imaginative illustrations" or, in Francis Crick's terms, "don't worry" theories.[11] (Another phrase is "just-so stories"—often used negatively.[12]) They are intended to show that the events in question cause no fatal difficulties for evolutionary theory and that evolutionary theory has the theoretical resources, power and potential necessary to account in principle for the events in question, rather than to reveal the exact historical truth of the matter.

But can inventing an imaginary series of events that one does not even pretend to be true really be scientifically useful? Yes. Consider this example. The police have circumstantial evidence that a murder has taken place, but unfortunately they cannot locate the body. The prime suspect had a terribly violent history, had a bitter grudge against the apparent victim, had made threats and had bragged about a killing, and in the suspect's truck were the victim's jewelry, credit cards, CD collection and left ear.

But as we all know from TV detective shows, getting a conviction requires establishing that the accused had the *means* to commit the crime. The accused, as it turns out, owned a pistol and a machete—both now missing. So we probably cannot discover the actual means employed (remember, the body is missing too). But if we can make a plausible case, consistent with what is known, concerning how the accused *could* have done it, if we can cite a sensible possible means that was within the accused's capability—in short, if we can construct an adequate "just-so story"—that surely is enough, even if we never do or never can observe either the body or the weapons, never do or never can get the exact details and never do or never can discover whether or not our plausible construction was exactly the right one.

Similarly, although there may be no chance of ever recovering the historical data necessary to determine some exact evolutionary route and means by which, say, the eye developed (if it did), the viability of evolutionary theory is preserved, with respect to that specific issue, if it has sufficient explanatory potential, if some *possible* route and means—some "just-so story"—can be constructed out of resources and processes contained in the theory and consistent with what is otherwise known. Indeed, such demonstration of the theory's explanatory potential and power even constitutes some degree of rational support for the theory.

### Summation

Science is, then, an interwoven mix of humanly molded components. Empirical data, theories and various nonempirical shaping factors are all utterly essential for the existence and functioning of science. The interrelations of the components are substantial and deep, meaning that they are presented to nature as a system, as a unified conceptual grid. Nature's responses must be read in that context, although the situation is complicated by the fact that principles governing our interpretation of nature's responses are themselves part of the very system in question. Alterations to the system can come anywhere among the components. Data, theories and shaping principles all can be altered or even repudiated, but alterations will frequently have consequences elsewhere in the system. On occasion entire systems can be junked, and the history of science does exhibit a number of massive changes of that sort. And unfortunately, there are no hard and fast rules concerning when such responses are or are not appropriate.

Science is not, as it turns out, a rule-governed enterprise. The "rules of science" are a myth. Science still strives to be empirical, rational and objective, but it turns out that those characteristics have an irremovable human shading to them. Still, it is rationally possible to maintain that there is a core of objective truth in our scientific theorizing, resulting in part from features of the way we are made, the way nature is made and the way the two interact.

# 10 THE NATURE OF SCIENCE
## Popular Creationist Mistakes

**C**ombatants on both sides of the creation-evolution dispute frequently try for easy, shortcut victories by showing that the views of the other side fail to qualify as legitimate science. Such attempts typically involve citing either some formal definition of science or some characteristic claimed to be utterly essential to science, then arguing that positions held by opponents fail to satisfy the cited requirements. We will look in some detail at philosophy of science arguments of this sort from both sides, from the creationist side in this chapter and from the anticreationist side in the next. As will become clear, the popular arguments in this category from both sides establish very little, and most involve serious confusion.

### Definitions

Creationist attempts to disqualify evolution on grounds that it violates some philosophy of science requirement frequently begin with a formal definition of science, and the definition cited by several creationist authors is that contained in the *Oxford Dictionary:*[1]

A branch of study which is concerned either with a connected body of demonstrated truths or with observed facts systematically classified and more or less colligated by being brought under general laws, and which includes trustworthy methods for the discovery of new truth within its own domain.

From discussions in the previous two chapters, we can easily recognize this definition as a version of Baconian inductivism, and it has all the flaws that beset such views. The first difficulty is with the idea of science *demonstrating* truths, although this definition gives no clue as to how one should understand that term.[2] There is no rote method or mechanical procedure for discovering new truths in science either. If there were, scientific breakthrough would not require the creative activity of human beings. But perhaps most seriously, if one begins with empirical data ("observed facts") and then "systematically classifies" them and "more or less colligates" them by generalizing from them ("brings them under general laws"), one will never get beyond mere empirical generalizations to theoretical principles or explanatory theories. Going from the empirical to underlying theoretical explanations requires a leap of human creativity. There is no purely logical or mechanical procedure for making the jump, and classifying and colligating or generalizing empirical data is simply inadequate to the task.[3]

This definition of science, then, misunderstands what science can do and how it does it ("demonstrated" truths arising out of "trustworthy methods of discovery") and would destroy science by implying the illegitimacy of theoretical explanations. The fact that evolutionary theory fails to meet this definition of science creates no problems whatever. The dictionary definition is so inadequate that atomic theory and nearly every other interesting scientific theory fail to meet it as well.

Various Institute for Creation Research (ICR) authors have in recent years claimed that science is simply knowledge or even just truth, whether known or not.[4] Obviously, neither of those definitions is correct. It may be true and known to be true that George Washington was a general, but that hardly makes it science. These views sometimes come with the qualification that the knowledge (or truth) in question has been uncovered by scientific procedures, but that qualification does not help much. Newton was a scientist, and his theories of motion and gravitation were clearly scientific. As it turns out, however, none of his theories in those areas was quite right. They *looked* true for well over two centuries, but if Einstein's theories are right every one of Newton's major theories of motion and gravitation is subtly wrong, and thus on the above definition not science. (And of course, if Einstein is wrong then Einstein's theories are not science on this definition either.)

The mere fact that something is known or true does not make it science, and the mere fact that something turns out not to be true does not disqualify it from being science. These definitions are clearly mistaken.

### Characteristics of Science

Creationists cite a number of characteristics that they claim are requirements either of science or of truth, then argue that evolutionary theory fails
to meet one or more of those requirements, thus undercutting its legitimacy.
A number of such characteristics and discussion of them follows. Although
there is overlap between some, I will discuss them individually.

### Evolution Is Mere Theory—Not Fact

Creationists here trade on a distinction between mere speculative conjecture
on the one hand and established truth on the other.[5] But although the term
*theory* does refer to mere speculation in some contexts, that is not its primary meaning in connection with science. As discussed in the previous
chapter, when scientists refer to the theory of evolution (or gravity or other
scientific theory), *theory* refers to the structure of evolutionary (or gravitational) principles and the role those principles play in various scientific
processes, such as explanation. It has nothing whatever to do with whether
the theory in question is true, confirmed, scientifically accepted or anything
of that sort. There is thus nothing whatever in the mere concept of *theory*
that prevents a theory, whether gravitational or evolutionary or atomic,
from being true. Nothing detrimental to evolution's status with respect to
being science, truth or knowledge can be derived merely from typical references to the "theory of evolution." That it is obviously a theory in the
"explanatory structure" sense does not in any way show that it is a theory
in the "mere speculative conjecture" sense. It might be, but establishing that
would require a further case.

### Evolution Has Not Been or Cannot Be Proven

Some claim that the true scientific attitude is to believe only what is proven,
and that evolution cannot be, or at least has not been, proven.[6] As we have
seen, however, proof in any rigorous sense is simply beyond the capability
of science. If we accepted only theories that were or could be proven, we
could accept no theories. This requirement is clearly mistaken.

### Evolution Is Not Falsifiable

It is often claimed that no theory is legitimately scientific unless it is at least
in principle falsifiable, and that evolution is not.[7] A few creationists are a

bit inconsistent here, claiming simultaneously that evolutionary theory is defective in not being falsifiable and that various pieces of empirical science (gaps in the fossil record, the Second Law of Thermodynamics and so on) have in fact revealed its falsehood.[8] But all that aside, as we saw earlier genuine scientific theories are not conclusively falsifiable in any case. Thus a requirement of conclusive falsifiability, whether or not evolutionary theory fails it, is a mistaken requirement.

But why think that evolutionary theory is unfalsifiable in any case? Two popular sorts of attempts to establish this unfalsifiability have been made, but neither seems to work.

*1. Evolution is too flexible.* The first common attempt involves the claim that evolutionary theory is so flexible that it can be bent in any direction to cover anything.[9] For instance, if the males of one species of bird guard the nest, it is because nest-guarding enhances fitness and was selected for. If the males of another species of bird abandon the nest, it is because nest-abandonment enhances fitness and was selected for. But, the objection continues, any theory that can be bent around to be consistent with anything and everything clearly does not in itself say anything at all, and thus has no significant content of its own.

Now, it is not at all clear that evolution is as flexible as charged. Darwin himself, in the *Origin,* mentioned things that, in his view, if discovered would have destroyed evolution. In any case, the accusation is not quite fine-tuned enough. Suppose that someone were to charge that physics was too flexible to be good science because, after all, if something flies the laws of physics explain it, if something cannot fly the laws of physics explain it, if something falls rapidly the laws of physics explain it, and if something falls slowly the laws of physics explain it. But obviously these different cases would involve different types of objects with different characteristics perhaps in different circumstances, and those differences are absolutely crucial in the explanation of the different outcomes. In the proposed objection those crucial differences have been ignored, and the example thus does not show any unacceptable flexibility in physics.

Similarly in the nest guarding/nest abandoning case, a variety of relevant differences in circumstances or characteristics may be exactly why, according to the theory, fitness is served by one behavior in one case and by precisely the opposite behavior in the other. One cannot ignore such differences, and the objection as formulated—ignoring possibly relevant differences—does no damage to the theory whatever.[10]

*2. Evolutionary theory makes no predictions or is not testable.* The second type of popular attempt to establish unfalsifiability involves the claims that to be genuinely falsifiable, or even testable, a theory must make testable empirical predictions, and that evolutionary theory makes no such predictions. Evolution thus is not testable and not genuinely scientific.[11]

But it is not clear that evolutionary theory generates no predictions. Indeed, many creationists claim that evolution predicts transition fossils, and use their absence as one basis for the claim that evolution has been empirically falsified. And most evolutionary theorists would be perfectly happy to predict that no modern human fossil remains will ever be found in undisturbed Precambrian rock.

It is no doubt true that no evolutionary theorist can, on the basis of evolutionary theory, predict when the next new species will emerge, where it will emerge and what characteristics it will have. But that is not necessarily a problem for the theory itself. As we saw in chapter eight, predictions are always generated out of a mix that includes the theory in question, subsidiary theories, facts concerning various relevant conditions and so forth. Sometimes we are unable to make any relevant predictions because some of those additional matters are simply too complicated—either there are so many variables that the mathematics is beyond control, or some of the variables may just be unknown. For instance, at present scientists are unable to predict when, where or how powerful the next earthquake will be. There are simply too many unknowns. But that does not mean that the theories concerning what earthquakes are, what causes them, what factors determine their strength and so forth are not scientific. Theories about faults, plate tectonics and so forth allow us to understand a great deal about earthquakes. They do not yet allow us to predict very much. But they are quite clearly legitimately scientific theories. Thus the fact that no one can generate much in the way of prediction from a theory does not at all show that the theory is not scientific, that it is scientifically defective or anything of the sort.[12]

### "Anomalous Facts"—Facts Contrary to Evolutionary Theory

Many creationists cite particular facts, argue that evolutionary theory seems unable to accommodate those facts, then conclude that evolutionary theory is thus destroyed, falsified or at least in serious trouble.[13] Some creationists claim that all it takes to do in evolution is a single recalcitrant empirical fact. But as we saw in the last chapter, it is not quite that simple. Human theories are not perfect, and virtually every significant scientific theory faces empirical problems of one sort or another. That being the case, abandoning a scientific theory solely because of some body of problematic data would effectively destroy science. At some point, depending on the type, quantity and character of the anomalies as well as on various other features of the theory in question, abandonment may be the most reasonable thing to do. But the mere presence of awkward and even apparently contradictory empirical data does not of itself always provide compelling grounds for abandonment of a theory.

### Evolution Is Only One of Several Alternative Theories

As noted earlier, theories are always underdetermined by empirical data, implying that for any collection of empirical data there are always in principle innumerable possible alternative theories consistent with that body of data. Stated another way, any collection of data is always subject to a variety of interpretations. Some creationists have argued that since any data cited in favor of evolution can also be given other interpretations, such data do not constitute good evidence for evolution.[14]

This argument has at least three problems. First, if it were true, it would mean that there was no good empirical evidence for creationism either—a conclusion that many creationists would immediately reject. Second, the argument seems to presuppose that evidence is good evidence only if it is conclusive.[15] Since empirical evidence is never logically conclusive (as we have seen), the consequence would be that there was no such thing as good empirical evidence. That seems clearly mistaken. Third, it fails to take account of other factors and shaping principles that play roles in various scientific processes, including evidence assessment. Consider this simple example. The American tobacco industry professes the belief that the strong statistical links between smoking and various lung and heart diseases is purely coincidental. Their argument might go as follows. There are numerous alternatives to the theory linking smoking and these diseases. For instance, it is *possible* that every case of lung cancer is a result of some strange, undetected cosmic ray that happens to strike smokers vastly more frequently than nonsmokers. Given, then, that there is an alternative theory, the empirical, statistical evidence is not good grounds for thinking that there is a smoking-disease link.

Obviously, few would find that argument persuasive. Most of us take the evidence for such a link to be quite powerful, despite the existence of possible alternative explanations. For various reasons, most of us find the alternatives wildly implausible. Various principles concerning plausibility (which we probably cannot explicitly state) play important roles as shaping principles in scientific evaluations. (And the plausibility principles that we accept are themselves shaped in part by other theories and data we accept—which is another example of the blending interaction among the three basic components of science.) In any case, the mere possibility of alternatives to evolutionary explanations of specific empirical data does not by itself show that the data cannot nonetheless constitute strong evidence for evolutionary theory (whether they in fact do or not).

### Evolutionary Processes Are Unobservable

Some creationists claim that evolutionary theory is not legitimate science because it purports to deal with processes and events that are not observable.[16] For instance, the emergence of a new species might, according to evolutionary theories, take anywhere from forty thousand to millions of years—a span well beyond the direct observation capabilities of humans. In fact, some creationists claim that no theories concerning prehuman history are scientifically legitimate, since no part of such a history has been or can be observed by humans.[17]

One prominent creationist speaker advises creationists to respond to nearly every claim concerning prehistory with the question "Were you there?"—linking that position to God's similar question to Job.[18] Obviously none of us were actually there, and caution and humility are indeed required. But we have to be careful how far we push that. If mere absence of direct witnesses implied that a unique past event could not be investigated, much less known, no perpetrator of an (otherwise) unwitnessed murder should ever be tried, much less convicted, no matter how compelling the circumstantial evidence. (Of course, one might claim that evolution cases are not merely unobserved past cases but are unique in other important ways that remove them from science. We will consider such claims shortly.)

This sort of doctrine appears to grow directly out of inductivist or positivist conceptions of science and is, like such views of science, seriously mistaken.[19] Explanatory theories nearly always deal with unobservable objects or processes—atomic theory with atoms, for instance. Atoms simply are not observable by human beings. We observe only certain sorts of empirical and experimental phenomena that we interpret as resulting from the properties, activities and interactions of atoms. Scientists sometimes talk of "observing" atoms and other such entities, but they are using that term in a highly specialized way. They mean only that they are measuring observable effects that, if their theories are right, are the indirect consequences of the unobservable behaviors of hypothesized, not-directly-observable particles. If that counts as being scientifically observable, then prehuman history and eon-long processes are also observable, since scientists can measure observable effects that, if their theories are right, are the indirect consequences of various processes and events in that hypothesized, not-directly-observable prehuman history.

As with some of the previous alleged requirements of science, if science had to conform to this requirement and could not include theories involving things and processes not directly observable by humans, science could not function. Creationists can reply that with many theories involving unobservable theoretical objects (atomic theory and the atoms it postulates being a good example) the observable indirect consequences of the objects postulated by those theories can be experimentally controlled and are repeatable, which places atomic theory and its not-directly-observable atoms in a very different category from theories concerning unique, unrepeatable evolutionary processes and events. Let's consider that response.

### Evolution Is Unrepeatable/Unreproducible

The claim that what cannot be reproduced cannot be scientifically investigated or tested occurs frequently in creationist writing. Morris, for instance, claims repeatedly that since evolution allegedly took millions of years we cannot reproduce it in a laboratory, and that since we cannot reproduce it we cannot even test it.[20] But it simply is not true that we cannot test theories about phenomena unless those phenomena can be reproduced. In fact, many creationists argue that evolution not only is unreproducible but can empirically be shown to be false. And indeed, scientists routinely test theories about things that are not, or cannot be, reproduced. Contrary to frequent claims, Sherlock Holmes often tested theories (his own and others') about specific crimes. For instance, he once rejected the theory that a particular person committed a murder with a harpoon. He tested the theory by trying to throw a harpoon through some carcasses in a butcher shop, discovering how much force it took and ruling out the prime suspect on the grounds that the suspect did not possess the requisite strength. And in testing—and rejecting—the theory about the murder, he did not have to reproduce the murder (*that* murder could not be reproduced, after all) or commit another one.

### Tautologies, Short Circuits and Circular Reasoning

One of the most popular forms of criticism directed against evolutionary theory is that it is logically defective in its very structure.[21] According to one version of this criticism, the theory itself reduces to a mere tautology. According to other versions, the type of reasoning that underlies the assessment of empirical evidence in the theory is subtly, or maybe blatantly, circular reasoning. Dicussion of both types of objections follows.

### Evolutionary Theory Is a Mere Tautology

In one sense, this is a curious charge for an opponent of evolutionary theory to make. After all, tautologies are by definition true, so if the theory is a tautology it hardly makes sense to oppose it. But why think it a tautology? The usual argument proceeds as follows. The theory of evolution is nothing but the doctrine of the survival of the fittest. But who or what are the fittest? Obviously, those that survive. Therefore, evolutionary theory reduces to the empty tautology that the ones that survive are the ones that survive.[22]

Popular as this criticism is, it is seriously misguided. First of all, evolutionary theory is not *merely* the doctrine of the survival of the fittest. Suppose that no evolution ever takes place but there is variation within species, overproduction and consequent competition for limited resources. Given the variations within the species, some individuals within the species may be a bit better off in a given environment—some will be a bit faster than others, a bit stronger, a bit more attractive to the opposite sex, a bit more disease-resistant and the like. That, again, will be true even if there is no evolution, if there are absolute fixed limits to variability within a species and if there is an absolute fixed upper limit to fitness within the species. In that situation, the fittest will tend to survive at the expense of the less fit. Natural selection will execute the less fit—the sickly, the weak, the malformed, the disease-susceptible—and will preserve the more fit—the strong, the healthy, the optimally formed, the disease-resistant. So even in the complete absence of any evolution, the fittest will tend to survive. It follows, of course, that evolutionary theory must be more than just the doctrine of the survival of the fittest.[23]

Indeed, the above constituted a key early puzzle for Darwin. Natural selection alone (nature's preservation of the fittest) was, as Darwin saw, the executioner of the less fit, but it did not itself generate newer, higher levels of fitness or more fit descendants. A theory of *increased fitness being generated* had to be added to the idea of the fittest being favored to survive in order to turn the theory into an evolutionary theory. The survival of the fittest alone, again, simply does not constitute the whole of the theory. A crucial part of the theory is that in specific cases, species *A* was succeeded by descendent species *B*—and that doesn't even have the superficial appearance of a tautology.

But suppose that this one part of evolutionary theory—the principle of the survival of the fittest—was in fact a tautology. That would have no particularly important consequences. The fact that some part of a total theory is a tautology does not at all imply that the entire theory is either tautological or in any way defective.[24]

But the claim that there is a tautology here also depends on the premise that *fitness* is defined solely in terms of survival. That, as it turns out, is not quite true either.[25] Imagine a situation involving two species, one of which flourishes easily while the other has to fight and scrabble, only a few members barely survive to reproduce, and the species escapes extinction only by a hair virtually every month or so. In this situation, the one species seems intuitively better fit to its environment than the other, but both species are surviving—thus the concept of fitness must involve more than mere survival. Fitness may typically *result* in survival or in increased prospects of survival, but that does not imply that fitness just *is* survival. Indeed some creationists themselves seem to have concepts of fitness that are independent of survival.[26]

Thus the objection that evolutionary theory reduces to a more or less vacuous tautology does not seem to be well founded.

## Naturalistic Short Circuits

According to some critics of evolution, evolutionists accept evolutionary theory not on the basis of empirical data, but rather on the basis of an a priori philosophical commitment to naturalism—the doctrine that all that exists is the natural realm, that nature is reality.[27] If one accepts naturalism, then acceptance of some purely naturalistic theory of the origins of life, species and humans is virtually inescapable, and evolution is the only currently viable naturalistic candidate. Furthermore, acceptance of a materialistic naturalism nearly forces one to deny the existence of any overall purpose or guidance in the cosmos. This sort of naturalism, the objection goes, is built into the very core of contemporary evolutionary theory. Evolutionary theory's reliance on random mutations and variations, the denial of any purpose or guided direction in evolutionary processes, is thus not some philosophical appendage that can be removed leaving the biological theory intact. It is part of the very identity of the theory.

Worse yet, the objection continues, this naturalism constitutes the very core of the standard case for biological evolution. Once one accepts naturalism and is consequently forced to adopt some sort of evolutionary theory as truth, two consequences ensue. First, all empirical data *must* be interpreted in terms consistent with evolution, whether they lend themselves to such interpretation or not, in order to be in accord with the truth. Second, since acceptance of evolutionary theory is already forced by the previously accepted naturalism, the whole issue of empirical support becomes secondary anyway, since acceptance or rejection of the theory will not hinge on the quantity, quality or character of the empirical data. And surely that is at least a partial departure from legitimate scientific procedure. (More insidiously dangerous, even if that naturalistic worldview is not consciously accepted, one's science still will be forced into a similar position even if one accepts only the common idea that science is restricted to the purely natural.)

According to this objection, when the shaping effects of the naturalism are stripped from the data, and when the driving force of the naturalism is removed, not much genuine empirical support for evolution remains. The empirical data taken straight are woefully weak support for evolution. Trying to retain the data as support requires implicitly keeping the naturalism, however deeply buried. Dig the effects of naturalism out of the allegedly supporting data, and the data lose all semblance of supporting evolution.

This is, I think, an extremely interesting objection, and in the case of some evolutionists it is fairly plausible. Dawkins, for instance, says that "even if there were no actual evidence in favor of the Darwinian theory . . . we should still be justified in preferring it over all rival theories."[28]

But one has to be exceedingly careful here not to overstate this objection. First, as we have seen, no theoretical science can be completely purged of nonempirical, philosophical shaping principles, and there are no hard and fast rules concerning what the nature and content of such principles can or cannot be. If it is true that contemporary, mainstream evolutionary theory has naturalistic presuppositions built into its core, that by itself does not disqualify it as science. Nor is such a theory necessarily defective merely in virtue of dealing exclusively with natural processes in its descriptions and explanations.

Consider this analogous case. Most of us accept meteorological theories according to which the weather (and even origins—storm origins) are results of perfectly natural processes. Nothing whatever seems wrong with doing that. Suppose, however, that such theories had been constructed and most people had come to accept those theories in large part because they were committed naturalists and thus were forced to deny any nonnatural causes in their meteorological theories. That would have nothing to do with whether the theories themselves were scientifically legitimate. In fact, their meteorological theories might even be right despite the utter mistakenness of the naturalism that partially motivated them. Thus the fact that a theory was forced upon one by a prior philosophical commitment to naturalism does not at all show that the theory itself is not legitimately scientific, or even that it is not correct.

Of course, should it turn out that purely natural processes were in fact incapable of accounting for some occurrence and that the truth of that particular matter was nonnatural, then the committed naturalist, forced by that commitment to reject all nonnaturalistic theories, would be prevented from ever seeing that part of the truth. But the one-sidedness of the naturalist's approach does not imply that any theory produced by that approach is unscientific, or that no theory produced by that approach is correct. The scientist who believes a theory in such a way and for such a purpose may be partially self-blinded, but being blind does not automatically imply that one is on the wrong road or on no road at all.

Nor does mistaken—or even reprehensible—motivation for believing a theory imply, by itself, that there is something defective about the theory itself. In some historical circles people accepted early versions of atomic theory in part *because* they believed the theory to be inherently atheistic. But none of us—including creationists—have any particular theological hesitations about atomic theory.

Thus the facts that naturalism is behind evolution and that a prohibition on any nonnatural factors is built into evolution (if they are facts) do not alone imply that evolutionary theory is not science, that it is defective in some other manner or even that evolutionary theory is not true. Of course, the theory might not be true. The evolutionary conceptual grid built around this naturalism may, as some claim, have failed miserably to fit nature. But that is a different issue, and must be established on other grounds.

### Circular Reasoning

*1. Phillip Johnson.* Closely related to the foregoing objection is the charge that supporters of evolution engage in circular reasoning when assessing evidence for evolution. The objection, which is a primary theme in Phillip Johnson's extremely popular book *Darwin on Trial,* runs as follows.

> [Gould] makes it sound as if Darwin proposed his theory because of the presence of an abundance of [specified data]. Of course what actually happened is that the theory was accepted first, and the supporting evidence was discovered and interpreted in the course of a determined effort to find [specified matters] that the theory demanded. . . . The question this sequence of events raises is . . . whether the Darwinist imagination might have played an important role in construing the evidence which has been offered to support Darwin's theory.[29]

After repeating the same sort of objection elsewhere, Johnson claims that employing the already accepted theory in the interpreting of data constitutes bias and means that the "true scientific question" of whether or not the data confirm the theory "has never been asked."[30]

So the objection is that evolutionists come to the empirical data already presupposing (because of their naturalism) that evolution must have happened and that evolutionary theory is thus roughly true. Their initial interpretation and analysis of the data is thus necessarily already from an evolutionary perspective—so what they consider to be data already has evolutionary theory built into it. Then they try to use this very data, with evolutionary theory already built into it, as evidence for evolutionary theory. But clearly, the objection continues, to assume a theory in interpreting data that is then in turn advanced as evidence for that very theory is blatantly defective reasoning.[31]

Although there are perhaps legitimate concerns in this area, this particular objection is not, I think, as powerful as it might initially appear. One does not just confront theories with "raw data" from nature. (And in any case, as we have seen, data are not as raw as positivists, inductivists and others once believed.) One is in a sense trying to see if data as interpreted according to the dictates of a theory can fit into a system, a conceptual grid, which can be fit onto nature as one is confronted by it. In fact, it is difficult to see how theoretical science could operate any other way. For instance, chemicals typically combine in constant ratios. How can one explain that? Well, if one interprets the chemical data as being the result of interactions of individual atoms of various types, the data fall into place nicely and make sense. But why should one think that chemicals are composed of individual atoms of various sorts? One important bit of evidence is the way chemical substances combine in constant ratios.

If we took something $A$ as evidence for $B$, and that same $B$ as evidence for $A$, that would be grounds for criticism. And if we took $A$ as the explanation of $B$, and $B$ in turn as the explanation of $A$, we would also be in deep logical yogurt. But given science's character as an interwoven system with which we approach hidden levels of nature, we have to take nature's interpretability in the terms of a theory—the theory's explanatory power—as a source of evidential support for the theory. And there is nothing logically pernicious about that. That $A$ explains $B$ while $B$ evidentially supports $A$ is not, on the face of it, a logical circle. Or if it is in some sense a circle, it might be what one philosopher has called a virtuous, rather than a vicious, circle.

For instance, what is our evidence that there used to be a huge salt sea around Bonneville in Utah? The present salt flats. And how do we explain the presence of the salt flats? Well, there used to be this huge salt sea . . . If science rested on inference from data, it might be circular to interpret the data in accord with the theory and then to infer that very theory from the data into which the theory had already been built. But that simply is not the way science works. That theories are not inferred from data has been recognized since the demise of inductivism several decades ago.[32]

A related objection Johnson raises several times is that evolutionists assume naturalism, on the basis of that naturalism infer that evolution is true, then conclude from that alleged truth of evolution that any conditions and mechanisms required by evolution must also have occurred. They then cite those inferred conditions and mechanisms as evidence of evolution—the assumption of which was the real grounds for believing in those conditions and mechanisms to begin with. For instance,

> The prevailing assumption in evolutionary science seems to be that speculative possibilities, without experimental confirmation, are all that is really necessary. . . . Nature must have provided whatever evolution had to have, because otherwise evolution wouldn't have happened. It follows that if evolution required macromutations then macromutations must be possible. . . . The theory itself provides whatever supporting evidence is essential.[33]

However, any evidence for a theory is also evidence for whatever else that theory requires. Here is a simple example. If you have evidence for the theory that the dog tore up your slippers (the slippers are ripped up, covered with slobber containing flecks of dog biscuit, none other of your acquaintances has a taste for both dog biscuits and slippers, and so on), and if the dog could have gotten at the slippers only if someone had left the bedroom door open, then your evidence is also evidence for that necessary condition—that someone left the bedroom door open. And the very fact that the theory's requirements can be met is, if true, at least evidentially relevant to evaluation of the theory. And if, once the requirements of a theory are recognized as such, independent evidence for those requirements can be generated, such evidence also can constitute support for the original theory. For Johnson's objection here to carry much weight, one needs grounds for believing that the relevant conditions and mechanisms are cited *as evidence for evolution* while evolution itself is *the only evidence cited for them.* That does not seem to be the case.

None of this is to say that theories and their data cannot get too "inbred"—too mutually dependent. But the mere fact that theory and data have this sort of interaction does not necessarily constitute a problem.

Thus evaluating a theory in light of the pronouncements of nature while reading those pronouncements from the perspective of that very theory is perfectly legitimate. Indeed, that is in part how theoretical science works.

*2. Michael Denton.*[34] Evolution critic Michael Denton, in his influential book *Evolution: A Theory in Crisis,* makes a similar sort of mistake in several contexts. The following is representative. Discussing the problem posed for Darwin by gaps in the fossil record, Denton notes Darwin's "appeal to the 'extreme imperfection' of the fossil record," then says, "But this was largely a circular argument because the only significant evidence he was able to provide for its 'extreme imperfection' was the very absence of intermediates that he sought to explain."[35]

Similar sorts of circularity charges occur at least a half-dozen times in Denton's book—concerning molecular clocks and so forth.[36] But there is no circularity here at all. Darwin is attempting to deal with data that at first glance pose a problem for his theory. But any viable response must necessarily fit within the theory being defended, and if there is reason to believe that the theory is correct, that itself constitutes at least some rational grounds for thinking that whatever does happen can be fitted into the theory.

Theories often provide some guidance concerning how specific problematic pieces of data can be defused. Here is a simple historical example. The Copernican picture of the earth orbiting the sun led to the expectation of slightly different visual perspectives on stars from opposite sides of the earth's orbit, just as one gets slightly different visual perspectives on a speaker from opposite sides of an auditorium. No such differences were observed, and some sixteenth- and seventeenth-century scientists took this as refuting Copernicus. Galileo, however, proposed an explanation of the absence of perspective shifts—the stars were so vastly far away that even a 186,000,000-mile shift in position (from one side of the earth's orbit to the other) did not visibly affect perspective.

What suggested that explanation to Galileo? Well, if Copernicus was correct, then given the absence of perspective shift, given some elementary geometry and some other simple assumptions, a vast distance from earth to the stars followed nearly logically. Note that Galileo's explanation attempting to rescue Copernican theory is framed within the context of the Copernican theory itself. But Galileo's suggestion did not thereby represent circular reasoning. (Furthermore, he was right, although had he been wrong that would not have affected the legitimacy of his suggestion.)

That is precisely what Darwin was doing. His theory might reasonably lead one to expect numerous fossil transitional forms. Yet this did not seem to be the case, and Darwin tried to defuse that difficulty by suggesting that the fossil record was incomplete. What suggested that solution? Well, if evolution had happened smoothly, as Darwin envisioned, then given the gaps (absence of smoothness) in the fossil record, it followed nearly logically that the record was only an imperfect reflection of history. Darwin's reasoning was no more circular than was Galileo's. (Incidently, Darwin was not exactly grasping at straws. In fact, he discussed a variety of plausible reasons—some of them completely independent of any evolutonary considerations—that gaps, although from his perspective lamentable, were to say the least not completely surprising. The reasons were not, as Wayne Frair and Percival Davis claim, "lamely suggested."[37])

Of course, the fact that such a theory-saving attempt is legitimate and not viciously circular does not mean that it is a happy circumstance for the theory. Other things being equal, it is usually better for a theory if such moves are not necessary. But theory defenders are perfectly within their rational rights in constructing such attempts, and the history of science contains countless examples. And in the absence of further supporting evidence, opponents are also perfectly within their rational rights in rejecting such attempts, and in pushing the data as being genuinely problematic for the theory. At some point, it may become clear that one side or the other has the stronger case, but the mere logic of the situation does not offer either side any decisive weapon.

*3. Henry Morris.* Another favorite creationist circularity claim goes as follows. The primary evidence for evolution is the alleged progression in the fossil record according to the standard geological column. But the geological column itself is simply a theoretical construct. Strata are assigned their positions in that column according to the fossils they contain, and those fossils themselves are arranged and ordered according to evolutionary assumptions. Thus Morris: "The very structure of the geological ages is itself based on the assumption of evolution. Thus, the main *proof* of evolution is based on the *assumption* of evolution. . . . This is obviously a flagrant case of circular reasoning" (emphasis in original).[38]

If one did begin with the assumption of evolution, then constructed the entire geological column to match, then cited that column as primary evidence supporting the original assumption, one might indeed be reasonably investigated for circular reasoning. And Morris and some other creationists suggest that in fact geologists first decided that evolution was true, then proceeded to invent an orderly geological column based on that assumption.[39] But that is not quite accurate.[40] The fact that fossils seemed to show some sort of progression was one of the observations that prompted evolutionary theory. And "index fossils" were already being used as geological keys independent of any evolutionary assumptions two decades before Darwin was born (see chapter two).

Once the general outline of a geological column had emerged from prior geological investigation, use of that column as evidence for evolutionary theory was clearly not circular. (Whether or not the evidence should be taken to be very good evidence is an entirely different issue.) Furthermore, once one forms the general outline on an observational basis and accepts evolution as the explanation of that outline, it is not circular to use either that general outline or evolutionary theory itself as a key to organizing other parts of the column. Nor is there any logical problem with using either the column or any theory based on it to help sort out disturbed, jumbled or otherwise puzzling portions of that column. Indeed, the facts that previously accepted portions of the column could be explained by the theory and that newly discovered portions could be organized in conformity with the theory (if they could) would constitute some degree of evidential support for the theory, since it would exhibit the theory's explanatory, systematizing, sense-making power.

## Science Cannot Investigate Origins

Earlier in this chapter we surveyed a number of reasons often cited as showing that evolution is not genuine science. Some creationists make the broader claim that science cannot properly deal with any deep historical matter, and some argue in particular that science cannot handle any matter of initial origins. Such conclusions obviously would have significant implications for the creation-evolution debate.

The general intuition behind such claims is that essential characteristics in virtue of which something is an origin are, so to speak, at right angles to essential defining characteristics of science. Science thus simply cannot get a grip on origins. Some of the reasons cited overlap with those advanced as showing that evolutionary theory is not science. However, this issue is both important enough and distinct enough to warrant separate discussion.

Nearly all creationists wish to uphold the scientific legitimacy and indeed the high status of the bulk of science—most physics, most biology, most geology, most chemistry and so forth. Nearly all creationists are perfectly happy with and even ready to defend any science that deals with presently occurring, presently investigatable natural processes, no matter how theoretical, how far removed from direct observation or at what level of theoretical abstraction. For instance, few creationist groups have principial objections to atomic theory, quark theory, black hole theory, molecular genetics theory and so forth.[41] Most creationists accept as fair game for science, scientific theorizing and scientific investigation any presently occurring or repeatable natural events or processes, no matter how indirectly one must investigate them.

Most creationists, then, take the theoretical to be legitimate in principle, even in cases involving the unobservable (despite the fact that the inductivism often endorsed would imply the illegitimacy of the theoretical). However, the theoretical becomes scientifically illegitimate, they claim, when it is not properly anchored in the empirical. To be properly empirically anchored, on their view, a scientific theory must ultimately rest, either directly or indirectly, on what is observable. That observable foundation must consist either of presently observable natural occurrences (such as volcanoes) or of presently observable experimentally reproducible occurrences (such as chemical reactions in the lab).[42] Obviously, events that are unique, prehuman and unreproducible cannot be empirically anchored in these ways and thus cannot be scientifically investigated. And, on this view, theories about these events will be only unconfirmable speculation—not science.[43] We can indeed speculate and hypothesize all we wish, but where there are no empirical checks there will be no way of telling whether or not our hypotheses are even close. And we should not confuse such bouts of free-floating speculation with real science.

But clearly, the objection continues, the origins of the cosmos, the earth, life, species and human beings are unique. We did not and cannot observe them—we were not there. Further, since alleged evolutionary origins developed over millions of years, we obviously cannot reproduce them in a laboratory, and we certainly cannot reproduce supernatural creation. Thus it follows that science cannot even in principle investigate origins in any scientifically legitimate way.[44] Of course if science cannot investigate origins legitimately, then theories of the origin of the cosmos, of the earth, of life, of species and of humans will have no scientific legitimacy whatever.

This objection is a bit tricky, so we will edge up to it gradually. First, creationist practice itself sometimes appears to undercut some parts of this objection. No global floods are occurring now, we cannot reproduce a global flood experimentally, and the flood was utterly unique. Furthermore, other than Scripture, to which creation science does not appeal, there are no direct observational data of the flood itself. Yet creationists frequently advance empirical reasons for accepting a global flood and link theories and explanations about various aspects of the flood to empirical data.

What exactly is the procedure, since it cannot be direct observation, experimental reproduction or anything of that sort? Basically, it involves examining geological structures, strata, fossils, coal deposits and the like, then arguing that proper extrapolation in the light of present laws (from thermodynamics, hydrology and geology) points to a global flood as the rational explanation. But is that really science? The original event of the flood is forever unrecoverable, and decisive confirmation is thus completely out of the question. Given those limitations, creationists a couple of decades ago frequently denied that any investigation of the past—including their own—was science. Thus, Gish said, "science has no way of ever proving *anything* that has occurred in the past" (my emphasis).[45]

More recently, however, some creationists have softened the denial a bit. For instance, according to Morris and Parker, "scientific evidence can point to the fact of a creation period, for example, but there is no way that the specific duration of that period could be determined scientifically."[46] So the fact that there was a creation period representing a discontinuity in the natural order can be supported scientifically, but science cannot penetrate into that creative period and investigate events and processes involved within it. But if the fact of creation can be indicated scientifically, then, obviously, unique, nonrepeatable, unobserved events of the past are not totally out of the realm of science—at least, their occurrence can be a legitimate scientific conclusion. Although quite a few creationists still claim that such historical/scientific evaluations do not constitute true—that is, inductivist—science, some creationists agree that it is genuine science but maintain that we should be somewhat less confident concerning such unrepeatable matters than concerning ongoing, reproducible events and processes.[47]

In historical cases such as the flood, scientific conclusions must rest on empirical investigation of the expected natural consequences of the events in question. Thus even this indirect sort of empirical investigation is possible only to the extent that presently operating natural processes and laws were involved in producing those consequences. But to the extent that natural processes ran their course in the flood (no matter how the event was initiated), information about scouring, sedimentation and so forth provided by investigation of ordinary present local floods can be extrapolated into expected effects of the global flood, and those expectations can be empirically checked.

While natural historical consequences of even unique, historical, nonnatural events can be studied scientifically (confirming that such events took place), some causes and mechanisms operating within such discontinuities are by definition outside of the natural order and thus cannot be similarly studied. We simply have no empirically grounded guidelines for theorizing about, much less understanding, such processes. That is why, on this creationist view, despite the fact that the competing models can be evaluated scientifically (as discussed earlier), they are not themselves science.

In the case of the flood, creationists contend that many natural processes continued in operation while the flood was occurring—erosion, sedimentation, hydrodynamic sorting and so forth. The activity even during the flood of those presently observable sorts of processes is what allows investigation and conceptual reconstruction of some events within the flood itself. But with origins, creationists argue, the case is different, since origins were the results of laws and processes other than those presently operating. Thus we cannot extrapolate from present processes to origin processes, nor can we conceptually reconstruct origin events out of our scientific knowledge, all of which rests on present processes. So although scientific evidence can be advanced for the view that there *was* a creative origin (as Morris and Parker claimed above), there can be no *science* of that origin itself.

Now, it may well be true that *ultimate* origins required processes that are not presently operating. But that does not necessarily have any bearing on the origin of the earth, or the origin of life, or the origin of species, or the origin of human beings. There is more than one type of origin.

Consider, for instance, the origin of this year's tulip blossoms. This origin can be explained in perfectly natural terms, completely within the context of presently ongoing processes. Or consider the origin of the most recently produced volcanic island. Here again is an origin—but an origin that involves no processes that are either unique or beyond the reach (in principle) of scientific investigation. That origin is embedded in a context of present law and processes. Or consider a more novel case. At some point in the distant past, a number of rare, maybe even absolutely unique, natural circumstances all intersected at one point in Oklo in the African nation of Gabon, and a low-level nuclear reaction occurred for a period in some concentrated river sediments.[48] The origin of that "natural reactor" was, so far as is known, an utterly unique origin—and utterly natural as well. It was a unique, one-time origin, brought about by an incredible coinciding of a set of natural processes. Thus even unique, unlikely origins can be embedded in a context of present law and processes, can be brought about by those present laws and processes and thus can properly be investigated scientifically.

What all this illustrates is that not all origins are ultimate origins of a type that might involve processes science could not investigate. One cannot rule out scientific investigation of the origin of this year's flowers, the origin of volcanic islands, the origin of the Oklo natural reactor or the origin of the earth, life, species and humans *merely because they are origins*. To rule them out, one must make a case that they are origins of a type that cannot be placed within a context of present law and processes. Perhaps such a case can indeed be made. But that is a very different matter.

### A Final Note

The popular objections to evolution based on creationist conceptions of philosophy of science do not, then, seem to exhibit much promise. That is not to say that evolutionary theory is not in some way philosophically defective, but only that the major creationist attempts to show that it fails to be genuine science are themselves inadequate. Nor is it to say that evolutionary theory might not be utterly defective in some other way entirely—empirically or theoretically or theologically, for instance. But attempts to discredit evolutionary theory by employing any of the above philosophical claims look unsuccessful.

# 11 THE NATURE OF SCIENCE
## Popular Anticreationist Mistakes

**C**reationists are not the only ones who try for quick backdoor victories using philosophy of science. Charges that creation science violates the definition of science or otherwise fails to meet various criteria of science and is thus not real science at all are quite popular among many evolutionists and other critics of creationism. And just as creationists are not alone in employing this sort of tactic, they are not alone in being seriously confused about various philosophy of science matters. Indeed, a number of the same confusions show up.[1] Of course, there are professionally competent philosophers of science who are evolutionists. But in this chapter we will look at some of the influential popular philosophical attempts to establish the illegitimacy of creation science as science.

### Definitions
The charge that creation science is by definition not science is immensely popular among critics of creationism. Those who level that charge do not always provide a full, rigorous definition of science, but several prominent sources come close to doing just that, and they are the subject of this section.

*The National Academy of Science.* In 1984 the NAS published *The View from the NAS,*[2] intended to clarify several key issues in the creation-evolution dispute. One of those issues was the nature of genuine science. The characterization of science given, however, was a seriously confused, even bizarre, roughly Popperian picture. It contained claims that our "understanding of the universe is advanced by elimination of disproved ideas," that scientists keep testing "until one [theory] emerges as the most probable explanation," that this is "the scientific method," that a "hypothesis may develop into a theory" if it is well supported, that "verifiable facts always take precedence," that on the failure of expected test results a theory is "proved false"—and so forth.[3] By now, reasons that each of those claims is mistaken should be familiar. (Despite pronouncing authoritatively on philosophy of science, the committee that wrote the NAS statement included four lawyers but no philosophers of science.)

Note, incidentally, that if Popperism were correct, advocates of evolutionary theory ought to be trying ferociously to falsify evolutionary theory, since on that view proper science consists of attempts to subject bold theories to stringent, potentially falsifying tests. That, of course, simply is not what one sees within either the evolutionary community or science as a whole.

*National Science Teachers Association.* In 1985, largely in response to creationism, the NSTA board of directors endorsed the following three criteria that any theory must meet to be "included in the system of science":

(a) the theory can explain what has been observed;

(b) the theory can predict what has not yet been observed; and

(c) the theory can be tested by further experimentation and modified as new data are acquired.[4]

There are, of course, problems here. First, as we have seen, no theory ever explains all of the relevant data, and virtually every theory, including creation science, can provide explanations for some portion of the data. Second, predictions emerge only out of a mix of background theories, instrumentation theories, boundary conditions, the theory in question and so forth. It is relatively easy to construct background theories that can be used in conjunction with nearly any theory to produce new predictions. In any case, creation science does produce empirical predictions—for instance, that there will always, eventually, be exceptions to any alleged hierarchical order in the fossil sequence, that almost no significant transition fossils will ever be found and so forth. Third, the flat claim of theory modification in light of new data is a bit off key. Recall the earlier discussion of the principle of tenacity. But in any case, creationist theories change as well. For instance, gap theory was superseded by flood geology, and absolute fixity of species has essentially disappeared as creationists have widely accepted microevolution. (We will discuss this issue in more detail shortly.)

So it looks as though the three criteria are woefully oversimplified and in some degree mistaken. And as vague as they are, if they *were* correct, they would pose no problem for many creationists, whose theories meet all three criteria.

*Judge William Overton.* Overton, in his 1982 decision striking down the Arkansas "balanced treatment" legislation, adopted as a first approximation the position that science is whatever is "accepted by the scientific community."[5] If that is all there is to it, then the old objectivity aim of science is in rather serious jeopardy. A self-certified group of humans—not nature—becomes the final arbiter of science. Worse yet, from the perspective of those who oppose creationism, should some future sociological tidal wave, political swing, massive fundamentalist revival or selective natural disaster result in the bulk of the scientific community holding creationist positions, then on this definition creationism would *be* science. This definition does not rule creationism out of science on principle, but only on the basis of the contingent, and changeable, outlook of a particular group of human beings—scientists.

But Overton did accept and advance the following as "essential characteristics of science":

(1) science is guided by natural law;

(2) science is to be explanatory by reference to natural law;

(3) science is testable against the empirical world;

(4) science's conclusions are tentative, i.e., they are not necessarily the final word; and

(5) science is falsifiable.[6]

This definition does not look particularly promising. We have already seen that the matter of testability (3) is nowhere near the simple matter that definitions like that above tend to assume; that tentativity (4) does not in any straightforward way characterize science (recall the principle of tenacity, and, in fact, try to find any tentativity in the commitment of many scientists to the idea that species evolved); and that the requirement of falsifiability (5) is fraught with pitfalls.

Requirement 2 is worth brief examination. The content of this requirement, that science must be explanatory by reference to natural law, depends on what *explanation* means, which is a philosophical issue—and a disputed one at that. But events in recent decades in physics have driven some physicists to the view that in any traditional sense, there simply is no explanation for events on the quantum mechanical level. For instance, on one definition, to explain something is to make it understandable in terms of familiar experiences, just as one might intuitively understand the behavior of gas molecules by visualizing them as miniature billiard balls bouncing off each other, off the container walls and so forth.

But if that is what explaining involves, then according to some scientists, such as the Nobel physicist Richard Feynman, there just is no explanation of quantum-level phenomena, by reference either to natural law or to anything else. (Nobel physicist Niels Bohr once said that if someone claims that they can think about quantum phenomena without getting dizzy, it is a sure sign that they "have not understood anything whatever about it.") Quantum phenomena can be described—sort of—but not explained in any intuitive sense of the term. Overton's criteria would rule significant and crucial parts of present physics out of science. Clearly something is not quite right here.

Overton's definition is seriously inadequate on almost all counts and has come under intense criticism even from within the anticreationist community.[7] That creationism may fail to live up to this definition is no particular problem for creationism.

*National Center for Science Education.* The NCSE is a privately funded organization opposing creationist attempts to gain access to public-school science classrooms. (Ironically, the NCSE objects to the teaching of creationism in science classes in part on the grounds, paralleling Overton, that "the job of the teacher is to present the consensus of the discipline."[8] If this is true, then early teachers of evolution were not the praiseworthy leading edge of change—they were flouting their responsibility as teachers. Should creationists take over biology, that principle might then commit the NCSE to combating the teaching of evolution in science classes.)

In 1989 the NCSE published a book containing formal position statements concerning creationism and science from more than sixty scientific, religious and education organizations.[9] The organizations were virtually unanimous in declaring that science and religion do not overlap and that creationism of whatever form is religion—not science. Reasons varied, but among the more popular were that creationism either was not testable or had failed such tests, that it employed supernatural rather than exclusively natural concepts, that it was based on Scripture rather than on data and that it was held immune to revision. Of particular interest was the introduction, written by Isaac Asimov, which contained the following characterization of science:

Science is a process of thought, a way of looking at the Universe. It consists of the gathering of observations which can be confirmed by others using other instruments at other times in other ways. From these confirmed observations, consequences and conclusions can be reasoned out by logical methods generally agreed upon. These consequences and conclusions are tentative and can be argued over by different people in the field and modified or changed altogether if additional, or more subtle, observations are made. There is no belief held in advance of such observations and conclusions except that observations can be made, that consequences and conclusions can be reasoned out, and that the Universe can, at least to a degree, be made comprehensible in this fashion. (If these assumptions are not true, then there is no way of using the mind at all.)[10]

So data are utterly independent and objective. They are gathered with no preconceptions, prior theories or the like. Consequences and conclusions follow from data by logical methods. In that introduction Asimov also at least suggests (the prose is not totally clear) that theories are bodies of organized data and that the logic leading from observations to conclusions is so rigid that "it is hard, or even impossible" to keep scientific mistake, falsehood or imposture from eventual discovery. I was extremely surprised to find such utterly simplistic claims coming from Asimov (who as a science-fiction author was one of my adolescent heroes). With the possible exception of the point about tentativity, the view presented is very nearly straight 1620s Bacon, and virtually every one of the claims is seriously confused, for reasons discussed in chapter eight.[11]

### Naturalism as Essential to Science

Although the above definitions do not explicitly stress it, a major driving force underlying each is the conviction that proper science can make no reference to, no appeal to or no explanatory use of anything beyond the purely natural.[12] The supernatural, the miraculous, is strictly out of bounds in science. Doing science properly, on this view, requires that one formulate methods, concepts and strategies that would be appropriate for a universe in which there was no supernatural domain and that one then apply those methods, concepts and strategies in *this* universe, whether or not it is true that there is no supernatural domain, whether or not one has rational grounds for believing that there is a supernatural domain and even whether or not one *knows* that there is a supernatural domain. Science is *"forced* to function as if there is no such thing as a supernatural."[13]

As the "forced" in that last quote indicates, this policy of confining science to the natural is not proposed as a mere polite suggestion. For instance, the NCSE says that "by the very *definition* of science [scientists] cannot offer God's intervention as the cause for whatever they seek to explain" (my emphasis).[14] In addition, "science as practiced in modern times is *necessarily* naturalistic. . . . Explanations founded on miracles *cannot* be allowed" (my emphasis again).[15] Indeed, some take "supernatural explanation" to be a contradiction in terms.[16]

Of course one may impose any rules and restrictions on the investigation of nature that one wishes. After all, science is a human pursuit, and we humans are the ones doing it. But why this particular restriction? Why should the supernatural or the nonnatural be excluded from science so adamantly? This question has two standard answers. One answer rests on the philosophical doctrine of empiricism, and the other on a historical claim concerning the track record of nonnaturalistic considerations in science. We will look briefly at both.[17]

### Empiricism

It is frequently claimed that science, with its empirical methods, has no way of dealing with the supernatural, the superempirical or anything of that sort. Since it obviously would be pointless to try to handle anything for which one's methods were utterly inappropriate, science has no choice but to confine itself to the natural—the empirically investigatable. Thus according to Eugenie Scott, executive director of the NCSE, "Science has made a little deal with itself; because you can't put God in a test tube (or keep it out of one) science acts as if the supernatural did not exist. This methodological materialism is the cornerstone of modern science."[18] But if the limitations on science grow out of the limitations of empirical methods, why restrict ourselves to empirical methods?

One historically influential answer is that by definition knowledge must be based on empirical interaction with reality, and that whatever might be produced by any other approach is confusion at best, nonsense at worst. This doctrine of empiricism—that only what is ultimately based on sensory experience can be known or rationally believed or, in some versions, even thought—has a long, influential history going back perhaps as far as ancient Greece. Strong claims here are not uncommon. For instance, Strahler's third sentence is this: "By 'universe' I mean everything that can be observed and described by humans with reasonable assurance and general agreement that what is being observed exists as some recognizable form of matter or energy."[19] So what we humans cannot observe is just not part of the universe. Or what we do not have the concepts to describe is not part of the universe. This attempt simply to decree the universe down to our empirical and conceptual size is a fairly extreme form of empiricism.

Empiricism was updated and popularized in the eighteenth century by Locke and Hume and eventually was incorporated into late-nineteenth- and early-twentieth-century positivism. Although in stronger forms it has been pretty thoroughly discredited and abandoned within the professional philosophical and the philosophically informed scientific communities, it is still alive and well elsewhere. For instance, the NCSE defines science in terms of human *observation* (the term is used five times in Asimov's five-sentence definition), then defines the domain of science as "the realm of the rational," outside of which it is "impossible to prove or disprove" anything at all.[20] So the rational is what can be linked to empirical observation. Results of empirical scientific procedures are frequently compared with other alleged sources of knowledge, much to the detriment of the latter, which are mere "belief" or "faith."[21] Strahler, for instance, decrees that while empirical science is in the domain of knowledge, religion goes into the domain of belief—which he then later simply defines in terms of "faith without evidence," the very idea of "reasoned faith" being "another contradiction in terms."[22]

Popular as such views have been, simple empiricism faces serious difficulties. For instance, the doctrine itself is philosophical, not empirical, and thus if true would create severe difficulties for itself. And what empirical observations could be cited as indicating that anything outside the domain of the empirical is necessarily beyond the realm of the rational—especially since, on this view, the empirical would be totally blind to that whole realm to begin with? The claim seems arbitrary at best, if not simply self-defeating.

Beyond that, any strong form of empiricism would create serious, perhaps fatal, problems for science itself. As we have seen, science cannot work without a variety of philosophical, nonempirical principles. Unfortunately, such philosophical principles do not seem to be matters of human observation (at least, not any direct observation) and on empiricist views might thus be forbidden, thereby bringing science to an untimely halt. (And for that matter, as the archempiricist Hume himself pointed out, matters of *necessity* are beyond the empirical realm entirely. That would pose some problems for the earlier claim that science is "necessarily naturalistic.")

## Historical Track Records

The second answer to the question of why the nonnatural must be barred from science is the claim that as a practical matter of fact, purely natural (primarily empirical) methods are the only ones that have demonstrated any success and promise historically.[23] The nonnatural standpoints have such a dismal track record of unbroken failure that one's best bet is to do science as if naturalism were true and to ignore the possibility of supernatural intervention in the world's processes. Such an approach may conceivably go off track occasionally, if there are indeed supernatural interventions, but judging from the history of science the odds are still hugely in one's favor.

This is an interesting claim. It is, however, a historical claim, and in order to see whether or not it is correct, one would have to do some substantial historical work. The problem is, no one has done it. There are some obvious failures involving nonnaturalistic assumptions (geocentric theory is often claimed to be such a case) and some equally obvious failures involving purely naturalistic assumptions (such as Lysenko genetics).

But merely adding up failures and successes will not quite do, because historically essentially every theory, regardless of source, eventually gets abandoned as wrong. So in those terms, naturalistic and nonnaturalistic theories are even. One might attempt to determine which theories fell into which category, then try to determine which category—naturalism or non-naturalism—had the most theories that, although wrong, were somehow scientifically fruitful, useful or productive. Again, that would not be a trivial task and would involve some difficult historical and philosophical matters—and in any case it has not been done.

Some well-known attempts have been made to establish that religion has had a powerful negative effect on science,[24] but contemporary historians of science see that work as more propaganda than sober history.[25] In fact, although the topic is controversial, some historians argue that had it not been for Christianity there would be no science as we know it—that various mindsets and principles arising out of Christianity were essential to the birth of modern science.[26] Why, for instance, can *rational* investigation of nature be successful? Because nature is a creation of a Person who thinks, acts and created in the rationally orderly ways of persons. Why must our investigations of nature be *empirical?* Because nature is a creation of a *free* Person who could have created in any of an unlimited number of ways. So we cannot reconstruct reality just by pure reason—we have to look to see which option this free Person chose. Suppose that this is right. Would such a historical connection between Christianity and science mean that every theory that conforms to such requirements counts in favor of allowing religion to affect one's science?

And incidentally, some pretty respectable scientists deliberately built theological constraints into their scientific theorizing. Newton postulated absolute space and absolute time largely for theological reasons. It has been argued that the structure that Maxwell gave to his field theories was influenced by his views concerning the Trinity. Boyle rejected the medieval idea that nature abhors a vacuum because he thought he could show that such an idea was morally pernicious and subverted true Christianity. Newton's views concerning both the character and the quantity of matter in the universe had a theological basis. Pasteur rejected spontaneous generation in part on theological grounds. Herschel's theories concerning the nature of nebulae had direct links to his theology. And such theorizing was often productive and fruitful. Impetus theory, which was a crucial step on the road to modern views on inertia, was defended early on in part on grounds having to do with the character of the sacraments of the church. Early forms of some conservation principles in physics were initially defended on partially theological grounds.[27]

The point here, however, is not to establish any particular line on history. I merely wish to suggest that the claim about naturalism in science—that it can be justified through the history of science—will require historical support, that the necessary historical work has not been done adequately and that it may turn up some awkward surprises for the naturalist who does it. So whether this second claim stands is, I think, an open question.

### Imposing Restrictions

There is one other consideration here. Suppose it is true that building theological or scriptural concerns into science has not been terribly successful. But successful in what terms? Theoretical matters are never rigorously proven, so success is defined in the indirect terms of explanatory power, empirical adequacy, fruitfulness and other evaluative factors governed by shaping principles. In particular cases, shaping principles can conflict. For example, one theory may have greater explanatory power but be less empirically adequate than a rival theory. Unfortunately, there are no overall rules for resolving such conflicts. Thus there is room for rational disagreement over what constitutes success. A creationist for whom *conformity to Scripture* is a shaping principle may rank such conformity above other evaluative principles, may judge success accordingly and may hold that this shaping principle must take precedence over any other.[28]

And there is nothing inherently or by definition irrational in doing that. Indeed, the case can be made that Newton, Boyle and other major historical scientists did exactly that. One could argue that history has shown that policy to be irrational or incoherent, but, again, one will actually need to make the historical case, and that turns out not to be as easy as it might initially seem.

But suppose that a case for such restrictions could be made. Does the fact (if it is so) that empirical methods cannot get a grip on something constitute any reason for thinking that this thing does not or cannot exist, or that it does not or cannot have any effect on the operation of the cosmos? Obviously not; and therein lies a potential problem for such restrictions. For while we can indeed impose whatever restrictions we wish, what we cannot do is then without further argument claim that the results of following those restrictions will be truth, approximate truth, self-correction or anything of the sort.

The problem is that nature may or may not conform to our stipulations. For instance, suppose that some czar wishes to be a respected scientist but just cannot do much math. One solution to his problem would be to decree that mathematics could not be employed in science—that in what he means by *science* mathematical concepts are by definition prohibited. Well, the czar's scientists, and even the czar himself, might construct a pretty amazing system. But if nature is fundamentally mathematical, that pretty amazing system would still be pretty amazingly mistaken. The czar cannot both put a priori restrictions on science *and* claim that the results reflect reality. If nature itself violates those restrictions, the results are going to be wrong.

Those who simply stipulate a naturalism in science face exactly the same situation. If nature is not a closed, naturalistic system—that is, if reality does not respect the naturalists' edict—then the science built around that edict cannot be credited a priori with getting at truth, being self-corrective or anything of the sort. Now if we had some rational reason for accepting naturalism as in fact true, then stipulating that science had to be naturalistic in order to have a chance at uncovering genuine truth would make perfect sense. But that would involve making a case for naturalism—not simply decreeing that science was by definition or for convenience naturalistic, which is the path taken by various evolutionists. For instance, Stanley Beck endorses observational and naturalistic boundaries for science, then simply asserts that scientific "concepts and theories will improve, grow . . . and be constantly better approximations of the real natural processes."[29] Or consider the following, taken from the 1982 statement of the West Virginia Academy of Science: "Science limits itself to ways of reasoning that can only produce naturalistic explanations." And in the next paragraph, "There is an overwhelming consensus among scientists . . . that interpretation of all available evidence by *scientific* standards renders contrary claims [to old-earth evolution] highly implausible."[30]

Some people have recognized that confining science to naturalism would nearly guarantee that some truths were forever beyond science should it turn out that supernatural events or processes did at times intersect the empirical realm. And some, recognizing that and faced with the dilemma of either giving up stipulating naturalism in science or risking the possibility that science will be incapable of getting at such truth, have chosen the latter.[31] For instance, Niles Eldredge says, "It could even be true—but it cannot be construed as science,"[32] while Douglas Futuyma adds, "It isn't necessarily wrong. It just is not amenable to scientific investigation."[33] Michael Ruse agrees: "It is not necessarily wrong . . . but it is not science."[34]

So if, say, we want to know about origins, and if the truth is supernatural, that truth cannot be a part of our science, even if we had some alternative rational access to that truth. One characterization of science that has been popular among scientists is that it is "a search for truth, no holds barred." On the present view, though, if one had some rationally defensible grounds for thinking that God had instantaneously created, say, basic phyla full blown, one would evidently as a scientist by definition have to pretend that one really did not know that particular truth.[35] That particular hold *would* be barred.

But then, exactly what sort of project is science supposed to be, if truth is not *the,* or at least *an,* ultimate object? The answer given by a number of people is—it's a game.[36]

But if truth *is* the object, then why shouldn't anything that we have rational reason for accepting as truth be allowed in principle to have some bearing on science? If we have rational reason, from whatever source, to accept naturalism, and if we are trying to get at truth in science, then confining our science to naturalism is perfectly sensible. If we have rational reason, from whatever source, to think that the earth is young, and if we are trying to get at truth in science, then confining our science to that short span is perfectly sensible.

But what one cannot reasonably do is to stipulate naturalistic restrictions on science by definition and simultaneously just assume that any and all truths about the cosmos around us must necessarily fall within the limits of those restrictions, or that anything produced under those restrictions is truth.[37]

## Empirical Philosophy

As mentioned earlier, an ultimate underlying intuition is that the empirical cannot deal with the nonnatural, such as the theological, the philosophical and the immaterial. There is simply no way for any empirical method to get a grip on anything nonempirical. There is no way to test it, to experiment on it, to measure it or, as Scott said earlier, to get it into a test tube. Empirical method, when confronted by the nonempirical, the spiritual, the supernatural, has to just throw up its hands. That at least is the claim.

But we have seen that it is not true that empirical scientific method cannot deal with things beyond the realm of human observation as such, since science routinely deals with all manner of unobservable theoretical entities, events and processes. It does so, recall, by constructing an integrated conceptual grid that it attempts to fit on the cosmos as we experience it, or as it confronts us. Those grids are composed of data, theories and nonempirical shaping principles. Empirical challenges to the total systems arise when nature lodges some sort of objection to having such a grid forced onto it. Nature's objections—which, recall, are not direct but are mediated through the system itself by various shaping principles—can be and often are taken to be challenges to the theory in question. But they can also, as we have seen, lead to repudiation of what science had previously taken the data to be.

But now we need to push that same lesson one step further. When a grid refuses to fit adequately, we can indeed decide that either the theory in question or some of the data in question are the source of the difficulty, and we may modify or even eventually abandon them for that reason. When we do so, we take them to have been empirically challenged by nature. Allowing such challenges from nature to percolate into our scientific systems and allowing that percolation process to factor into the shaping of those systems is primarily what we mean when we claim that science is fundamentally *empirical.*

But there is also one other alternative response to the misfitting of a grid on nature. We can also decide that the problem lies ultimately somewhere in our philosophical shaping principles. Since the shaping principles, being philosophical, often lie deep within our worldviews, we often have a strong reluctance to tinker with them. And since they are in a sense not as directly in touch with the empirical realm as either data or our theories, the impact felt on them from the failure of a grid to fit the world adequately is much more indirect and muted. But the impact is there nonetheless. And that impact, being of the same general type as that affecting theory and data, is properly construed as empirical, just as it is in the cases of theory and data. So we confront nature with integrated conceptual systems. To the extent that nonempirical factors—shaping principles—are inescapably built into our scientific structures, and to the extent that those structures are at empirical risk before nature, nature can, in the long run, speak, however subtly and quietly, to the nonempirical, the philosophical, the metaphysical and even the religious, if they are built into our scientific systems. So the empirical and the nonempirical *can* interact, and both can be altered by means of their mutual incorporation into our human scientific constructions. The claim that even some creationists make, that "science is blind to metaphysics," simply is not true.[38]

Historical cases are not rare; here are three quick examples. For centuries, astronomers believed that descriptions of celestial motions had to be compounded out of systems of circular motions. That requirement was an explicitly embraced philosophical shaping principle within the Ptolemaic system. That system became increasingly unwieldy as it had to incorporate increasing and increasingly accurate data, and finally, when it was confronted with a mathematically more elegant alternative, that system *and its key philosophical shaping principle* were considered to have been repudiated by nature and were replaced.

More recently it was widely believed that the laws of nature were rigidly deterministic—given a specific cause in a specific context, a precise effect was completely inevitable. The grounds for that stipulation concerning the character of natural law were partly philosophical and had deep historical roots. But in the twentieth century, that philosophical decree has been abandoned largely because of difficulties posed by empirical results of quantum mechanics for systems incorporating that philosophical principle.

Or to take the most obvious current case, nearly every advocate of evolutionary theory believes that the nonempirical, even religious, principle that "science should conform to Genesis literally construed" has been thoroughly discredited by empirical failure of the creationist systems conforming to that principle. If that proposed creationist shaping principle *has* been discredited by empirical failure of the resultant systems, then, obviously, nonempirical principles built into scientific systems are at indirect empirical risk when the systems containing them are confronted by nature. Or if William Provine, James Birx and others are correct that Christian theism and contemporary science are logically incompatible, and if contemporary science is empirical, then obviously such theism must have the capability of coming into at least indirect conflict with the empirical—and that is all that is required for empirical testability.[39]

What all this means is that given the systems character of science, and given that those systems inevitably include nonempirical principles, there is a sort of feedback loop by which in the practice of science the empirical is brought to bear on anything—empirical, nonempirical, metaphysical or whatever—that is woven into science. That bearing can be tenuous, complicated and not directly empirical—but that is a very different matter from being nonexistent. One would thus anticipate that the nonempirical, metaphysical doctrines necessarily employed in the very conduct of science would be subject to subtle empirical pressures and in some instances might even be overthrown. And, again, that has happened repeatedly throughout the history of science. Such principles are not, of course, given up because of some specific piece of pure data. They are given up as the mixes, the grids of which they are a part, are seen to fail in ways thought to be important when brought into contact with nature.

In any case it is not at all obvious that attempts to legislate creation science out of contention by some sort of stipulative naturalism really work. Perhaps some objection in the region here will work, but the presently popular attempts do not, being based on confusion concerning philosophy of science, unsubstantiated claims about history or epistemologies known to be defective.

### Creation Science Is Really Disguised Religion

The charge that creation science is really just disguised religion is found in virtually every critical discussion of creation science.[40] One question that immediately arises is, Why should one think that this is a criticism? Even if true, it establishes that creationism cannot be proper science only if being religious or a religion automatically disqualifies something from also being proper science. Why think that this is true? One might try to establish that by definition or by appeal to some philosophical principles of rationality as discussed above. But given the infusion of theological concerns into scientific theorizing by Newton, Boyle and others mentioned above, we might end up having to conclude that Newton either did not know what science was or just did not understand rationality as well as we do.[41] Maybe one of those conclusions is true, but they certainly sound presumptuous. Or maybe allowing religion into science was all right back then, but we have since learned better and it is not legitimate now. Maybe so, but establishing that would require a difficult historical and philosophical case, and there are no compelling cases of that sort available at present. (In fact, it is not at all clear how one would establish that there is anything defective about taking theological principles as shaping principles in science. More later.)

But in any case, why think that creation science is actually religion? At least, why think that versions of it that neither make mention of nor base arguments on Scripture or theology are really disguised religion? The reasons found in the literature critical of creation science generally fall into one or more of four categories. We shall briefly examine each.

### Creation Science Is Ultimately Based on Scripture

The claim here is that the positions and theories advanced by creation science just happen to match exactly what fundamentalist creationists take Genesis to teach. Even if creation scientists do not overtly appeal to Scripture, it is the underlying source and inspiration, and they are tacitly conforming their theories to it even while giving selected pieces of data hernias as they stretch them to try to support those theories.[42]

This objection, however, carries no real weight. Suppose that it is true. That would mean at most that the *source* of creationist theories was religious. It would not at all imply that the theories themselves were religious and not scientific. It is as near a commonplace as one finds in science that the source of a theory is irrelevant to its legitimacy, status and truthfulness. Darwin, as some historians argue, may have structured parts of his theory as he did because of his commitment to various Victorian social values. But even if he did, that has no bearing whatever on whether or not his theory was scientific, whether or not it was well supported or whether or not it is true.

Of course, one might argue that that is the only reason creationists hold their theories, that there is virtually no empirical evidence for them, and masses of evidence against them. But even if that is true, that has to do only with whether or not the theory is well supported empirically—not with whether or not the theory fails to fit the category *scientific*.

So it may be true that no creationists would dream of pushing the sorts of theories they do were it not for their belief in a certain interpretation of Genesis. But that is, even if true, utterly irrelevant to the scientific status of the theory.[43]

### Creation Science Is Motivated Solely by a Religious Agenda

This objection is similar to that just discussed, and it fails for essentially the same reason.[44] Suppose it were true that creationists would not have the faintest interest in any of the relevant issues were it not for a fundamentalist missionary zeal, or were it not that they thought creation science was a slick way to sneak their religious agenda into public-school classrooms. That would not in any way establish that the theories themselves were not legitimately scientific.

Newton's stated motive in constructing some of his theories was to promote belief in God.[45] The stated motives of some Enlightenment thinkers in adopting Newtonian theories was to destroy religion. It seems perfectly clear that neither of those contradictory motivations had any bearing whatever on whether or not Newton's theories themselves were religious, antireligious or genuinely scientific. Similarly, there seems no good reason to think that creationists' allegedly religious motivations make the theories themselves religious or have any bearing whatever on whether or not their theories are legitimately scientific.

### Creationist Theories Are Not Held Tentatively

This is a particularly popular objection. The idea is that creationists hold their views far too strongly, in defiance of the "rule of science" that theories be held tentatively. Indeed, the NCSE claims that having such a firm grip on one's views disqualifies them not only from being genuinely scientific but even from being genuine theories.[46]

It is relatively easy to see why this objection is misguided. First, most who voice this objection misconceive the normal operation of science, having missed the principle of tenacity, discussed earlier. But more immediately, it surely is not the fault of a theory that it inspires such dogged loyalty. One can hold any theory in an inappropriate way, but that says something about the holder—not about the theory. Some hold evolution far from tentatively, and perhaps far more firmly than they ought. But inflated claims for the status of evolutionary theory do not at all show that there is something wrong with the theory. They only tell us something about certain of its advocates. Similarly, if creationists hold their theories in inappropriate ways, that tells us nothing about their theories.[47]

### Creationists Never Change Their Views

This related objection is one of the most popular criticisms of creationists. Being truly scientific requires that one be prepared to modify, and in fact modify, one's views over time in the face of new data. Since creationists never do, creationism is not genuinely scientific.[48]

The two biggest problems here are that the underlying philosophy of science is not quite as straightforward as apparently thought, and the claim about creationism is simply mistaken. As we saw earlier in the discussion of the principle of tenacity, scientists often hang on to theories (even troubled theories) for surprising lengths of time. The basics of Newtonian physics, once considered the ultimate in science, were essentially unchanged for well over two centuries, despite the fact that Newton in his original publications pointed out specific empirical difficulties with his own theory (as would Darwin with his theory a century and a half later). Creationism in modern form has been around for significantly less than half that time, so even if it had remained fundamentally unchanged, it is not clear why that length of time alone should be seen as problematic.

One could argue that there was good reason for loyalty to the basics of Newton, but that there is not adequately good (or even any) reason for loyalty to creation science. Perhaps so—but that changes the issue from one of mere refusal to change. The criticism now becomes that there is compelling reason to modify or abandon creation science but its adherents improperly refuse to do so. Again, maybe such a case can be made, but it cannot be made merely by claiming that creationists never change position.

But it simply is not true that creationists never modify or abandon positions.[49] Gap theory gave way to flood geology. Absolute fixity of species has essentially disappeared as virtually all creationists have accepted microevolution. Many creationists now accept mutation and natural selection as being the mechanism for microevolution. The earlier belief in mingled human and dinosaur tracks in the Paluxy River formation has, on further investigation, been repudiated by nearly every major creationist group. Some leading creationists have abandoned earlier claims concerning geological overthrusting. Some major creationist groups have modified positions concerning the source and implications of the laws of thermodynamics. On the other hand, the creationist case against evolution has been significantly expanded over the last two decades, as at least some creationists have incorporated developments in genetics, cellular biology, biochemistry and other areas into their systems.

Of course, one could argue that these changes were not of the right sort,[50] that the theoretical expansions of creationism were confused, unjustified, incompetent or otherwise defective. Perhaps so. But even if so, that constitutes a different objection, and one that requires a different sort of case. The original charge—that creationists never change their views regardless of the advance of data—is simply not true. (Oddly enough, at least one evolutionist seems to hold it against them that they *have* made some changes.[51])

There is an interesting addendum to this particular criticism of creationism. If correct, the above objections would create difficulties for evolutionary theory also, since few of its advocates are prepared to give up or abandon the idea that all of life is related through ancestry. For instance, James Skehan (and presumably the NSTA) apparently wants to insist both that evolutionary theory has become rationally unchallengeable and that creationists' resistance to change and lack of tentativity violate requirements of true science. There is an obvious dilemma here. How can one declare the basic idea of evolution to be beyond rational challenge on the one hand, yet avoid having evolution being thereby scientifically disqualified for not being sufficiently tentative and subject to change on the other? Skehan's solution is to declare that the *"general* validity" of evolution is *"logically demonstrable"* (my emphasis)—so the basic idea of evolution is preserved immune from challenge—while "our understanding of the theory itself evolves"—thus evolutionists are still within the bounds of science because their *understandings* are tentative and subject to change.[52] But if that is a legitimate ploy, creationists can use it as well.

### Key Concepts of Creation Science Are Inherently Religious

As we saw in an earlier chapter, some creationists tried to make their views legally more acceptable by purging them of all references and appeals to religious principles, theological doctrines and scriptural citations. Creationists believed that their theories, if rid of all explicit supernatural references, would be legitimate candidates for scientific consideration. That strategy has not been well received in major portions of the evolution community. Why not? One objection is, roughly, that the very concept of a complex entity coming into sudden existence is religious. For instance, Overton, in the Arkansas decision, asserted that "the idea of sudden creation from nothing, or creatio ex nihilo, is an inherently religious concept."[53] The NCSE concurs, claiming that a teacher would "cross the line [into religious advocacy] by teaching that the universe was in fact created all at one time, and that this was scientifically demonstrable." One might think that perhaps the term *created* is the source of the problem. Not so, according to the NCSE: "Not using 'the C-word' is an attempt to avoid entanglement with the First Amendment. But the *content* of what they would teach qualifies as religious advocacy" (NCSE emphasis).[54]

Evidently, then, the claim that things came into sudden existence at one time is itself an *inherently religious* claim. But surely that is a bit peculiar. Consider this hypothetical case. Scientists manage to construct a time machine and proceed to trace life backward in order to settle the origins issue once and for all. They are tracing the lineage of, say, mammals when at some moment there is an abrupt change. One instant there are no mammals, and the next instant there a bunch of them are. Films of the moment, run frame by frame, show the same thing. One frame contains no mammals, the frame instantly following shows some. And suppose (what is in fact true) that scientists could not remotely imagine any natural process, law or combination of laws by which that could happen. What should those scientists do? According to Overton and the NCSE, they could not in the next biology textbook say, "Well, mammals simply appeared at one point in time and we can't imagine how that happened." They could not put that in a *science* text, if the admission of instant appearance is *inherently religious*. But surely something has gone dreadfully wrong here, if what would in that case be an empirically observed truth about mammals would be simply defined as religious and if being religious means that science must pretend not to know it.

One might claim, of course, that in this hypothetical case the instantaneous appearance was *observed,* making the fact no longer religious but scientific. But to claim that is to claim that whether the concept is religious or scientific depends on its source. And if that is true, then the religious character of the claim is obviously not inherent—it depends on how the claim arose. That, if true, destroys the objection entirely.

We do not, of course, have time machines. But the necessity of indirect, theoretical investigation does not destroy scientific character. If it did, nearly everything theoretical within science—atoms, fields, entropy, quarks— would be scientifically illegitimate. Thus if a claim based on direct time-machine observation is legitimately scientific, then that exact same claim, advanced as a theoretical postulate indirectly based on empirical evidence, is also of legitimately scientific character—whether well supported or not.

Creationists, of course, believe that empirical evidence—the character of the fossil record, probability arguments, "irreducible complexity" arguments and so forth—provide empirical grounds that, while not as direct as time-machine observations, rationally support the conclusion that some things appeared in history on earth full blown. A decree that it is impermissible to construe empirical evidence, *no matter what it is,* as supporting such a view must be backed by some sort of an argument. The flat claim that any such view is inherently religious does not provide the necessary support. One could try to establish that such sudden appearance was somehow impossible (although the historical track record of impossibility claims is singularly dismal). In any case that would be a different objection. Or one could argue that the creationist empirical case for sudden appearance was woefully inept. Perhaps so, but again, that would be a different objection— one having nothing to do with creationism being inherently religious. But in either of these last two cases, some real work is required. The mere "inherently religious" label is unable to bear the weight of the objection.[55]

It is also worth noting that evolutionists almost universally separate the *fact* of evolution from questions or ignorance concerning the *mechanism* of evolution. And that is a perfectly legitimate distinction. Presumably, one could make the same distinction in the creationist case. Thus the fact that there is no understood or even imaginable *mechanism* for sudden appearance, or even that any mechanisms for divine instantaneous creation might in principle be beyond human understanding, would have minimal implications for the scientific legitimacy of the *fact* of sudden appearance or instantaneous creation, contrary to some evolutionists.[56] Morris on one occasion at least hints at this.[57]

### Other Popular Philosophical Criticism

Scientific theorizing and acceptance of theories, some claim, must be governed not by authority but by empirical data.[58] But for creationists, it is charged, authority takes precedence over data. Thus creationism is not genuine science. (Although the authority referred to here—Scripture—is in fact considered to be supernaturally inspired, the core of this present objection is not that supernatural authority is illegitimate in science but that any authority not ultimately subject to data is forbidden.)

This objection is a bit tricky. First, authority plays a profound role in any scientific endeavor. The overwhelming bulk of the scientific theories most of us believe, we accept on the authoritative word of teachers, texts (by authors we do not know), journals (by authors we do not know) and so forth. Scientific articles typically contain more references and citations—that is, appeals to the authoritative word of other authors—than any other sort of literature. And even the NCSE advises teachers who have creationist colleagues but who do not have "sufficient understanding of evolution to point out the flaws in [the creationists'] arguments" that one option is to "point out to the teacher that the scientific establishment is firmly on the side of evolution."[59]

The crucial assumption, though, is that if one tracked down each scientific reference, each reference cited within each reference and so forth (which is virtually never done), at the ultimate end of each trail one would discover some collection of empirical data, some set of observations, some group of direct experimental results. But creationist authority, it is charged, never tracks completely to the empirical in that manner. Tracing creationist authority eventually brings one to some nonempirical barrier (typically called "revelation" or "inspiration"). Thus the authority employed in real science ultimately rests on the empirical, whereas the authority appealed to in creationism ultimately does not.

Perhaps so. But a bit of caution is needed here. For one thing, the picture of all science ultimately resting on the pure empirical is, as we have seen, not quite accurate. For another, many creationist attempts within recent years deliberately have avoided appeal to authority—especially scriptural or other theological authority. For yet another, it is probably inaccurate to say that authority has precedence over data for creationists. The more responsible among contemporary creationists do try to respect all empirical data. Indeed, they often have an extremely high view of data, viewing them as one means by which God speaks through the creation. (On this view, God's speaking though the creation is "general revelation," in contrast to God's "special revelation," which is spoken through Scripture.) One cannot play fast and loose with data having that sort of status.[60] One might, however, let one's theorizing about those data be governed by authority (such as Scripture), as many creationists do. But that would constitute letting authority have precedence over data only if data in and of themselves tried to advance certain theories while authority overrode those attempts. But as noted earlier, that inductivist and positivist conception of data is mistaken.

## A Final Note

The popular philosophy-of-science objections raised against creationism do not work. In fact, some of the objections are rather surprising. One critic claims that one cannot even tell whether or not a theory is scientific unless one can discover such things as "the names of the people who have spent years of time developing and testing the theory."[61]

In any case, all this is not to say that creation science is not in some way philosophically defective, but only that the most prominent of the attempts to show that it fails to be genuine science themselves fail. Nor is it to say that creation science might not be defective in some other way entirely—empirically or theoretically or theologically, for instance. But attempts to discredit creation science by employing any of the above philosophical claims appear unsuccessful.

# 12 THEISTIC EVOLUTION
## Catching It from Both Sides

**C**reationists and naturalistic evolutionists agree on very few things. But they do seem to agree that theistic evolution is woefully—even perniciously—confused. Surprisingly enough, their reasons sometimes overlap. That *naturalistic* evolutionists should be unhappy with theistic evolution is perhaps not surprising. Nor might it be surprising that creationists should be unhappy with theistic *evolution*. But what does seem initially surprising is the bitterness with which some creationists attack theistic evolution. After all, isn't the dispute between creationism and theistic evolution only over the *means* of creation, with both firmly allied not only on the conviction that God is the Creator but also on the deeper issues of Christian faith?

### Creationist Objections to Theistic Evolution
That is not how most creationists tend to see it. Creationists not only apply many of their criticisms of evolution itself to theistic evolution but raise deeper objections as well. These deeper creationist accusations against theistic evolution begin with charges that it is incoherent, compromising, self-contradictory and vacuous, and once past that point get downright negative.[1] The fundamental objections are that theistic evolution is internally inconsistent and that it is also contrary to important scriptural doctrines. (Some naturalistic evolutionists make exactly these same claims.) We will examine objections of both sorts.

### Internal Inconsistency

The internal inconsistency charge comes in two varieties. The first involves the popular creationist "two model" picture briefly discussed earlier, while the second derives from the view that theistic evolution attempts to unify irreconcilables.

*1. The two-model picture.* Popular creationists nearly unanimously believe that ultimately there are only two basic perspectives on reality. Ultimately, the very existence and character of the universe derive either from impersonal, blind natural forces and from them alone or from creative activity residing outside of the natural realm. Either the cosmos is self-contained (and self-explained or unexplained) or it is not self-contained (and must be explained from beyond itself). Every possible worldview is, in the final analysis, a variation on one or the other of those two perspectives. That implies, creationists argue, that in the final, deepest sense there are only two perspectives on the world. And each is "essentially a complete worldview, a philosophy of life and meaning, of origin and destiny." Creationists call these two models the "evolution model" and the "creation model."[2]

Both models, creationists claim, are beyond the reach of human proof—and consequently are not parts of *real* (inductivist) science.[3] (Gish, though, sometimes appears to subsume both theories under "faiths," then claims that there is overwhelming evidence both for creationist and against evolutionist faith.[4]) This does not mean that we cannot bring scientifically relevant considerations to bear on the two models, however. We can generate predictions from each, see how those predictions fare in the face of proper scientific investigation of the cosmos and partially evaluate the models in terms of this sort of indirect, circumstantial evidence. And given that the two models are mutually inconsistent, evidence for (or against) either one will thereby constitute evidence against (or for) the other.[5] Morris, for instance, claims that the evolution model would predict that not only life but galaxies, stars and even the laws of nature themselves all would be constantly changing, whereas the creation model would predict that not only life but natural laws, galaxies and stars all would be constant.[6]

But since indirect, circumstantial evaluation does not either constitute proof or measure up to creationist definitions of science, the acceptance of either will constitute only *belief.*[7] One must choose, and the choice between them ultimately will arise out of "philosophical or religious preference." Thus, says Morris, "the ultimate choice is between God and the cosmos as the ultimate reality from which all other things derive their existence. . . . It is the choice between creation and evolution, between theism and atheism, between supernaturalism and naturalism."[8] Pretty clearly, the two models deal with global worldviews and not just with biological theories.[9] And on the other side, Richard Lewontin, speaking of "the fundamental contradiction between evolution and creationism," characterizes them as "irreconcilable world views."[10]

Although creationists have endured some criticism for linking the dispute over biological theories to deeper worldview themes, there is some sociological evidence that for many of the combatants on both sides the dispute really is worldview-driven.[11] Although the geological and biological issues have served as the emotional flashpoints of the dispute, for many on both sides the dispute ultimately goes far deeper. Thus many on each side see attempts to carve out a middle ground as a weasel compromise at best, but more bluntly as betrayal and as rationally (or spiritually) corrupt.

If we understand the evolution model to be, basically, that the cosmos is self-existent and the creation model to be, basically, that the cosmos is not self-existent, then much that creationists say about the two models is certainly reasonable. Those two options do, pretty clearly, about cover it— they are exhaustive. And they are mutually exclusive—only one can be true. Evidence for one would constitute evidence against the other. The evolution model would be inherently naturalistic and would indeed be flatly inconsistent with the Christian doctrine of creation.

But contrary to many creationists, nothing whatever follows from any of that concerning the *biological theory* of the origin of species and their diversity by means of mutation, natural selection and so forth. Many creationists note the logical incompatibility of the theistic creation model and the naturalistic evolution model, then apparently on that basis conclude that theism and biological evolutionary theory must be similarly incompatible— an inconsistency fatal to theistic evolution. Thus Ham considers theistic evolution to be "inconsistent." Morris calls it a "contradiction in terms," a "semantic confusion." Similar claims from others are common.[12] But the fact that the evolution *model* is inherently contrary to the creation *model* and that biological evolutionary theory is perhaps absolutely indispensable to the evolution model does not by itself suggest in the slightest that there is any logical tension between theism and the biological theory of evolution. That two worldviews are mutually inconsistent as *wholes* does not imply that every specific *part* of each must be inconsistent with the other. To argue so is to make the logical mistake known as the "fallacy of division."[13]

Consider this simple example. A complete naturalistic worldview must contain some meteorological theories concerning the origin of thunderstorms. Those theories, to fit into the naturalistic worldview, must be purely natural theories—theories that cite only natural laws and conditions such as fronts, hydrological cycles, temperatures and so forth and make no reference whatever to any sort of supernatural intervention or nonnatural processes. But such theories can also fit perfectly well into theistic worldviews. There is nothing atheistic about such theories. Accepting the theory that last week's storm was brought about by purely natural processes does not render one's Christian worldview internally inconsistent. Nor does that acceptance represent a compromise with naturalism.

Or as an even simpler example, if your plumber gave you an explanation other than a purely natural one for why your water heater did not work, you would hire another plumber. But that would not represent a compromise of your Christian principles.

Creationists may be perfectly right that Christians should be open to the possibility that God has directly acted in geological and biological history or has at specific points even altered the governing principles of the world. And maybe creationists are right that Christians should not uncritically accept some uniformitarian outlook that automatically rules all that out. But this would not by itself imply that Christians are obliged to conclude that God has in fact directly acted in those ways. Nor would it by itself imply that acceptance of a theory that could be true only had there been no such intervention is a compromise of Christian principles.

The fact, then, that a theory might be an essential part of an overall naturalistic model does not by itself say anything at all about the effects of incorporating that theory into a theistic model. Thus the facts that mainstream biological evolutionary theory appeals only to natural processes and that evolutionary theory may be an utterly essential part of modern naturalistic and atheistic worldviews do not by themselves show that there is anything inconsistent or compromising about theistic evolution. Perhaps theistic evolution can be shown to be inconsistent and compromising, but that will have to be shown on other grounds. And it cannot be shown simply by trading on the fact that the model and the biological theory have the same word—*evolution*—in their names. Nor can it be shown by arguing that the two *overall* models in question are inconsistent with each other or by simply defining biological evolution in worldview terms.[14]

This sort of slide, transferring conclusions from a cosmic philosophical evolutionism to the biological theory of organic evolution, is particularly clear in the following passage from Morris. Morris says that a universal philosophy of evolution "is a religion. . . . It is not a science in any proper sense of the word at all. And the same must *therefore* be true for the system of evolutionary historical geology which both supports it and is supported by it" (my emphasis).[15] So what is true of a universal *philosophy* of evolution is applied to theories of historical *geology*.

There is an extremely important, related, but often overlooked logical issue here as well. Suppose that there are two general alternatives that between them exhaust all of some range of possibilities. If one adds further conditions to either or both of those general categories, then the altered categories will typically no longer between them exhaust the possibilities. Here is a simple example. With respect to material things in the world, the two categories *red* and *nonred* pretty much between them exhaust the possibilities. Everything will fall into one or the other of those two categories. But suppose that we add a further stipulation to the first category—that things in this category must also be *round*. The two categories—*red and round* and *nonred*—no longer exhaust the possibilities, because anything *red and nonround* will not fall into either category. In general, any additional specification of conditions for either or both categories will result in the new possibility of some things falling outside of both of the newly altered categories.

How is that fact of logic relevant to present considerations? Obviously, either the universe is completely self-existent or it is not. Suppose we call the first alternative "evolution" and the second "creation." Those two broad options are mutually inconsistent, and every possibility must fall into one or the other of those two categories. But once one adds further defining conditions to either or both, they typically cease to exhaust the possibilities, and the situation is no longer a simple "either-or."

Unfortunately, creationists often cite two relevant categories as exhausting the possibilities, add further conditions to one or both and continue to claim that the altered categories are the only two possibilities. Here are some typical examples. Morris begins one discussion with the claim that "the universe was either created or it was not—one or the other."[16] Those two options obviously cover the possibilities (they are exhaustive), and only one can be true (they are exclusive). But within a page, quite a number of more specific conditions have been added: "the choice becomes one of believing either in a Creator—an omnipotent, transcendent, personal God who creat-ed the cosmos itself, with its magnificent array of complex systems and living beings—or in the external cosmos evolving itself into this array of complexity."[17]

A number of possibilities now exist that those two newly altered cate-gories no longer cover. Two obvious ones are (1) a Creator who created the initial primordial cosmos and let complex systems and living beings evolve according to laws he implanted in that cosmos and (2) an eternal steady-state cosmos that has always had complex systems and living beings. The two original alternatives, which were exhaustive, cease to be so with the addition of the further specified conditions. Yet in the next paragraph when speaking of the altered categories, Morris still claims that "there are only these two basic choices."[18]

Here is another example. Near the beginning of their discussion of the two-model idea, Morris and Parker note that "[there are] only two possi-bilities—simply stated, either it happened by accident (chance) . . . *or it didn't* (design)" (ellipsis and emphasis theirs).[19] It may well be that those two alternatives are exhaustive. But two pages later, these two alternatives ("evolution" and "creation," respectively) are further defined, and the def-initions contain additional conditions that again remove any exhaustiveness present in the original two alternatives. The "chance" model is now stipu-lated to contain uniformitarianism. The "nonchance" model now con-tains the principle that "particles, chemicals, planets, stars, organisms, and people were all created, so that long ages were not required for their devel-opment."[20] Obviously the possibility that organisms and people are results of deliberate design brought about through designed processes over time is no longer covered by either of the altered alternatives. Yet three pages later, Morris and Parker again claim that "there are only two possible models."[21]

Again, this sort of argument is fairly widespread in creationist writing.[22] But nothing detrimental to the coherence of theistic evolution follows.

*2. Randomness, law, guidance and design—an allegedly inconsistent set.* This objection can perhaps be best understood as a dilemma posed to the theistic evolutionist. Theistic evolution is often described as evolution guided by God. But if it is genuine evolution, then the theory itself demands that the processes be governed by natural law and random chance. That is part of the very structure of Darwin's theory, and abandoning it would make the "evolution" in "theistic evolution" a bit dishonest. On the other hand, if it is genuinely guided, then the processes must involve not chance but deliberately designed intervention. That is what divine guidance is, and abandoning that makes the "theistic" vacuous. Obviously, the objection continues, one cannot have both genuine evolution and genuine guidance. Theistic evolution, which attempts to have it both ways, is clearly in trouble.[23]

This objection is a bit tricky, and evaluating it will take a bit of doing. But it seems to me that it fails, although for fairly subtle reasons.[24]

*2.1. Guidance and intervention.* The first question we must ask is whether or not guidance truly demands deliberate intervention. It is not clear that it does. If development was built in from the very beginning, if it was deliberately and designedly precontained in the very laws, structures and initial conditions of the cosmos, then we might reasonably say that this preprogrammed development was deliberate, designed and guided. The guidance would not be interventive during the development, but does that mean that it would not be guidance nonetheless? Given that God ordained the laws by which a single cell develops into a newborn child, is it inappropriate to say that this development is guided, even though it is governed by the outworking of preset biological laws? If not, then guidance does not necessarily entail intervention.

*2.2. Probabilistic laws.* One of the most significant scientific developments within twentieth-century physics is the emergence of irreducibly probabilistic laws—laws describing events whose occurrence is not the result of any deterministic processes. According to contemporary physics, on the quantum level there are gaps not just in our knowledge of causation but in the very causal fabric of the cosmos itself. For instance, there is no determining law for whether or not and when an atom of some radioactive substance emits, say, an alpha particle. It simply happens or it does not, with a certain probability in any specified period of time. If that is true, then for a process to be law-governed is consistent with its containing elements of fundamental randomness.

Guidance and planning are compatible with some degree of randomness in any case. Suppose, for instance, that after a winning touchdown the coach says, "That pass play worked exactly as planned," whereupon a reporter asks, "Exactly how many air molecules did you intend for the ball to disturb while in flight?" Such a question is obviously inappropriate. There is usually some level of detail below which a plan does not go. If so, then a wide range of random variation below that level is perfectly consistent with the plan's working exactly as laid out.

Of course, one might argue that there is something in God's nature that would prevent God's plans from having any such looseness. His concern, after all, extends to the number of hairs on our heads. But keep in mind that God brought the animals to Adam to see what Adam would call them, and the original term for "see" has the sense of "discover." That certainly makes it sound as though the plan had space to accommodate a wide range of names that Adam might have come up with.

But probabilistic law opens another interesting possibility. If there are causal gaps in the ultimate physical processes of the cosmos, those gaps provide space for intervention that would still be *wholly within the boundaries of natural law.* For example, God could either bring about or prohibit the radioactive decay of a particular atom at a particular time, but given the way probabilistic laws function, either of those would be totally within the bounds of all of the relevant physical laws.[25]

Let us take it one step further. Suppose that whether or not some mutation arises depends on whether or not some radioactive atom incorporated into some organism's DNA decays at a specific moment. And suppose that the mutation is essential to the next step in the evolution of the species in question. The atom's decaying and not decaying are both consistent with physical law. Thus, were God deliberately to intervene and decree the decay of the atom for the very purpose of triggering the next evolutionary step, that purposeful intervention would be an instance of divine guiding intervention and *also* would involve no violation or suspension of any law of nature. Counterintuitive as it might initially seem, in the context of fundamentally probabilistic law an event's being wholly within the boundaries of natural law while simultaneously being the result of deliberate divine intervention is perfectly logically consistent.

So it is far from clear that the attempt in question to establish the internal inconsistency of theistic evolution works. But suppose it did. Suppose contemporary evolutionary theory had blind chance built into it so firmly that there was simply no way of reconciling it with any sort of divine guidance.[26] It would still be perfectly possible for theists to reject that theory of evolution and accept instead a theory according to which natural processes and laws drove most of evolution, but God on occasion abridged those laws and inserted some crucial mutation into the course of events. Even were God to intervene directly to suspend natural law and inject essential new genetic material at various points in order to facilitate the emergence of new traits and, eventually, new species, that miraculous and deliberate divine intervention would by itself leave unchallenged such key theses of evolutionary theory as that all species derive ultimately from some common ancestor. Descent with genetic intervention is still descent—it is just descent with nonnatural elements in the process.

Consider this partial parallel. Suppose the environment had become so toxic that the only way to ensure the survival of the next generation of humans was to artificially introduce an inheritable genetic alteration in utero to that entire generation. Suppose, further, that either intentionally or as an unavoidable side effect, those children when mature were fertile among themselves but were infertile with all previous human beings. That being the case, this new generation would constitute a new species. Deliberate intervention, then, would have resulted in a discontinuity in the human line. But it would obviously be the case that one's children, although members of a different species as a result of deliberate intervention, were still one's children. This means that intervention, discontinuity and divergence of species simply do not settle the issue of common ancestry. One apparently could believe, for suitable reasons, that God intervened in the course of history to generate new traits, new species and so forth, and that those traits and species could not have emerged by purely natural means, yet still accept all the usual evidences of relatedness, descent with modification and so forth, and maintain that the basic evolutionary thesis of the common ancestry of all species was perfectly true. Nothing whatever seems to be inconsistent about that.

Many of the popular creationist arguments against evolution would not apply to this sort of theistic evolution. For instance, probability arguments and arguments concerning processes going "against the flow" of nature would have no bearing on this type of view. And such a view would be no more incoherent or insidiously naturalistic than is the view that meteorological laws drive weather patterns but that God can and sometimes does intervene to bring rain in answer to need or prayer.

### External Inconsistency

As we saw earlier, the mere fact that a theory appeals only to purely natural laws and processes in its descriptions and explanations has no direct bearing on whether or not that theory is acceptable within a theistic worldview. Indeed, our theories of gravity, planetary orbits, chemical bonding, erosion—not to mention our practical theories about automotive, electrical and plumbing matters—all seem to be of exactly this sort and to fit perfectly comfortably into a theistic model. However, many creationists believe that the specific *type* of laws and processes evolutionary theory incorporates generates inconsistencies between the theory and various specific doctrines contained in Scripture.[27] Evolution simply is not the sort of means that God, as revealed in Scripture, would use even were he to use natural means. A brief discussion of one category of such objections follows.

*1. Original creation as good.* In Genesis 1, God repeatedly pronounces what he has created to be good and ends by pronouncing the whole of creation as very good. No Christian picture can abandon this aspect of the doctrine of creation—this initial, unfallen goodness. Yet theistic evolution would have us believe that prior to the Fall, when the world was as God intended and planned, the world was filled with violence, suffering and death. Death, after all, is an essential grease for the wheels of evolution. But how could a world filled with death be divinely perceived as *good?*[28]

Worse yet, how could God have deliberately chosen evolution as a method of creation? Evolution is fueled by predation and death. Evolution is prodigiously wasteful. Billions of creatures die waiting for some key mutation that may or may not emerge. Whole species, whole kinds, are done to death—roadkill on the evolutionary highway. Evolution is grossly inefficient. It works only by accident, by chance, and even if it works, it takes zillions of years to get anywhere. Would God as we know him from Scripture be expected to choose such a hit-or-miss method and call the resultant suffering, death, failure and extinctions *good?*[29]

To be perfectly honest, I do not know the answer to that question. But we have to be extremely careful here not to put undue weight on our own constructions of what *good* means. Creationists understand *good* as automatically implying lack of animal death, animal suffering or animal predation and as implying efficiency, economy and so forth. But it was God who saw the creation as good, and just as his thoughts are not ours and his ways are not ours, his judgments of good might be a bit beyond ours as well.[30] In fact, when God speaks of providing prey for young lions, the tone is not one of regret. It is part of God's glory—not some distasteful task—that he provides the young lions with their prey.[31]

Nor is it obvious that wastefulness would be a concern to God. Nature produces a lavish profusion of everything from beetles to grass blades to rocks to stars. Indeed, what would *wasteful* even mean in the context of omnipotent ability to create anything and everything from nothing with a word? And the creation does not seem to be defined by ruthless efficiency.

Why would efficiency be a concern to the eternal God? He is not going to run out of time, energy or resources. Rather than emphasizing efficiency, Scripture tells us that he created leviathan for his enjoyment. Leviathan was perhaps just a delight to watch. And again, God brought the animals to Adam, we are told, in order "to see what he would call them." The original word for "see" has the sense of "discover." Finding out what Adam would call them by bringing them to him, then waiting for him to name them is certainly inefficient compared to the instant foreknowing available to God. But efficiency does not seem to be the governing principle here.

And maybe God enjoys watching his creation operate. Maybe he delights in seeing processes he has designed unfold. Maybe a few billion years watching an incredibly intricate, complex, beautiful creation in exquisite operation does not strike him as a waste of time. And maybe we should be a bit cautious about humanly decreeing that it would be.[32]

Creationists typically see theistic evolution to be in conflict with Scripture in other, more specific areas.[33] For instance, creationists frequently note that the order of appearance of things in Genesis 1 differs from that postulated by most evolutionary theories. These more specific objections, however, depend on certain interpretations of Scripture—in particular, on "literal" readings of the early chapters of Genesis. I will not pursue those matters here.

### An Evolutionist Objection to Theistic Evolution

According to the naturalistic evolutionist Richard Dawkins, any attempt to bring God into the scientific picture, whether in a "supervising role [or merely] influencing key moments [or] meddling . . . in the day to day events that add up to evolutionary change," is "transparently feeble."[34] In fact, he thinks, it is far worse than feeble—it is logically pernicious. Why so?

As Dawkins sees it, there are two reasons. First, any reference to divine guidance or intervention is superfluous since normal evolutionary processes, neither guided nor interfered with, can do the job quite well themselves.[35] But second, and more serious, any appeal, whether direct or indirect, to divine activity logically short-circuits the entire process. The argument goes as follows. The object is to explain the existence of *organized complexity*— life, the eye, echolocation and so forth. But "a deity capable of engineering all the organized complexity of the world . . . must already have been vastly complex in the first place."[36] Thus to appeal in any way to any deity is to presuppose the very thing—complexity—whose explanation is at issue.

This, Dawkins thinks, gets us nowhere at all.

As Dawkins sees it, "explanations" of complexity that appeal to a deity already possessing complexity will be completely vacuous unless we can take the next step and provide an explanation for the deity's complexity. Ultimately, he thinks, no explanation of any complexity has been provided until that complexity has been tracked back directly or indirectly to the emergence of complexity out of simplicity.[37] Of course, few if any orthodox theists of the last few centuries—evolutionist, creationist or whatever— would buy the idea that divine complexity somehow emerged out of some more fundamental state of simplicity, but rather would consider the "vast complexity" Dawkins refers to above as eternal and not even a possible object for explanation. That is perhaps why Dawkins claims (as noted earlier) that we would be rationally justified in preferring naturalistic Darwinian evolution to views incorporating divine activity, guidance or oversight "even if there were no actual evidence in favor of the Darwinian theory."[38] An implication of Dawkins's position here is that while there is at least the possibility of an explanation of complexity in Darwinian terms, there is no possibility of such explanation even in principle on a theistic view that makes complexity—divine complexity—a fundamental and eternal given.

Dawkins's argument is interesting, but exactly how does it bear on the issue? Were someone attempting to explain the ultimate origin of complexity, then obviously appealing to a deity already possessing complexity would indeed be logically corrupt. But theistic evolutionists are not doing that. (Nor are creationists, for that matter.) The issue is the much more restricted one of the origin of biological complexity. And there is absolutely nothing wrong with explaining one sort of complexity by reference to some other sort of complexity. For instance, one can properly explain automotive complexity by reference to human design, human needs, human economic systems and so forth. And the fact that humans are themselves complex does not in the least render such explanations circular, devoid of explanatory content or anything else of the sort. Although such an explanation would not be a complete and ultimate explanation, neither would it be empty. Dawkins seems to be presupposing that if explanations are not ultimate they are vacuous. But that does not seem to be true.

In fact, Dawkins may be presupposing something even stronger. In a related discussion, he says, "To explain the origin of the DNA/protein machine by invoking a supernatural Designer is to explain precisely nothing, for it leaves unexplained the origin of the Designer."[39] He seems to be assuming that no origin has been explained unless the ultimate origin of anything appealed to in the explanation has also been explained. In addition to being mistaken, that principle is surely as dangerous for the naturalist as for the theist. To take the parallel case, one could claim that to explain the origin of species by invoking natural processes is to explain precisely nothing, for it leaves unexplained the origin of natural processes. And, of course, attempts to explain natural processes by invoking the big bang— or anything else—will generate an exactly similar problem with anything appealed to in *that* explanation.

Any explanation has to begin somewhere, and the principle that no explanation is legitimate unless anything referred to in the explanation is itself explained immediately generates a regress that would effectively destroy any possibility of any explanation for anything. That is surely a high price to pay just to undercut theistic evolution.

### Design, Divine Activity and Gaps

Considerations of design sometimes figure into theistic evolution, and arguments involving design constitute the unifying theme of the newly emerging "upper tier" of creationism referred to earlier. Objections have flown from all directions and involve charges that appealing to deliberate, intelligent divine design is somehow inappropriate in science, that the concept is not thoroughly enough naturalistic, that it has no legitimate place in explanations of origins and so forth. What is one to make of this?

First, it is perfectly clear that there is nothing inherently unscientific or subversive in employing the basic *concept* of deliberate design, plan and so forth in scientific explanations. Suppose that we land on some alien planet. There would be nothing in principle wrong with concluding, after careful scientific examination, that some of the objects found on that planet were artifacts—that they had been designed and produced deliberately. We might even conclude that via genetic engineering far beyond our capability, natural organisms had been altered to produce some of those artifacts—we might discover some fruit whose juice contained vodka and whose seeds were extremely high in aspirin.

Or suppose that our earlier time-machine explorations had revealed that aliens (however they came to exist) had artificially created life in a test tube and had engineered it to earth specifications, then had planted it here. There is nothing inherently nonscientific, antiscientific or religious about that, even though in that case the very existence of life on earth would be the result of intelligent design and deliberate activity.

But lacking time machines, how might we scientifically discover whether or not design had played some role in the existence of life or in the diversity of life on earth? We intuitively rely on several indicators when we take something to be the result of intelligent design (human or otherwise). Such indicators can include considerations of improbability, meaning, type of complexity, pattern and the like. But perhaps the most fundamental such factor is that production of artifacts always involves going sufficiently "against the flow" of what nature typically produces. In producing an artifact, nature must be subdued in a way that left to its own devices it would not or did not choose, and the further from nature's normal path the production is, the more unmistakable is the designedness of the artifact. William Paley was right—not even a complete stranger to civilization, upon discovering a watch, would wonder what sort of plant it had grown on.

So concluding design or intelligent activity after scientific examination of some object or process is not unscientific in the slightest.[40] Caution, however, often is appropriate. Determining that something goes sufficiently "against the flow" of nature requires knowing the details of that flow, and science has a long history of changing its mind about that at historically short intervals. Furthermore, saying what *sufficient* means here is nearly impossible. So we are fallible on such issues, but mere fallibility does not preclude rational judgment.

The real objection arises, however, when the design or intelligent activity postulated is divine. Appeals to divine intelligent activity are often pejoratively labeled "God of the gaps" explanation—whenever one cannot figure out how to plug some gap in a scientific explanation, one blithely claims that God acted in that processes or event, and then goes on to the next easy problem. Not only is that widely perceived as having a debilitating effect on science,[41] but of course many argue that any reference to the supernatural in science is illegitimate in principle. Thus in this context it typically is believed that an explanation in terms of intelligence is scientifically legitimate if "it seeks *natural* intelligence [but] any theory with a supernatural foundation is not scientific."[42]

But such objections do not seem compelling. If there are no gaps in the fabric of natural causation, then obviously appeal to divine activity will get us off track. On the other hand, if there are such gaps, refusing on principle to recognize them within science will equally get us off track. We should perhaps be wary of both ways of going wrong. If in our intellectual endeavors we are attempting to get at truth as best we can, then if we have *rational* reason—from whatever source—to believe that God has taken a hand in the origin or ongoing operation of the cosmos, arbitrarily excluding that belief needs some justification. Appealing to some definition of science will not work here (for reasons discussed earlier), and insisting that proper scientific strategy demands rejection of divine design requires some justifying case.[43]

Some advocates of a design theory claim that their appeals to design are not God-of-the-gaps appeals. The idea is not that design is a theistic scientific safety net deployed in areas that we do not understand, but rather that what we indeed *do* know about some aspects of the world reasonably allows for an intelligent design explanation.[44] Here again is one stripped-down example. The biochemistry of life is vastly more complex than anyone ever suspected, and within that complexity life requires that key reactions go in exactly the opposite direction—against the flow—from where they would go spontaneously. Living cells have catalysts, templates and specific conditions that facilitate these "wrong-way" processes and reactions. But it is vastly unclear how those catalysts, templates and conditions themselves developed. One problem is a sort of chicken-and-egg situation. There is no presently understood way of constructing DNA (and probably RNA) without the crucial involvement of very specific protein structures that push key steps against the flow. And there is no known way of generating such protein structures independently of DNA (or RNA) activity that directs key steps against the flow. Given either the DNA or the structures, the task is perhaps manageable by purely natural processes and life can get under way and perpetuate itself. But the initial origin of either is not just given. Construction of each of the key components also has to be pushed "against the flow" of ordinary processes (in ways that can be defined fairly technically).

This complexity, and others in living organisms, may be an *irreducible* complexity in that (at least, so far as can be seen at present) construction cannot involve a series of small steps—especially involving only purely normal-flow processes.[45] Each of those steps would require prior components and structures, the production of which themselves had to be driven against the flow. As a simple analogy, think of a sterile nutrient solution. Nothing much is going to happen in it spontaneously, but if it is infected from the outside with live bacteria, life gets off and running and takes over the solution. But it has to be infected from outside of itself. Similarly, some theistic evolutionists (and creationists) argue, given that nearly all life-essential biochemical processes go against the natural flow and cannot be initiated by any normal-flow biochemical processes, getting life on earth up and running required an "infection"—of design—from outside of the natural system.

Keep in mind that the intent of such arguments is not always to show that the evidence forces one to a belief in design, but sometimes merely that reference to such outside design is legitimate when proper evidence warrants it and that some presently available evidence can be taken as pointing in that direction.[46] (And the question of whether or not evidence warrants a conclusion of design can at least in principle be addressed independently of questions about the immediate means of actual production—whether evolutionary or creationist.[47])

Regardless of whether one finds the design arguments persuasive, one cannot simply rule consideration of design out of scientific bounds, either arbitrarily or definitionally.

### Where We Are to This Point

None of the above objections to theistic evolution seems to work very well. That is not, of course, to say that theistic evolution is not in some way fatally flawed—only that the foregoing popular objections to it do not really establish any such things.

Creationists, however, typically advance one further type of objection, and that is that theistic evolution cannot be reconciled with many of the details taught by the early chapters of Genesis (such as the order of appearance of created organisms).[48] Underlying this type of objection are two presuppositions: first, that a faithful and responsible reading of Genesis requires that it be understood literally, and second, that understood literally, early Genesis actually teaches what creationists think it does. I will not address those issues here. However, I do not think that either presupposition is inherently improper or incoherent.

# 13 CONCLUSION

**I** *mentioned a number of dimensions of the creation-evolution dispute in* the introduction—historical, philosophical, theological, scientific and others. As we have now seen, popular assaults from both sides in some of these areas are frequently inconclusive, irrelevant or defective. Many creationists have failed to understand some of the basic distinctives of Darwinian evolutionary theory, much less the precise details that render many of the popular easy criticisms irrelevant. Many evolutionists have likewise simply failed to investigate the contents of the creationist case, are unfamiliar both with specific positions and with developments in recent decades, and confidently repeat criticisms that are similarly irrelevant. It is difficult to fight an effective battle when one does not know what the opposition even looks like.

And philosophy of science offers neither side easy victory, although such attempts are mainstays in both arsenals. Neither the core concepts of creationism nor the core concepts of evolution violate defensible definitions of science or principles of rationality. Compelling cases against one or the other side can perhaps be made, but not merely on the grounds that they assume naturalism, assume supernaturalism, theorize about the unobservably deep past, deny the normativity of uniformity and so on—even if such accusations are true. Contributing to the failures in this area is the fact that both sides frequently employ conceptions and definitions of science that are seriously inadequate.

The foregoing chapters contain no extended discussion of theological dimensions of the dispute. This is not because theology is irrelevant. In fact, I have argued that such matters cannot be barred even from science itself without better arguments for that prohibition than are usually presented. Creationists, theistic evolutionists or both may be muddled in their theology or their hermeneutics. But the irrelevance or illegitimacy of theological and scriptural considerations in science—much less in the broader creation-evolution debate—cannot be established either by sheer edict or by inadequate stipulative definitions and concepts of science. In any case, broad-based clarity on the larger issue is going to require that both sides abandon their respective favorite muddles.

I have not engaged in purely scientific evaluation, either. However, the scientific aspect of the dispute is not completely separate from some of these other dimensions, and to the extent that there may be legitimate and rational disagreement on those fronts, there is at least the potential for legitimate and rational disagreement within the scientific area as well.

For instance, materialists have no viable choice but to view the world through evolutionary spectacles of some sort, and their theorizing, assessment of evidence and other scientific procedures are not unaffected. That is not to say that such effects are illegitimate or that the ensuing results are scientifically mistaken. But it does mean that many evolutionists are forbidding themselves to consider certain classes of possible theoretical options— and that can in principle affect assessment of evidence and other scientific procedures. Worldviews do have effects, and any clear-eyed view of the situation will recognize that. Such effects can be legitimate. But legitimacy is a vastly different matter from normativity. Even when built into a science, such worldview matters are not automatically universally normative.

On the other hand, creationists who accept the authority of Scripture and take it to be relevant to the issues also will have unique input into their view of the cosmos, its origin and its workings. And there is nothing inherently irrational merely in the holding of such views—at least not on any definition of *rational* that can plausibly claim to be normative. Some critics will, of course, refuse to grant the honorific title *science* to the results of such views, but that is at best a mere semantic nicety. If the aim is genuine truth, the mere fact that a system purporting to display that truth does not meet the conditions of some stipulative, worldview-laden definition of the term *science* can hardly carry serious weight.

It seems in principle perfectly possible that there might be elements within the sciences—the sciences partially and legitimately shaped by these conflicting worldview thrusts—that will generate ultimately irreconcilable theories, evaluations of theories, assessments of evidence, estimates of probabilities and other differences between the two sides. What all that suggests is that the two sides may be unable to find a common ground on which all the details of their scientific differences can be hashed out. But the mere fact of that inability does not of itself count against either side.

However, if various acts were cleaned up, the area of commonality—or at least of sensible discussability—probably could be substantially enlarged compared to what it now is. And even if some differences are so foundational that ultimate reconciliation is clearly impossible, that of itself does not justify embracing rationally slipshod cases either for defending the views of one side or for dismissing those of the other side.

The caricatures, the easy criticisms, the propaganda, the familiar commonplaces of the various sides are comfortable—but they have become costly both within and for the Christian community. So what should we do? On all sides we need to unhitch our egos and do some hard, maybe even painful work. And maybe the various sides should talk. Not debate—talk. It is just possible, neither side being omniscient, that both sides could gain something from serious contact with competent practitioners on the other.

And in any case, we should keep in mind that in this entire area we see through a glass darkly, and that when looking through a glass darkly it is almost impossible to see well enough to remove a mote from someone else's eye.

# Notes

**Chapter 1: Introduction**
[1]Morris [1967] preface.
[2]Dawkins [1989] 35.
[3]I know of no creationist who would deny that God has the power or knowledge to create an evolutionary world, but many argue that employing a system operating so indirectly and requiring death, as evolution does, would be contrary to God's nature. See discussion in chapter twelve.
[4]Denton, Macbeth and Bethell seemingly do not classify themselves as creationists of any sort. There are claims in the literature that neither Wysong nor Bird is a creationist, although I find such claims implausible. Johnson and Geisler both belong somewhere in the old-earth creationist category.

**Chapter 2: Darwin: The Historical Context**
[1]Nearly any good history-of-science survey covering this period may be consulted for further details. Such works are widely available, and include Bowler [1989]; Brooke [1991]; Greene [1959]; Toulmin and Goodfield [1965]; Gillespie [1979]; Young [1982]; Dijksterhuis [1961]; and Randall's classic [1926]. See also Burkhardt [1977].

**Chapter 3: Darwin's Theory: A Brief Introduction**
[1]In recent decades a "Darwin industry" has arisen in the academic community, the result being a huge—and growing—bibliography concerning Darwin and the background to, the development of and the reception of his theory. There is, I think, nothing controversial in this chapter, so since treatments are both widely available and familiar I will again forgo extensive footnotes. Those wishing to pursue details further might wish to consult any of the following: Darwin [1859]; Wallace [1858] (which some take to be a better summary statement of the theory than any of

Darwin's); Darwin [1871]; Darwin [1892]; Wallace [1855]; Desmond and Moore [1991] (the most recent, definitive biography of Darwin); Bowler [1989]; Himmelfarb [1959]; Greene [1963]; and Greene [1959]. Among the versions of the Darwin/ Wallace episode, the one that reflects most negatively on Darwin (including a charge that he plagiarized a key element in his theory from Wallace) is that of Brackman [1980]. The case strikes me as inconclusive.

## Chapter 4: Darwin's Theory: Popular Creationist Misunderstandings

[1]Some nice discussion of some similar points is contained in Alexander [1983].

[2]Letter to Joseph Hooker, cited in the editor's introduction to Darwin [1859]. See also Desmond and Moore [1991] 231. Criswell [1957] 96 quotes this line, but simply ends it with the word *nonsense*. See also Wallace [1855] 319.

[3]For example, Lubenow [1992] 76; Saint [1993] 15-16; Wilder-Smith's presentation in the film *Origin of Species* is to say the least misleading. See also Morris, Boardman and Koontz *(Teacher's Handbook)* [1971] and Myers [1988] 6 for standard confusion of a Lamarckian adjustment mechanism with the total theory.

[4]Gish [1985b] 64, 74; Morris [1946] 50-51; Morris [1974c] 265; Wysong [1976] 56, 287-88; Huse [1983/1993] 4; Denton [1985] 136; Davis and Kenyon [1993] 88; Gish [1993] 134. See also Ouweneel [1971] 113. However, such resistance to change by the bulk of species has caused some upheaval—in particular, it has given rise to punctuated equilibria theories. See also Gingrich [1993] 218. See also Desmond and Moore [1991] 702 n. 44. Rusch [1984] 51 says that for evolution, time is "the great creator."

[5]Darwin [1859] chap. 4. See also Francis Darwin [1897] 209 and Darwin's comment quoted in Dawkins [1989] 244. See also Desmond and Moore [1991] 702 n. 44.

[6]Morris [1974e] 83; Saint [1993] 27, 36; Ian Taylor [1989] 10-15; Snelling [1993] 40ff. See also ads for *Creation* magazine. See also Morris [1984b] 32; and Wysong [1976] 287. Crofut [1992] 149, 155 comes close to this. Klotz [1985] 124 argues that living fossils are a problem for creationists, since they imply that, for example, 100 million years of absence from the fossil record does not demonstrate nonexistence, which may undercut "fossil gap" arguments.

[7]Darwin himself was aware of at least one case of a "living fossil" genus that last appeared in the fossil record 65 million years ago—and was discovered still to be around in 1802. See Gould [1985] 17. See also Desmond and Moore [1991] 702 n. 44.

[8]See, for example, Lubenow [1983] 225; ReMine [1993] 263.

[9]Gish [1993] 216-27; Morris [1974e] 13; Davis and Kenyon [1993] 88; Brown [1983] 212; Wilder-Smith [1981] xiii. This charge is also frequently made at workshops by, for example, Ham and Parker; the latter makes a similar claim in [1987] 62. Some—such as John Morris—do get this right.

[10]Morris [1974e] 78, 13, 70, 72; Morris [1974g] 84; Morris [1971] 83-84; Morris, Boardman and Koontz *(Living World)* [1971] 23; Niessen [1980] 221 point 13. Ouweneel [1971] 114 comes close to this. See also Lubenow [1983] 211; Brown [1983] 211; Moore and Slusher [1970/1974] xviii. This is also suggested in Morris [1977d] 30; Morris [1974c] 254; and John N. Moore [1983] 3. See also Tinkle [1970] 86-87. See also Desmond and Moore [1991] 312.

[11]Morris [1974e] 31-32, 70; Morris [1967] 22-23; Morris [1985a] 29; Gish [1993] 216-17, 65; Wysong [1976] 279; Saint [1993] 21; Colson (no. 3) [1993]; Davis and

Kenyon [1993] 88; Denton [1985] 137, 139, and see also 132-36.

12Denton [1985] 281ff. Davis and Kenyon [1993] 139-40.

13Darwin [1859] 207.

14Huse [1983/1993] 123; Morris [1976c] 95.

15Taylor [1984] 254.

16Wysong [1976] 345-47. See Darwin [1871] 444. Wysong has reportedly denied being a creationist (McIver [1988] 317). Whether or not that is true, his work has become such a landmark for creationists that I include him here.

17Kitcher [1982] 72 contains a similar point.

18Morris [1974e] 83. See also Morris [1974c] 266; Gish [1993] 131; Wysong [1976] 326-28; Lubenow [1992] 153-54, 179; Lubenow [1983] 225; Paul Taylor [1992] 38.

19Darwin [1859] 165, 206, 211. See also [1871] 525. Lubenow offers a response in Wieland [1995] 17-18, but the response is defective in explicitly ignoring geographical isolation, which is a crucial part of the case.

20Morris [1977a] 39; Morris [1974g] 17, 85, 97, 110; Whitcomb [1986] 13; Gish [1993] 157; Morris [1963a] 11; Ham [1986] 34; Hallonquist [1987] 25. See also Niessen [1980] 221 point 9; Ouweneel [1971] 112.

21Ham and Taylor [1988] 66, 68; Huse [1983/1993] 4; Matrisciana and Oakland [1991] 15-16; Ham [1987] 141; Morris [1946] 51; Gish [1985b] 101, 106, 208. Morris [1966] 147, 164. In this connection see also Lubenow's discussion of reversals in [1992] 159-64; Patten [1970b] 40; Williams [1975] 449. E. H. Andrews is also quoted to this effect in Poole and Wenham [1987] 61.

22In fact, even Darwin occasionally lapsed into such language; Darwin [1859] (6th ed.) 669, quoted in Poole and Wenham [1987] 62, and Darwin [1871] 511.

23Some creationists, such as Bergman, consistently miss this point; see his [1992b] 148, 155, 157. Bergman [1992a] 10-11 also misconstrues Darwin concerning linearity. A particularly clear case is Gish's discussion of teeth in [1985b] 114.

24Wysong [1976] 271-72, 324; also Sunderland [1988] 154. Klotz [1985] 179-80 discusses the same sheep. See also Frair and Davis [1983] 101; Gish [1973b] 24. Ironically, short-legged sheep are briefly discussed in Wallace [1858] 334.

25See Denton [1985] 222-23; Wysong [1976] 328; also Morris [1974e] 75; and Coppedge [1973] 88. See also Lubenow [1983] 16; Bergman [1992b] 149.

26Darwin [1859] 183-85, 227, and [1871] 407, 427, 442, 583, 613, 615, 777-78, 846, 851, 903-4, 908. But see also 581, 653 and 910. Harper [1978] 84 is the only place in any creationist writing that I have ever seen this point of Darwin's even mentioned.

27Wysong [1976] 320, 332-34; Morris [1974e] 53-54; Morris [1974d] 40; Morris [1967] 28; Morris [1977a] 40; Saint [1993] 37; Brown [1983] 214; Pearcey [1987a] 8; Bergman [1991] 39; Pearcey [1990] 8; Gish [1977] 55; Macbeth [1971] 4. Paul Taylor [1992] 32 cites and endorses Wilder-Smith on this point. See also Gish [1985b] 106-7, 236. Some evolutionists also make this mistake. See John A. Moore [1983] 120.

28Wysong [1976] 321-23.

29For example, Gould [1977a] 32-37.

30The example is Darwin's [1859] 220.

31For example, Dawkins [1987] 80-86.

32Wysong [1976] 320, 310 and also 332-33. See also Darwin [1859] 212-14, 229. Creationist construals of evolution based on need have a long history—for example, as early as Rimmer [1937] 258. Bergman repeatedly pushes this objection, such as in [1992b] 151-56. Criswell refers to protoplasm's "ambition" [1957] 67.

[33]Ricki Lewis [1992] 625.

[34]Ward [1992] 53.

[35]For example, Colson (no. 1) [1993]; Davis and Kenyon [1993] 78-79; Sunderland [1988] 115. See also Johnson [1993a] 100, 158; see Morris and Parker [1987] 91 for the allegedly creative nature of natural selection.

[36]See Wysong [1976] 57, 320 for some possible confusions here.

[37]ReMine [1993] 189-90.

[38]Bowler [1989] 139.

[39]Wysong [1976] 162, 178; see also Morris [1967] 43; Steinhauer [1975b] 85-86.

[40]Gish [1993] 15; see Whitcomb and Morris [1961] 96, 123-24, 139, 142-43, 154, 158, 160-61, 164, 172, 200, 250, 293, 312, 439, 451-52; Morris [1974e] 91-92, 97, 99, 101, 110; Morris [1985a] 31, 45, 207; Morris [1974g] 21; Morris [1977a] 108-9; Morris [1963b] 61; Morris [1989b] 99; Morris [1977d] 28; Morris [1974c] 271; Morris [1976c] 47, 199; Gish [1985b] 37, 46-7; Gish [1973b] 37, 41; Gish [1978] 54; Gish [1993] 302; Kofahl and Segraves [1975] 40; Morris [1967] 36-37, 59; Morris and Parker [1987] 171-73, 192, 244-45; Wysong [1976] 156, 355-62; Sunderland [1988] 111-14, 157; Huse [1983/1993] 50-51; Ankerberg and Weldon [1993] 32; Sylvia Baker [1976] 11, 12; Colson (no. 6) [1993]; Ian Taylor [1982] 309; Pearcey and Thaxton [1994] 246-47; Ham, Snelling and Wieland [1990] 175; Ham [1985] 25, 29; Whitcomb [1966] 12-13; Boardman, Koontz and Morris [1973] 15, 19; Kofahl [1977] 85; Morris [1984a] 261; Morris [1974d] 100, 107; Morris [1972b] 23; Morris [1966] 102-3, 109, 139, 145, 165-66; Morris, Boardman and Koontz *(Teacher's Handbook)* [1971] 13, 24; Morris, Boardman and Koontz *(Man and His World)* [1971] 24; Chittick [1984] 79; Lubenow [1983] 31; Austin [1971] 34; Austin [1984] 2; Morris [1970] 25; Paul Taylor [1992] 10; Morris [1972a] 13, 68-69. Morris [1988a] 36-37 suggests this also.

[41]For example, Bowler [1989] 12.

[42]Whitcomb and Morris [1961] 137-39, 168, 216; Morris [1974e] 91; Morris [1984a] 304-5; Morris and Morris [1989] 25l; Frair and Davis [1983] 66-67; Moore and Slusher [1970/1974] 420-22; Austin [1976] 205 is relevant here too. But see Morris [1974d] 100. See also Morris, Boardman and Koontz *(World of Long Ago)* [1971] 10.

[43]Morris [1974e] 97; also Morris [1984a] 343; Morris, Boardman and Koontz *(Teacher's Handbook)* [1971] 25-26.

[44]Morris [1984a] 182, 346; Morris [1971] 110; see also Gish, Bliss and Bird in Morris and Rohrer [1982] 136.

[45]Wieland [1994] 8, also 9-12.

[46]Wysong [1976] 367-68.

[47]Morris and Parker [1987] 172; Whitcomb and Morris [1961] 160-61; Morris [1974e] 100, 110; Wysong [1976] 359; Morris [1967] 37; Morris [1972b] 91; Ankerberg and Weldon [1993] 32; Whitcomb [1973] 142; Morris [1970] 27, 89; Morris [1976c] 685; Austin [1986] 219; Austin [1989] 36; Snelling [1989] 12; John Morris [1980a] 58-59. Brown [1983] 211-12 is close to this. See also Cox [1976] 157; Ouweneel [1971] 112.

[48]Whitcomb and Morris [1961] 139, 147, 155-56, 161, 168-69, 200, 203, 312; Morris [1977a] 110; Morris and Parker [1987] 172-74; Morris, Boardman and Koontz

*(Teacher's Handbook)* [1971] 56; Morris [1963b] 63; Morris [1968b] 109. Scale also figures into some of the objections of others, for example, Parker [1994] 177-79, 188; Huse [1983/1993] 48; Gish [1973b] 40; Gish [1993] 302; Wysong [1976] 361; Frair and Davis [1983] 66-67; Whitcomb [1973] 87; Morris [1946] 69; Moore and Slusher [1970/1974] 428; Whitelaw [1975] 42. On other occasions, creationists are perfectly happy to extrapolate across scale differences. See, for example, Arries [1991b] 5-7.

49Morris [1956] 67-69; Morris [1963a] 9; Morris [1968b] 108. Davidheiser [1971] 66 says that geologists have seen the need for catastrophes since the end of World War II. Both Morris [1974e] 93 and Wysong [1976] 361-62 quote geologists advocating the change as early as 1956. And in 1970 or earlier Morris said, "That geological process rates are subject to wide variation—all the way from zero to catastrophic intensities—has in recent years been *widely recognized* even by historical geologists"; Morris [1970] 26, my emphasis. Klotz [1966] 6 and [1985] 131 also notes this. See also Livingstone [1987] 43 and Bowler [1989] 46.

50The terminology is found in Gould [1965] .

51Morris and Morris [1989] 64-65; Morris [1984a] 304-5; Morris [1974d]; Morris and Parker [1987] 244-45. See also Morris [1974e] 139; Morris [1985a] 207-9. John N. Moore [1976a] 47-48 refers to the distinction but has it somewhat confused. See also Steinhauer [1975a].

52As one example, Morris sometimes seems to take process uniformity and law uniformity to be the same thing, for example, Morris [1974d] 107 and Morris [1972b] cf. 23 and 91; Morris [1966] 30, 152. Whitcomb and Morris [1961] contains a slightly more subtle equating of the two. See Austin [1986] 219. Whitcomb [1973] 105 claims that he and Morris had the concept straight all along, then nineteen pages later simply asserts that "Uniformitarians *must* believe that oil was formed gradually" (my emphasis). Morris [1946] 60 makes the same shift in a single paragraph. But see also Morris [1970] 26; Morris [1966] 156-58, 165.

53Morris [1974d] 107, 109; Whitcomb and Morris [1961] 161, 224; Morris [1984a] 77, 305; Morris [1967] 43, 53-54; Morris [1966] 43, 69, 135; Wysong [1976] 405.

54For example, Morris [1966] 43; Morris [1984a] 305; Morris [1974e] 150.

55Morris [1974d] 107-9; Morris [1985a] 209; Whitcomb [1973] 102ff., especially 103; Whitcomb and Morris [1961] 227-28; Morris [1966] 158. See also Morris [1976c] 38.

56Lewontin [1983b] xxvi. He says essentially the same thing in [1983a] 22. See also Strahler [1987] 62, 193-94.

57Morris [1974e] 92; Morris and Parker [1987] 192; Whitcomb and Morris [1961] xx n. 1, xxiii; Morris [1966] 44. This is, I think, related to some of Johnson's points concerning the role of naturalism in evolution. See, for example, Johnson [1993b].

58Morris [1981c] 179; Morris [1974f] 106-7. See also Morris [1984a] 107, 318; Frair and Davis [1983] 67. Similar sorts of claims—for example, that "the 'theory of evolution' itself is . . . a philosophical dogma of continuity"—are found in Arthur Jones [1971] 46 and Hedtke [1981] 8. See also Ouweneel [1971] 110.

59Morris and Morris [1989] 27.

60Whitcomb and Morris [1961] 224.

61Steinhauer [1975b] 88; Austin [1970] 91. See also Chittick [1970] 60, 62, 73. And although he may mean this to apply only to science and not more broadly, the evolutionist Edwords [1983a] 7 says that "uniformity is a naturalistic premise. One uses [it] precisely because one is not admitting miraculous, mysterious or other processes into the argument."

[62]For example, Morris and Morris [1989] 65; Morris [1966] 43-44, 169; Morris [1963a] 12; Morris [1984a] 77; Morris [1970] 35; Morris [1976c] 198; Morris [1974e]; Whitcomb [1986] 135-36. John N. Moore [1976b] 21 may also be suggesting this. In fact, Morris even says that "the reign of *naturalism* and uniformity in the present cosmos is thus quite Biblical"; Morris [1970] 36 (my emphasis). See also Steinhauer [1975b] 94.

[63]See chapter six.

[64]Morris and Morris [1989] 72; Morris [1970] 30. See also Whitcomb [1973] 103-4; Whitcomb and Morris [1961] xxi, 227.

[65]Colson (no. 3) [1993]; Matrisciana and Oakland [1991] 99; Ham in Kennedy [1988] 5. See van Inwagen [1989] 32 for some interesting comment on this issue.

[66]Wysong [1976] 320, also 57; suggested in Morris [1985c] iii. Lamarck maintained that extinctions typically did not occur, but Darwin's theory does not imply that.

[67]Morris [1974e] 75.

[68]Sylvia Baker [1976] 14; Criswell [1957] 73-74.

[69]Morris [1967] 23; Morris [1974e] 70; Gish [1985b] 214. See also Gish [1993] 131 for a related confusion.

[70]Wysong [1976] 332-33. Hedtke [1979] 94 contains a partial variant of this.

[71]Morris [1974e] 54. See also Wysong [1976] 275-76, 321 for confusion on this point.

[72]Bethell [1978] 91. This description would fit an eternal steady-state system, and in any case if there were a *first* evolved organism *it* did not have parents. See Bethell [1977] 14 for a related misconstrual.

[73]Lubenow [1983] 164, see also 167; Gish [1984] 32-33; see also Gish [1979] 190-91.

[74]This is fairly popular, as in Morris [1974e] 56-57. Wysong [1976] 275-76 even goes so far as to claim that "evolution demands pollution." Evolutionist answers in the literature go back at least thirty years; see, for example, Dobzhansky [1962] 293-95.

[75]This not a complete list. Some are surprising. See, for example, Jonathan Jones [1990] 11; and Gish [1977] 42.

[76]This charge is often made only implicitly—for example, Lubenow [1983] 223. See again the Morris quote in chapter one.

## Chapter 5: Twentieth-Century Creationism: The Historical Context

[1]Numbers [1992] 3. The definitive history of the creationist movement is Numbers [1992]. The work is substantial and fascinating, and received dust-jacket blurbs ranging from Henry Morris to Martin Gardner. Much of the present chapter is based on Numbers's book. For a sociological treatment of the contemporary creationist movement, see Eve and Harrold [1991]. See also McIver [1989], Webb [1994] and Toumey [1994].

[2]Numbers [1992] x, 36, and chap. 1.

[3]Numbers [1992] 11, 14.

[4]Numbers [1992] 38.

[5]Numbers [1992] 32-35 and chap. 3; Marsden [1980] 119; Marsden [1991] 155; Synan [1988] 325.

[6]Numbers [1992] 49; Marsden [1980] 118-64. Riley himself dates the founding to 1918; Riley [1922a] 9.

⁷See, for example, Cole [1983] 30-31 for a typical accusation. Morris [1984b] 59; Marsden [1980] 31, 121-23, 152; Marsden [1991] 41, 176; Numbers [1992] 20-25, 34-35, 72.

⁸Marsden [1991] 116-17; Marsden [1980] 120-23, 219; Synan [1988] 326.

⁹Numbers [1992] 43, 50-53, 57-59; Numbers [1982] 539; Marsden [1991] 162 and see also 167-68; Marsden [1980] 217.

¹⁰This was also a view held by Hodge. See Livingstone [1987] 103; Marsden [1980] 217.

¹¹Numbers [1982] 539.

¹²Numbers [1992] 66-67, 45; Morris [1984b] 58-59, Marsden [1991] 176.

¹³Morris [1984b] 58-59; Numbers [1992] 45-46, 66, 71.

¹⁴Numbers [1992] 31, 68 and also 109-12; Morris [1984b] 59-61; McIver [1989] 66; Webb [1994] 156.

¹⁵See chapter ten below. Numbers [1992] 50, 65, 90-91; Marsden [1980] 121, 217; Marsden [1991] 213-14; Marsden [1984] 97ff.; McIver [1989] 19ff.

¹⁶Numbers [1992] 50; Livingstone [1987] 167; Marsden [1991] 37.

¹⁷Numbers [1992] 20, 27-32, 35-36, 38-43, 72; Marsden [1991] 138-39, 155-56, 160, 173, 176-77; Morris [1984b] 61; Livingstone [1987] 103, 115-21, 147-51, 159; Numbers [1982] 540; Larson [1985] 40-43, 65; McIver [1989] 61, 444ff.

¹⁸Marsden [1980] 122; Livingstone [1987] 150, 152-54; Larson [1985] 43.

¹⁹Marsden [1991] 120; Larson [1985] 43-44.

²⁰Marsden [1991] 138; Hodge had earlier maintained this position; see Livingstone [1987] 105, and see also 166-67.

²¹Numbers [1992] 28; Marsden [1991] 148, 178, 181.

²²Morris [1984b] 62; Numbers [1992] 42, 46-47; Marsden [1980] 153-75, 209; Marsden [1991] 174; Numbers [1982] 538; Larson [1985] 47; Eve and Harrold [1991] 21-22. See also McIver [1989] 71ff.; Webb [1994] 56ff.

²³Marsden [1980] chap. 17; Morris [1984b] 55; Numbers [1992] 33, 36, 39; Livingstone [1987] 167; Larson [1985] 45; Numbers [1982] 539; Riley [1922a] 16-20, 22; Bryan [1922] 28-29; McIver [1989] 68; Webb [1994] 66ff.

²⁴Numbers [1992] 41-44.

²⁵Marsden [1980] 185-89. See Larson [1985] chap. 3 for an account of the Scopes trial. Eve and Harrold [1991] chap. 8 also discusses a number of creation/evolution court cases.

²⁶Marsden [1980] chap. 21, 212; Larson [1985] 72ff.; Morris [1984b] 66ff.

²⁷Numbers [1992] 102-3; Morris [1984b] 76; Marsden [1991] 149; Numbers [1982] 540-41; Webb [1994] 93ff.

²⁸Numbers [1992] 60-71; Morris [1984b] 88ff.

²⁹Numbers [1992] 65-66, 69; Marsden [1980] 212-13; Numbers [1982] 539.

³⁰Numbers [1992] 73-74; Morris [1984b] 60ff.

³¹Numbers [1992] 75-76, 81, 88; Livingstone [1987] 157; Marsden [1991] 159; Numbers [1982] 539.

³²Numbers [1992] 79-81, 88, 94.

³³Numbers [1992] 80, 76-77, 107; Numbers [1982] 540.

³⁴Numbers [1992] 81-84.

³⁵Numbers [1992] 96-101, 90-91.

³⁶Numbers [1992] chaps. 6 and 7, 216; Morris [1994] 112-30.

³⁷Morris [1994] 130ff.; Numbers [1992] 133, chap. 9; Numbers [1982] 541.

38Numbers [1992] 167-81; Numbers [1982] 541-42.

39Morris [1984b] 80, 97, 115, 129-30, 133, 136, 328; Numbers [1992] 194.

40Numbers [1992] chap. 10; Morris [1984b] 141ff., chap. 5.

41Numbers [1992] 209-13, 338; Numbers [1982] 542. See also Toumey [1994] 21ff., 144, 257.

42Numbers [1992] chaps. 11 and 14; Morris [1984b] 141, 160, chap. 6, 212ff.

43Morris [1984b] 225-34, chap. 8; Numbers [1992] chap. 14.

44See Gallup Poll results reproduced widely—for example, Milner [1990] 100. For the history of the legal battles from Scopes to the present, see Larson [1985].

45Lewin [1981] 635-38; Eve and Harrold [1991] 135ff. See also Matrisciana and Oakland [1991] chap. 9; Bird (vol. 2) [1989] 351-56, 405-6; Gish [1993] chap. 2; Geisler and Anderson [1987] 20ff.; Webb [1994] 217ff., 237ff. See also McCollister [1989] for several dozen of the resultant official statements.

46Patterson [1983b] 137; Larson [1985] 178. Eve and Harrold [1991] 200 n. 7 even suggest that under creation science, we perhaps could not have landed on the moon. Asimov [1984] 193 suggests that under creationism we would not be able to run industry.

### Chapter 6: Creationist Theory: A Brief Introduction

1Whitcomb and Morris [1961] 440-41, 450, 471-73.

2Ibid. 219, 441.

3Ibid. xx, xxvii, 44, 227, 329, 356-57, 443-53, 451-53, 471-73. This is a continuing theme. See, for example, Morris [1974e] iii.

4Whitcomb and Morris [1961] xx, 119, 327.

5Ibid. xx, xxvi, xxvii, 118, 213, 330, 438-40. This last theme is even more pronounced in subsequent works—for example, Morris [1974e] 15 says "*at every point,* the creation model is superior to the evolution model" (my emphasis).

6Whitcomb and Morris's discussion specifically on Scripture and the flood occupies the first three chapters. See also [1961] chap. 5, 219, 222-28, 228-29, 344-45, 439-40. The inadequacy of uniformitarian principles is a major theme of the book.

7Ibid. 214-15, 220-21, 229, 240, 243-49, 253-58.

8Ibid. 229-32.

9Ibid. 232-39, 343-46, 350, 354-55, 359, 366, 378-79.

10Ibid. 215, 466.

11Ibid. 239-40, 242.

12Ibid. 375, 399-405; 25, 306.

13Ibid. chap. 1, 122-23, 126-27, 242, 258, 264-65.

14Ibid. 265-66, 273-77, 283-85.

15Ibid. 123, 128-30, 275-85.

16Ibid. 127-28, 243, 429-36.

17Ibid. 268-70, 287-311, 306, 311.

18Ibid. chap. 5, 217, 439-40. This is one of the basic themes of the entire book.

19Ibid. 131.

20Ibid. xxiii, xxvi, xxi, 130-31, 213, 227-29, 331, 345-46, 378, 391, 439.

21Ibid. xxi, 76-77, 216, 391.

22Ibid. xix, 217, 444-47. See also John Morris [1995] 37.

23The book's title page says that the text was "prepared by the technical staff and consultants" of the ICR and "edited" by Morris. However, according to page i the "basic text of the manuscript was prepared by" Morris, while others "reviewed" it, their suggestions being "incorporated in the revised text." I am consequently treating the book as Morris's.

24Whitcomb and Morris [1961] xxiii, xxvi, xxi, 217.

25Morris [1974e] iv, 4-6.

26Ibid. iv-v, 3.

27For example, Whitcomb and Morris [1961] 81.

28Some creationists come close to admitting this. See Howe [1985] 141-42, points 2, 3, 5, 6, 7. Whitcomb's comments in [1984b] 22-23 are also of interest here.

29Morris [1974e] 124-25, 185, 188.

30Ibid. chaps. 2-6, 181.

31Ibid. 116-17, 129.

32Ibid. 23. Morris made the same sort of claim in other works during this time; see, for example, Morris [1974f] 188-89.

33Morris [1974e] 3, 4-6, 8-13, 19.

34Ibid. 228, 243. Morris makes that claim also in Mackay [1984] 17.

35Morris [1974e] 13, 203, 8, 149-50.

36Ibid. 4-6, 8-13, 17-19, 33.

37Purported predictions of the two models are found throughout the book, for example [1974e] 12-13, 17-18, 37-38, 56-57, 69-75, 78-79, 83, 122-23, 152ff., 158, 167-69, 182, 201. See also iii. That the data favor creationism is, of course, the main theme of the book.

38Although the Creation Research Society required science degrees for membership, such degrees were not always in relevant fields (the movement did not get its first member with a doctorate in geology until 1979), and thus their members did not always have the problematic precise details in hand. The one notable early exception in the movement was Frank Marsh. That many noncreationist professional scientists were unimpressed is not difficult to understand.

39Morris and Parker [1987] 36-48. Similar arguments have come from noncreationists as well—for example, Popper, cited in Bird (vol. 1) [1989].

40Morris and Parker [1987] 52-73.

41Ibid. 299.

42Ibid. 243, xii.

43Ibid. 297.

44In 1989-1990 the Australian creationist journal *Creation Ex Nihilo* published a three-part series in which twenty prominent creationists gave general, nontechnical, one- or two-paragraph statements of their favorite arguments for creation. These were described as "powerful ammunition," and readers were encouraged to "learn the arguments yourself—and use them." *Creation Ex Nihilo* 12, no. 1 (December 1989-February 1990): 35-37; also see vol. 11, no. 3 (June-August 1989): 22-24; vol. 11, no. 4 (September-November 1989): 29-31.

45This split has even been remarked by opponents of creationism; see Schadewald [1989b] 23; Schadewald and Hastings [1990] 23. See also Numbers [1992] 282. Tactics of the two tiers may differ as well; see Eve and Harrold [1991] 187-93.

46I have personally seen this in Ham's presentations. For another sort of example, see Morris [1976c] 196.

47Barrow and Tipler [1986] 130.

48Denton [1985] 191-92, also 117. See also ReMine [1993] 325.

[49]*The Creation Hypothesis,* however, does contain an appendix (written by two people, neither of whom has an advanced degree in science or philosophy) that pursues the popular creationist technique of trying to establish cases by assembling quotations. As evidence that "some scientists today are almost embarrassed by the theory of evolution," they give a single thirty-two-year-old quote from Loren Eisley. Morris and Parker are cited as establishing that "the scientific case for creation [is accepted] as legitimate [by] hundreds of other established scientists." What this is doing here is a bit puzzling.

### Chapter 7: Creationist Theory: Popular Evolutionist Misunderstandings

[1]Ward and Ricki Lewis were mentioned earlier. See also, for example, John A. Moore [1983] 120; Ralph Lewis [1981] 9. Actually, Darwin sometimes lapsed into such talk. Oddly enough, creationist John N. Moore comes close to this same mistake in [1986] 111.

[2]Gish, Bliss and Bird [1982] 130; Gish [1973b] 18, 21-23; Gish [1985b] 31-32, 44; Morris and Parker [1987] 118-19; Morris [1967] 26-29; Morris [1972b] vi, 41; Ham, Snelling and Wieland [1990] 106-13; Lang [1972] 35, 91-92; Johnson [1993c] 177-78; Johnson [1993a] 117-18; Lubenow [1983] 43; Sylvia Baker [1976] 5; Brown [1983] 208. Also Marsh [1933] 29, 207-20, 295ff., 306-9. Marsh took the mechanism to be hybridization. See also Whitcomb and Morris [1961] 226-27.

[3]Acceptance of natural selection is now orthodoxy among such creationist speakers as Parker and Ham. See also Frair and Davis [1983] 138; Parker [1994] 123; Morris [1974g] 86; Morris [1977a] 40. Anonymous [1991b] 50 says that "survival of the fittest . . . is a fact of life." See also Numbers [1992] 132.

[4]Moore and Slusher [1970/1974] xix; Morris [1946] 48-49. Elsewhere Morris [1970] 20, [1977a] 40 and [1966] 146 seems inclined toward the "pre-created resources" view, below. See Frair and Davis [1983] 29, 34-36, 89; Rimmer (well over a half century ago). See also Ham and Taylor [1988] 36; Ham, Snelling and Wieland [1990] 106 and 113 n. 1. With respect to the ark animals, the abilities to hibernate and migrate may have resulted from "divinely ordered genetic mutations" according to Morris [1977a] 98. See also Carson [1988] 19.

[5]For example, Murris [1986]; Wilder-Smith [1981] 124-25; Frair and Davis [1983] 101; Morris [1970] 20; Morris [1984a] 145; Morris [1988d] 15; Ham, Snelling and Wieland [1990] 111-13, 114 n. 5; Gish [1973b] 25; Gish [1993] 34; Whitcomb [1966] 16.

[6]Marsh held this view.

[7]For example, Morris [1974g] 80. Some creationists take the principle that "living beings remain within their kind, although lmited variation is allowed" to be a "Fourth Law of Creation"—for example, see Colin Brown [1982].

[8]For example, Gish, Bliss and Bird [1982] 134; Morris [1972b] 72; Morris [1974e] 53.

[9]For instance, the Field Museum of Natural History in Chicago in a recent evolution exhibit defined *clade* as a group composed of an ancestor and all and only descendants.

[10]Hoover [1977] 35; Frair and Davis [1983] 129; Morris [1946] 49, 79; Morris [1984a] 129; Morris [1956] 46; Morris [1977d] 29. One theologian even refers to phyla here, but does not seem to be using the biological definition—J. Vernon McGee [1981] 15-16—although McIver [1988] 162 takes him to be. Whitcomb [1966] 16-17 is one

of the few to suggest that kinds are species.

[11]Gish, Bliss and Bird [1982] 132-33. John N. Moore [1983] 203 contains a similar definition.

[12]For example, Lubenow [1983] 34: "By this definition, *all of us* are evolutionists."

[13]Birx [1991] 26-27; Dobzhansky [1973] 127; Beck [1982] 738. Birx has creationists accepting microevolution "below the species level."

[14]Morris [1974e] 71; Klotz [1966] 3; Kenyon, cited in Bird (vol. 1) [1989] 242; Bergman [1992b] 150-51; Gish [1978] 40.

[15]Ruse [1982] 299; Scott [1993] 41; Eve and Harrold [1991] 198 n. 3.

[16]Dobzhansky [1973] 127; see also Scott [n.d.]; Thwaites [n.d.]; Newell [1974] 207; Milner [1990] 99; NAS [1984]; McKown [1993] 72; John A. Moore [1975] 413. A very few creationists may hold this view, for example, Chittick [1984] 67; Criswell [1957] 72.

[17]For example, McCollister [1985] 44-45 and the New Orleans Geological Society. For an example of rejection of the extrapolation see ReMine [1993] 258.

[18]This is roughly Kitcher's characterization in [1982] 90.

[19]Morris [1966] 145-47; Morris [1963b] 35; Morris and Parker [1987] 5, 12, 193, 197, 204, 214; Morris [1977a] 13, 63; John N. Moore [1977] 35; Morris [1972b] 19; Morris [1974g] 17; Morris [1980a] 10, 111; Morris [1984a] 204ff.; Gish [1993] 151, 157-58, 160-61, 164-65, 205; Morris [1985a] 150, 154; Morris [1967] 45, 47; Kofahl and Segraves [1975] 35, 156; Whitcomb and Morris [1961] xxi n. 2, 226-27; Morris [1974e] 10, 23; Morris [1970] 127; Morris [1974b] 123-24; Morris [1971] 81; Morris [1977d] 16; Gish [1985a] 145, 148; Morris [1972a] 55-56; Morris [1991] 126; Hoover [1981] 22, 66; Morris [1985b] i.

[20]Morris [1980b] ii refers to the theory that there is a "net present increase in complexity." Virtually no one may hold that view, but that is a different matter. See also Morris [1974f] 188.

[21]Eldredge [1992] 88ff.; Kitcher [1982] 82-83, 91-96; Dawkins [1987] 94; Jukes [1984] 398; Ruse [1982] 306-7; Futuyma [1983] 223; Harris [1981] 24-25; Asimov [1984] 187-88; Pollitzer [1980] 329; Patterson [1983a] and [1983b]—see below. This is only the tip of the iceberg.

[22]Morris [1974g] 99-100; Morris [1974e] 42-46; Morris [1978c]; Morris [1984a] 207-11; Morris [1985b]; Morris [1985c]; Morris [1981a] iii; Morris [1982c] 24; Morris [1986a] 60; Morris [1980a] 114ff.; Morris [1972b] 19-20; Morris [1985a] 155-58; Morris [1971] 87; Morris [1977d] 16-17; Morris [1989b] 129-30; Morris [1976a] 17, 20; Kofahl [1977] 42ff.; Williams [1975] 445ff. See also Morris in Steele [1983] 334-35. There are hints at this in Morris [1967] 46-47. See also Morris and Parker [1987] 205-14; Gish [1993] 177-85, 194; Gish [1985a] 146; Wysong [1976] 246ff.; Mehlert [1987] 24; John N. Moore [1985b] 22; Malcolm [1988-1989] 34; Wieland [1993a] 46-47. Morris sometimes claims that the codes and mechanisms must come from *outside* of the system; see Morris [1985c] iii; Morris [1986b] ii-iii.

[23]Morris [1980a] 117.

[24]Morris [1974g] 101.

[25]Ibid. 99.

[26]Morris [1984a] 207. The identical sentence appears in Morris [1970] 127.

[27]Morris [1966] 146; Morris [1984a] 207; Morris [1980a] 114; Morris [1985b] i-iv.

[28]Morris [1985a] 155-56.

[29]Morris [1972b] 20.

[30]Morris [1974g] 100.

[31]Morris [1986a] 60.

[32]Morris [1974g] 101.

[33]Gish [1993] 175-77, 194; Wysong [1976] 251-53; Bird (vol. 1) [1989] 316; Kofahl and Segraves [1975] 35-37; Pearcey [1987b] 8; and Morris elsewhere, for example, Morris [1970] 129-30; Morris [1974b] 123; Morris [1977d] 19; Morris [1985b] i, iv; Morris [1985a] 29. Morris [1971] 88 and Gish [1974a] 131 are also relevant in this context. Paul Taylor seems to take this position in [1992] 7-10. This is also a prominent theme in Wilder-Smith's books—for example, [1981] 7, 61-66. Many of the above would be extremely skeptical of even the possibility left open by Morris.

[34]Morris [1974e] 45; Morris [1985a] 258; Morris [1980a] 209. Sometimes he says "seems precluded"; see Morris [1977c] 73. See also Morris [1970] 123; Morris [1976c] 19; Morris [1982c] 23.

[35]Huse [1983/1993] 63; Sylvia Baker [1976] 28. Morris early on apparently thought that there *was* a direct contradiction between biological evolution and the Second Law; see Morris [1956] 54. But in a revision of that book—Morris [1986a] 60— he dropped that claim. However, Morris did claim on one occasion in 1970 that the questions raised by the Second Law were not only unanswered but "unanswerable"—Morris [1970] 128-29—and later claimed that the issue with respect to the origin of life could "really only be resolved by recognition of the omnipotent creator"; see Morris [1981d] 37 and Morris [1978c] iv; see also Morris [1990c] 35. Whitcomb and Morris, Gish, Morris and Parker and perhaps Wysong take the odds of a workable mechanism to be so huge as to amount to a practical contradiction; see Whitcomb and Morris [1961] 225-26; Gish [1981] 39, 45; Morris and Parker [1987] 13-14, 269-73; Wysong [1976] 259; and possibly Ackerman [1986] 213. Creationists who seem to believe that there *is* a direct contradiction include Ian Taylor [1984] 305, Bliss [1992] 9; Whitcomb [1986] 129; Whitcomb [1966] 15; Heinz [1970] 46; Bliss and Parker [1979] 40-41; and John N. Moore [1977] 36. In fact, Gish himself sometimes sounds like this; see Gish [1979] 186; Gish [n.d.].

[36]Morris [1980a] 120; Morris [1981d] 33; Morris [1978c] ii. Compounding possible problems, Morris on one occasion claimed that the First Law implies "that *nothing* is being either 'created' or 'evolved' by present processes"; see Morris [1990b] iii.

[37]Patterson [1983b] 100.

[38]Morris [1974g] 99.

[39]Ibid. 100.

[40]Patterson [1983b] 103.

[41]Ibid. 101; Patterson [1983a] 134.

[42]McKown [1993] 60-61.

[43]Huse [1983/1993] 62; Wysong [1976] 259; Morris [1972b] 20; Morris [1980a] 114; Morris [1974g] 123; Morris [1985a] 155; Morris [1974e] 43; Morris and Parker [1987] 206, 221. The point is also implicit in Morris [1986a] 60, and in Morris [1970] 128-29 and Morris [1984a] 209-10, which contain essentially identical passages. The point may also be intended in Wysong [1976] 248, 252 and Morris [1967] 47.

[44]Morris in [1988e] *seems* to take a harder line on a number of issues. For instance, he again claims that the Second Law can be derived from the principles of creation (with no essential reference to the Fall, 44). He also claims that the Second Law precludes "evolution . . . in the living world" (41), and in the context of a *biological*

discussion claims that "the entropy principle squarely refutes even the possibility of vertical upward evolution" (47). And instead of his usual claim that the "open system" response concerning the earth is _inadequate,_ he now claims that it is _irrelevant_ (45). I say that Morris _may_ be changing his position, because Morris [1988e] concerns evangelism and missions, and he may simply have thought that greater precision here would be a counterproductive, needlessly complicating distraction.

[45]For example, Whitcomb and Morris [1961] 232-33, 238; Morris [1963b] 56; Morris [1963a] 10; Morris [1966] 42-43; Morris [1967] 62-64; Morris [1976c] 63; Whitcomb [1986] 40, 43.

[46]Morris [1972b] 61-62; Morris [1976c] 65-66; Morris [1972a] 46; Whitcomb and Morris [1961] 369.

[47]Whitcomb [1986] 43, 46 thinks that only the unavoidable appearances of age were present. Thus, for example, created trees had no growth rings. Whitcomb would probably be delighted with recent reports of fossilized wood showing "no evidence of tree rings"; see Sereno [1995] 44. See also Whitcomb [1966] 7. Not all creationists agree, such as Rusch [1991] 42.

[48]Morris [1972b] 94; Morris [1970] 70. Whitcomb and Morris [1961] 345-46, 354; Morris [1972a] 70. See also Ackerman [1986] 102; Wilder-Smith [1986] 14-15.

[49]Dawkins [1987] 293. See also Poole and Wenham [1987] 73; McGowan [1983] 89.

[50]Sonleitner [1991] chap. 6. See also Anderson [1991].

[51]Anderson [1991].

[52]Humphries [1985] 16-17.

[53]Weiner and Maizels [n.d.] 560; Gould [1981] 36; Gould [1987a] 68; Asimov [1984] 189; Futuyma [1983] 199; Brush [1981] 31-32; Dobzhansky [1973] 126.

[54]Note, incidentally, that although the case may be tremendously compelling, nearly all stars—the _sources_ of the light points we see—are theoretical explanatory entities nonetheless. Whitcomb [1979] 28 argues that our theories' being mistaken is not evidence for deceit, as does Niessen [1983] iii.

[55]Whitcomb and Morris [1961] 238; Morris [1963b] 57-58; Morris [1966] 43; Morris [1977a] 25; Ham, Snelling and Wieland [1990] 195 n. 6; Whitcomb [1986] 45, 160; Dressler [1990-1991] 19; Whitcomb [1979] 28; Whitcomb [1966] 8. In fact, some creationists argue that God would be guilty of deceit in Scripture if evolution _had_ taken place—Ham and Taylor [1988] 63, 68—or if the earth really was old—Morris [1984c] iv.

[56]Harris [1981] 26-27.

[57]Ecker [1990] 92; Scott [1985] 28. See also Key [1985] and Rice [1985], as well as Teeple [1978] 66-71.

[58]For example, Morris [1974d] 97; Morris [1972b] 29; Morris [1978b] 71; Chittick [1984] 195; Brown [1983] 225; Whitcomb and Morris [1961] 83. McGowan [1983] 61, misses the fountains of the deep and cites problems with accounting for the water purely by rainfall. He also ignores the claim of topographic changes.

[59]See, for example, Asimov [1981] 157; Teeple [1978]; McGowan [1983] 56.

[60]Diamond [1985] 86; Scott [n.d.]

[61]Whitcomb and Morris [1961] 65-70; Morris [1986a] 87-88; Whitcomb [1973] 22-23; Ham, Snelling and Wieland [1990] 27; Parker [1987] 25. Others argue that juveniles or even eggs of larger kinds such as dinosaurs might have been taken; see, for example, John Morris [1980] 66; John Morris [1989].

[62]For example, Morris [1946] 79; Morris [1971] 106; Whitcomb and Morris [1961] 67, 87. See also Numbers [1992] 109. For evolutionist confusion here see, for example, Jukes [1984] 399; John A. Moore [1975] 415.

[63]Kitcher [1982] 141-42.

[64]Fezer [1993b] 48. Some creationists believe that animals were vegetarian until after the flood, in connection with Gen 9:3; see Ham and Taylor [1988] 60. Teeple [1978] 71 claims that Noah's postflood sacrifice (representing each kind) would have been too huge to accomplish. That obviously depends on the number of kinds. In any case, the sacrifice included only *clean* animals and birds (Gen 8:20). See also Asimov [1981] 158; Jukes [1984] 399.

[65]Frair and Davis [1983] 72 refer to "a few marsupial founders" in Australia. See Boardman [1986] 219ff.

[66]Quoted from Kitcher in Schadewald [1985] 15. See Milne [1981] 240; Fezer [1993b] 48; Tiffin [1994] 117; Appleman [1994]. Schadewald [1983b] 451 contains a related confusion.

[67]Robert A. Moore [1983] 5-9; Fezer [1993b] 48; Scott [n.d.].

[68]See Fezer [1993a] 6; Harris [1981] 27. For the creationist claim see, for example, Morris [1974c] 239; Morris [1976c] 78; Gish [1990] 35.

[69]Milne [1981] 239. See also Harris [1981] 22.

[70]See, for example, Dawkins [1987] 92-93. Gould has particularly stressed this sort of argument. See also Arduini [1987] 23; Thwaites [1984] 209.

[71]For example, Ham [1967] 12; Morris and Parker [1987] 88. This also includes disease organisms; see Morris [1976c] 125-26; Gish [1990] 35; Parker [1994] 93, 95.

[72]Harris [1981] 23-24, 26.

[73]Schadewald [1983a] 289; Schadewald [1985] 15.

[74]Ruse [1988b] 290-91; Morris [1974e] 5-6, 9-10. This claim is standard among creationists.

[75]Strahler [1987] 63; Eldredge [1982] 95; Denton [1985] 22; Patterson [1978] 184; Birx [1991] 288; McCollister [1989] 115; Webb [1994] 2.

[76]For example, Dobzhansky [1973] 126; see Strahler [1987] 82. See also Birx [1991] 242; Brush [1982] 39; Eldredge [1982] 92-93; Price [1980]; McIver [1988] 237-38. Some creationists explicitly reject Gosse but accept apparent age. See Whitcomb [1966] 7.

[77]Godfrey [1983b] xiii, xiv.

[78]Edey and Johanson [1989] 291.

**Chapter 8: Philosophy of Science: The Twentieth-Century Background**

[1]There are a number of good general histories of this period. See, for example, relevant sections of Dijksterhuis [1961] 164-70; Crombie (vol. 2) [1959] 3, 27, 35, 46; Randall [1926] 219ff.; and Blake, DuCasse and Madden [1960] 7.

[2]Thackray [1970] 191 ; Cassirir [1951] chap. 6; Randall [1926] 254, 265ff.; Brinton [1963] 110ff., 119ff.

[3]See Ratzsch [1986] 14-20 for further discussion.

[4]Bacon [1620/1955]. See especially bk. 2, beginning with section 10.

[5]For brief outlines of Bacon's method, see, for example, Dijksterhuis [1961] 399-400; Blake, DuCasse and Madden [1960] 54-62.

[6]Nearly every philosophy-of-science survey contains discussion of this point. See, for example, Ratzsch [1986] chap. 2; Suppe [1977] 3-118.

7Suppe [1977] 9ff.

8Standard explications can be found in Hempel, Suppe, Salmon and nearly any other standard philosophy-of-science survey.

9See virtually any philosophy-of-science survey—for example, Ratzsch [1986] 24, 32, 78-79.

10This point, while surprising to many, is no longer even controversial. See, for example, Ratzsch [1986] 24.

11Popper [1959] 40-41.

12Ibid. 108-9.

13Ibid. 111.

14For more detailed discussion of Kuhn's views and difficulties with them see, for example, Ratzsch [1986] chap. 3; Suppe [1977] 135-50, 636ff.

15Kuhn [1962] postscript, 182-87.

16Ibid. chap. 3; 10, 24-34, 37; chap. 4; 52, 64.

17Ibid. chaps. 7-8; 79, 82-84.

18Ibid. chaps. 6, 10; 56, 64-65, 102, 109-10, 148-50; Kuhn [1970] 231-78; Kuhn [1977]. See Ratzsch [1986] 49-56.

19Kuhn [1962] 106, 110-14, 117-18, 120-21, 125, 129, 134-35, 150; Kuhn [1970] 270. Ratzsch [1986] 51-55.

20Kuhn [1962] 170-73, 206-7, 94, 103, 122, 148, 150, 158, 199; Kuhn [1970] 259-68, 234-35; Kuhn [1977] 332, 338, chap. 13.

21See Ratzsch [1986] 59-61; Suppe [1977] 617-730.

### Chapter 9: The Nature of Science: A Contemporary Perspective

1Shapin [1982] 160; Gould [1978] 18.

2Shapin [1982] 160.

3Irving Klotz [1980] 168ff.

4See Forman's [1971] study.

5Pope [1989] 51.

6Hartmann [1989] 74. See also Gould [1981] 37.

7This occurred with both Newton and Darwin, whose theories were received very differently in England and France.

8Dirac [1971] 39. In a similar context, Gould [1978] 22 says, "Orthodoxy can be as stubborn in science as in religion."

9This is nearly a defining trait of some "sociology of science" views.

10See, for example, Crick [1988] 138-39. Some philosophers of science are suspicious of simplicity considerations as well.

11Darwin [1859] 138; Darwin [1871] 770; Crick [1988] 97, 114-15, 141; see also 160.

12For instance, Gould [1977b] 28.

### Chapter 10: The Nature of Science: Popular Creationist Mistakes

1Gish [1973b] 2; Gish [1993] 261; Gish [1985b] 12; Gish [1973a] 132; Gish [1978] 12; Matrisciana and Oakland [1991] 100; Wysong [1976] 40; Ankerberg and Weldon [1993] 9; Morris [1984a] 302; Morris [1966] 151; John N. Moore [1976b] 11-12; John N. Moore [1973] 23. Morris [1988e] 13, 99 very nearly endorses Bacon, as does Morris [1982b] i, iii and Rusch [1991] 9-10. See also Morris [1966] 144-45; Morris [1980a] 8-10; Arndts [1991b] 8; Nelkin [1982] 76; and Eve and Harrold [1991] 61-62, 176, 179ff., 190.

²In an older sense, *science* included mathematics and other disciplines for which reference to "demonstrate truths" was appropriate. However, popular creationists who use the quoted definition seem without exception to take the entire definition to apply to the natural sciences. See, for example, Morris [1966] 151.

³Morris and Parker [1987] xi, xii, 37, 179, 254, 286-87; Morris [1984b] 24; Morris [1967] 19, 42-43; Ian Taylor [1984] 315-16; Sunderland [1988] 25-26; Gish [1985b] 176. Hartwig and Meyer [1993] 156-57, 162 n. 13 speak repeatedly of inferences from data, as does Bird (vol. 2) [1989] 14, 56, 486. The *Bible-Science Newsletter* 30, no. 3 (1992): 13, takes Gould's recognition of some non-Baconian aspects of science as an "unintentional admission that evolution is religion, not science." See also Chittick [1984] 38, 139; Frair and Davis [1983] 16, 22; Pearcey [1993] 2; Bartz [1984] 3-4; Paul Taylor [1992] 48; Bergman [1983] 40-41; Klotz [1966] 4; Ouweneel [1971] 111; ReMine [1993] 32; John N. Moore [1983] 5; Ham [1989]. Some creationists present hypothetico-deductivism as the proper view; see, for example, Moore and Slusher [1970/1974] chap. 1. Ham—possibly reflecting some postempiricism—emphasizes the role of "bias" in scientific procedures; Ham [1987] 8-12. Bird (vol. 1) [1989] 8 and elsewhere cites Kuhn but does not seem to recognize the implications. For an odd twist on this, see Frangos [1991] 18. John N. Moore repeatedly refers to the theoretical as "imaginary"; see John N. Moore [1986a] 110-11; John N. Moore [1976b] 104; John N. Moore [1974] 5; John N. Moore [1976a] 46; John N. Moore [1983] 68, 79, 81, 83, 88, 127. He does, however, think that we can have "excellent" indirect evidence of actual existence of *nonhistorical* theoretical entities; see John N. Moore [1983] 83, 86, 88-89.

Creationist journals have contained a few articles displaying some more philosophical sophistication—for example, Ancil, Ferst, Schoepflin and Arthur Jones. It is not entirely clear, however, that all of these authors are creationists. There are a few professionally competent philosophers of science in the creationist upper tier. Probably the most prominent is J. P. Moreland.

⁴Morris [1974e] 1; Morris [1967] 24, 42; Morris [1966] 108, 111; Morris and Parker [1987] 191; Morris [1974d] 111; Morris [1981b] i; Morris [1982d] i; Morris [1982c] 23; Morris [1984a] 260; Morris [1974c] 229, 249; Morris [1971] 82; Morris [1980a] 69; Morris [1977a] 12; Gish [1993] 261. Bartz [1984] 4 at least suggests this as well.

⁵Johnson [1993a] 67, 100; Gish [1985b] 11; Gish [1993] 210; Gish [1973b] 1-2; Sylvia Baker [1976] 30; Bird (vol. 1) [1989] 141-42, 155; Segraves [1973] 13. Hartwig and Meyer [1993] sometimes comes close to this—for example, 156; Chittick [1984] 266. See also Lindsell [1977].

⁶Gish [1985b] 19; Morris [1985a] 147; Morris [1990a] 40. See also Whitcomb and Morris [1961] 131 and Morris [1984a] 303; Wieland [1994] 4, also see 5; Frair and Davis [1983] 23. See Morris [1970] 69 for a related claim.

⁷Morris [1984b] 24; Gish [1985b] 13; Frair and Davis [1983] 17, 64; Riemen [1987] 142. See also Sunderland [1988] 26, 153 and Lubenow [1992] 57. The discussion in Arthur Jones [1971] 46 is a bit more nuanced.

⁸As one example, see Morris [1981a] ii and iv.

⁹Gish [1993] 39, 52, 216, 328; Gish [1973b] 5, 17; Gish [1985b] 15; Morris [1974e] 7; Sunderland [1988] 39, 139; Bartz [1993b] 8; ReMine [1993] 94, 137, 459, 462; Whitcomb and DeYoung [1978] 63; Bergman and Howe [1990] 16. Johnson is quoted to this effect in Pearcey [1990] 8.

¹⁰Oddly enough, some creationists seem to think that modifications of evolutionary

theory in response to data count against the theory—see, for example, Matrisciana and Oakland [1991] 111; Lubenow [1992] 75. See also ReMine [1993] 102, 462.

[11] Morris [1974e] 9; Morris [1984b] 24; Morris [1983a] 3; Gish [1973b] 2; Gish [1985b] 14, 19; Sunderland [1988] 26-28; Ian Taylor [1984] 392; Matrisciana and Oakland [1991] 79; ReMine [1993] 129, 138. See, for example, Dawkins [1987] 225.

[12] Some creationists seem not to recognize the evidential status of explanatory power, for example, ReMine [1993] 25. See also n. 31 below on Johnson and others. ReMine [1993] 145 is relevant here as well. Mistaken correlation of explanation and prediction can be found in Macbeth [1971] 104.

[13] Whitcomb and Morris [1961] 209; Sunderland [1988] 38-39; Ouweneel [1971] 113. See also Chittick [1984] 184. Arthur Jones [1971] 48 seems to recognize problems with this objection. See also Torrey [1907] 11-12.

[14] Gish [1993] 314; Whitcomb and Morris [1961] 51; Morris [1967] 16-19, 21-22; Morris [1974e] 74; Lubenow [1983] 141; Frair and Davis [1983] 61; Arndts [1991a] 8; Bird (vol. 1) [1989] 92ff. See also Lubenow [1992] 74-77 for a related discussion. Davis and Kenyon [1993] sometimes gets close to this objection; see, for example, 133, 138. Hoover [1977] 55 perhaps intends this as well. Ankerberg and Weldon [1993] 7, 45 n. 17 contains a variant version of this mistake.

[15] This move is made explicitly in Morris [1989b] 114, where in two sentences he goes from someone having no evidence to prove something, to that person having no evidence.

[16] Gish [1993] 232; Gish [1985b] 14; Gish [1973a] 132; Gish [1983b] 177; Gish [1978] 13; Sylvia Baker [1976] 29; Wysong [1976] 45; Colson (no. 1) [1993]. Bartz [1984b] 20 demands *complete and repeatable* observation.

[17] Ham and Taylor [1988] 11; Ham, Snelling and Wieland [1990] 25; Morris [1984a] 261, 302; Morris [1946] 27; Morris [1966] 151-52; Morris [1956] 29-30; Gish [1974b] 19; Austin [1970] 78, 96. Chittick [1984] 59 comes close to this. John N. Moore [1982] 196 claims that studies of the deep past cannot be proper science because it deals with "objects and/or events of the past where human experience is totally impossible." See also John N. Moore [1985a] 192. Moore's characterizations of science are generally hyperempirical. He not only frequently links the theoretical to the imaginary (see n. 3 above) but is even reluctant to call evolutionary theories *theories;* see [1982] 197 n. 1.

[18] Ken Ham [1991a], Job 38:4. See also his [1987] 19. This theme appears also in Ham's interview in Pearcey [1989] 9. See also Bliss [1989] 9, 11. Ham is completely open about the role that Scripture plays in his views and has suggested publicly that other creationists also ought to be.

[19] See, for example, Gish [1993] 232; Gish [1985b] 14; Sylvia Baker [1976] 29; Morris and Parker [1987] xi, xii, 37, 179, 254, 286-87; Morris [1984b] 24; Morris [1967] 19, 42-43; Ian Taylor [1984] 315-16.

[20] Morris [1973] 69, 70; Morris [1971] 83; Morris [1974a] 109; Morris [1974c] 271; Morris [1974f] 188; Boardman, Koontz and Morris [1973] 13, 118. See also John N. Moore [1985a] 190; John N. Moore [1982] 196; Gish [1973b] 4. Creationists also almost universally claim that even if one could, for example, generate life in the laboratory, that still would not show much, because that production would involve human intelligence and thus would not be a reproduction of natural processes. See, for example, Morris [1974c] 262; John N. Moore [1985b] 24. It is not clear that this argument works.

21In addition to the more specific versions discussed below, blanket claims that evolution is simply incoherent can be found in, for example, the preface of Morris [1967].

22Gish [1993] 38; Gish [1983b] 182; Morris [1974e] 7; Wysong [1976] 344; Bethell [1976] 14. Some evolutionists cheerfully accept this charge, for example, Harris [1981] 188-92. See also Patterson [1978] 147.

23At least one creationist seems to admit this; see Bergman [1992b] 147.

24Gould [1983] 141-43; Kitcher [1982] 60. Oddly enough, ReMine [1993] 98-101 seems to recognize this, and claims that only natural selection (not the whole theory) is a tautology, but he still claims that evolutionists "need a way out" of the objection.

25Gould [1983] 141-43. For an explicit claim that fitness must be defined in terms of survival see Bethell [1994] 18.

26For example, Morris [1946] 40 refers to "the great dinosaurs and huge and fierce mammals of the past, which were certainly better fitted to survive than their modern descendants." Since their descendants survived while they, although better fitted, did not, fitness and survival obviously are not equivalent on this view. Bergman [1993] 93-94 argues that extinction typically is not related to lack of fitness and cites that as a problem for evolution. For either Morris or Bergman to be correct, one cannot understand *fitness* in terms purely of survival. Some creationists accept "survival of the fittest [as] a fact of life"; see Anonymous [1991b] 50. Wallace [1858] 330-31 discussed degrees of fitness. One might argue that *fitness* must be defined in terms of *prospects* of survival, but if so the alleged circle seems to collapse.

27Johnson [1993a] 117, 127, 153, 163; Johnson [1993b] 292; Wysong [1976] 44-45; Morris and Parker [1987] 18; Arndts [1989] 4. See Bethell [1978] 91. Van Inwagen [1989] 50ff. at least suggests this as a possibility. Similar earlier objections can be found in Dawson [1873] 339-43 and Hedtke [1981] 8-13, 26; Ouweneel [1971] 109, 111. For a related charge see Arthur Jones [1971] 46. There are few nuanced popular creationist discussions of the role of philosophical principles in evolutionist or other scientific thinking, but see Ancil [1985] 118-22 and Schoepflin [1972].

28Dawkins [1987] 287. See also Dawkins [1987] 142 passim and Dawkins [1988] 219. See also Savage [1963] v and Dawson [1873] 339-43, quoted in Gillespie [1979] 151-52, for earlier examples and discussion of this point.

29Johnson [1993a] 82.

30Ibid. 101. In fact, Johnson identifies this as the main issue of his book, 14.

31In addition to ibid. 82 and 101, see 85-86, 93, 99. This may also be behind 73 and 154. See also Gish [1993] 312, 345; Gish [1985b] 90-91. See also Lubenow [1992] 57, 71-73 and Denton [1985] 351-53. A related argument is in Bethell [1978] 91. Hummer [1980] 27 gives a similar argument, as does Ouweneel [1971] 114. See also Hedtke [1981] 10-11.

32Johnson's apparent inferential picture may be linked to a possible suspicion of the force of explanatory power; see, for example, Johnson [1993a] 66. Morris [1980a] 8-10 at least presupposes that explanatory power is not a factor, as does Arndts [1991b] 8; Moore and Slusher [1970] 441; and perhaps Bergman [1992b] 153. See also Rusch [1984] 21. Oddly enough, Morris does seem to recognize the value of explanatory power concerning theories of Genesis authorship; see Morris [1976c] 30. See also Bartz [1992] 5; Gish [1993] 220. There is one interesting hint in

Boardman, Koontz and Morris [1973] 33-34, and Anderson and Coffin [1977] 80 claims that the creationist view gains support from its role in a "broad, unifying and coherent worldview."

33Johnson [1993a] 43; see also 48, 100 and, possibly, 78. Bergman [1992b] 149 also makes this charge, and a related claim is in John N. Moore [1982] 194, 197 n. 14.

34Denton is not himself a creationist, but since his work has been adopted almost wholesale by creationists, he is included here. Another noncreationist critic of evolution whose criticisms have been influential among creationists is Norman Macbeth. I will not discuss Macbeth except to note that his work contains signif-icant philosophy of science mistakes as well as some inaccuracies about evolution-ary theory. On philosophy of science, Macbeth accepts the old, roughly positivist idea of the inseparability of explanation and prediction, accepts the idea that theories facing difficulties should be junked, and comes close to endorsing some form of inductivism. See Macbeth [1971] 6-7, 100-101, 104, and possibly 77-78. On evolutionary theory, Macbeth fails to distinguish competition between species from competition between individuals within a species, and accepts various forms of a number of the misconstruals discussed in chapter four. See Macbeth [1971] 47, 60 62ff., 83-84, 92-93, 116, 121. I think he also has problems at 4, 97, 99-100. Still, Gish [1993] 56 classifies the Macbeth book as one of the best recent anti-evolution works. Bird also reportedly claims not to be a creationist—Eve and Harrold [1991] 202 n. 4—although Morris [1987] 1 sounds otherwise.

35Denton [1985] 57.

36Denton [1985] 192, 291, 294-96, 300, 306, 346. Frair and Davis [1983] 61-62 makes a similar point.

37Frair and Davis [1983] 62. Criswell [1957] 69 calls them "feeble." For a creationist explanation of the absence of preflood human fossils, see Snelling [1991].

38Morris [1967] 34-35. See also Lubenow [1992] 71.

39For example, Whitcomb and Morris [1961] 132, 136, 203-7; Morris [1974e] 95-96, 229; Morris [1986b] ii; Morris [1977b]; Morris [1980a] 154ff.; Morris [1977a] 111-12; Whitcomb [1986] 82; Morris [1967] 34-36; Morris [1985a] 222, 254; Morris and Parker [1987] 240; Wysong [1976] 348-50; Huse [1983/1993] 14; Morris and Mor-ris [1989] 58; Morris [1956] 60; Morris [1984a] 312; Morris [1946] 62; Morris [1970] 27; Morris [1966] 66, 159-63; Morris [1956] 60; Gish [1985b] 91-92. Morris, Boardman and Koontz (Teacher's Handbook) [1971] 25; Hoover [1977] 40; Morris [1972b] 22, 27, 76-77; Wilder-Smith [1986] 102-3; Lubenow [1983] 93; Frair and Davis [1983] 66; Lubenow [1983] 93; Moore and Slusher [1970/1974] 424. See also Marsh [1933] 271-76, 367-68. This same general sort of argument is also sometimes advanced in other areas—see Brown [1983] 217 #53.

40For criticism of Morris's argument see Raup [1983a] 153-54; Schafersma [1983a] 221ff.; Brush [1982] 49ff.; and Abbot [1984] 167-68. Some other creationists reject Morris's type of claim here also; see Sylvia Baker [1976] 15; Sunderland [1988] 42.

41Morris may object to black holes; see Morris [1981c] 183.

42Gish [1993] 32; Morris [1974e] 4; Morris [1967] 19, 42; Ham [1987] 16-17; John N. Moore [1976b] 21-22; Morris [1972b] 57-58; Chittick [1984] 50.

43Gish [1993] 232; Gish [1985b] 14; Gish [1990] 21; Gish [1972] 1; Kofahl [1977] 18-19; Sylvia Baker [1976] 29; Morris [1984b] 96; Lubenow [1992] 57, 146; Ham [1987] 16-17; Ham [1991b] 62; Ackerman [1982] 15; Whitcomb and DeYoung [1978] 55; Gish [1977] 45, 57. See other citations in n. 16 above. John N. Moore has probably pushed this objection harder than anyone. It occurs in nearly all of his writings. On one occasion, Morris—[1983c] iv—even puts catastrophes in the category of unobservable.

44Gish [1993] 32, 33, 254, 263; Gish [1983b] 176; Whitcomb and Morris [1961] xxvi, 213, 227, 331, 378; Morris [1967] 19ff.; Morris [1966] 103-9, 145, 168; Morris [1984a] 138; Morris [1974d] 35; Morris [1977a] 39; Morris [1974f] 188; Gish [1974b] 19; Morris [1973] 69, 70; Morris [1974a] 109; Morris [1989b] 23; Morris [1971] 83; Morris [1974c] 249, 271; Huse [1983/1993] 126; Thaxton, Bradley and Olsen [1984] 8, 204; Morris, Boardman and Koontz *(Teacher's Handbook)* [1971] 7; Hoover [1977] 48, 57-58; Andrews [1986] 46-47; Moore and Slusher [1970/1974] xvii, 80; John N. Moore [1976a] 46; John N. Moore [1982] 196; John N. Moore [1986b] 95; John N. Moore [1983] xii, 86-87, 159; Anderson and Coffin [1977] 15. Some noncreationists may also agree; see, for example, Patterson [1978] 144-46. See also Morris and Parker [1987] 191. For further criticism of this view, see Plantinga [unpublished] 24.

45Gish [1974b] 19. See also John Morris [1991b]; Rusch [1984] 19; Rusch [1991] 11. See again references in n. 17 above. One of the few nuanced creationist discussions in this area is Ancil [1985] 119-21.

46Morris and Parker [1987] 298.

47Geisler and Anderson [1987] 13-18; Geisler [1989] chap. 6; Sunderland [1988] 29-30. See also Lubenow [1992] chap. 2 and Hartwig and Meyer [1993] 157-59; Ancil [1985] 118-21; Arthur Jones [1971] 46; Hoover [1981] 2-4.

48Cowan [1976] 36-37. For creationist discussion of this case see Chaffin [1982] and Chaffin [1985].

## Chapter 11: The Nature of Science: Popular Anticreationist Mistakes

1Various critics of creationism invoke the fact-theory issue, appeal to inductivist and Baconian sorts of principles and to "rules" of science, charge creationism with being unprovable, untestable, unfalsifiable, overly flexible, overly inflexible, too tenaciously held, held for underhanded motives and with involving unique and unrepeatable events, and assert the illegitimacy of worldview considerations in science. Perhaps the most extended discussion by other than professional philosophers of science is Strahler (part 1) [1987], which despite some references to more recent work still has a pre-1960s flavor. For various examples from others, see Newell [1982] xxx-xxxi; Harris [1981] 97; Shapiro [1993] 12-14; Harold I. Brown [1986] 21; Birx [1991] 35; Albert [1986] 26-27; Edwords [1983b] 172; McKown [1993] 27, 59; Edwords [1983c] 308; Scott [1993] 41; Fezer [1991] 17; Mirsky [1988] 11; Eldredge [1982] 10, 22, 27-28, 40, 87; Morowitz [1982] 54; Denton [1985] 75, 255, 260; R. W. Lewis [1981] 8, 10; Scott and Sager [1992] 47-48; Shmaefsky [1991] 23; Diamond [1985] 92; Pine [1983] 10-13, esp. 12; McCollister [1989] 134; Hanson [1980] 5; Beck [1982] 739-40; Eldredge [1981] 16; Scott [n.d.]; Gingrich [1993] 211, 215, 218, 228; Newell [1985] 16, 20; Cloud [1983] 138; Asimov [1981] 7-8; Fezer [1984] 12; McCollister [1989] 33; Tiffin [1994] 131-32; Siegel [1981] 98-99; Smith [1989] 700. Futuyma [1983] 166 cites the *Oxford Dictionary* definition.

2NAS [1984]. Also partially reproduced in McCollister [1989] 34-42.

3NAS [1984] 9-10; McCollister [1989] 33-42.

4*The Science Teacher* 48, no. 4 (April 1981): 33. Reproduced in Skehan [1986].

5Overton [1982] 218. Kehoe [1983] 10 even takes facts to depend on the beliefs of scientists, and Futuyma [1983] 166 says something similar.

[6]Overton [1982] 218-19.

[7]See, for example, Laudan [1982] 149-54; Quinn [1984]. Overton was following Ruse here. For further discussion, see also Ruse [1988c] and [1988a]; Quinn [1988]; Burien [1986]; and Laudan [1988]. See Plantinga [unpublished] 23ff. for further criticism of Ruse's position.

[8]NCSE, "Keeping Creationism out of Education." Also Scott [1993] 46; McCollister [1989] 22; Scott quoted in Arries [1991] 2; and Futuyma [1983] 216.

[9]McCollister [1989].

[10]Asimov gives the same views in Asimov [1981] 7-11.

[11]Others endorse Baconian positions as well, for example, Shapiro [1993] 14.

[12]That conviction is widely held. Representative examples include John A. Moore [1991] 7; Scott [1993] 43; Albert [1986] 27; Pine [1983] 10; Jones and Leise [1987] 1681; Levin [1992] 31; McKown [1993] 95; Fezer [1984] 12-13; R. W. Lewis [1981] 10, 11; Patterson [1983a] 142-43; Sonleitner [1991] "Science" section p2; Fezer [1988] 19-20; NCSE, "Keeping Creationism out of Education." NAS [1982] contains related claims. Fezer [1991] 16-17; Schadewald [1989a] 9; NCSE, "Evolution and Creationism"; Birx [1991] 56, 98, 259; Denton [1985] 35, 41, 355-56; Gould [1987b] 34; Eldredge [1981] 17; Gingrich [1993] 215-18; McMullin [1993] 303-4; Ruse [1982] 322; Heckenlively [1993] 236; Walsh and Demere [1993]; Strahler [1987] vii, 1, 4, 62, 73-74, 193-94; Ruse [1988d] 301; Futuyma [1983] 217. See also Dawkins [1987] 141—more later. Even some creationists agree, for example Thaxton, Bradley and Olsen [1984] 202-10; also Kofahl [1989] 12-13; Kofahl [1990] 41; Gish [1993] 66. Indeed, any inductivist definition of science would have this consequence. For additional criticism of this view, see Plantinga.

[13]Pine [1983] 10.

[14]Walsh and Demere [1993].

[15]NCSE, "Keeping Creationism out of Education." Others advance this point as well, for example, Birx [1991] 27.

[16]Some take the phrase *creation science* to be self-contradictory—for example, Gould [1987a] 64; Gould [1981] 35. For related points, see Jukes [1986] 22; Siegel [1981] 98.

[17]Duhem [1954] 274-75 and others argue for naturalism in science on practical strategic grounds—that science will thus involve only things on which we can all agree, whatever our persuasion. That, of course, will provide no grounds for making such naturalism normative, and will not bypass issues discussed below in any case. See Plantinga [unpublished] 42. See also McMullin [1993] 303.

[18]Scott [1993] 43. See also Lewontin [1983a] 22.

[19]Strahler [1987] 1.

[20]Walsh and Demere [1993].

[21]For example, Shmaefsky [1991] 23; Walsh and Demere [1993]; Strahler [1987] 7, 36, 43, 76. Birx is filled with such comparisons, for example, "The splendid advancements of modern science [vs] the reactionary tenets of myopic theology"; Birx [1991] 274. See also Birx [1991] 102; Ruse [1982] 322; NAS [1984] 10; Scott [n.d.]; Asimov [1981] 8; Arnold Clark [1987] 4; Newell [1985] 20; Kenneth Baker [1987] 18; McKown [1993] 39, 41.

[22]Strahler [1987] 7, 36, 43, 76.

[23]Fezer [1984] 12-13; Scott [1993] 43; Fezer [1985] 7; Walsh and Demere [1993];

NCSE, "Keeping Creationism out of Education"; Scott [1988] 269.

[24]White [1896]. See also J. W. Draper [1874]. Some evolutionists still explicitly appeal to such sources; see, for example, John A. Moore [1983b] 126.

[25]Lindberg and Numbers [1986]; Kalthoff [1993]; Livingstone [1987]; James Moore [1979]; Marsden [1991] 139-40.

[26]A number of historians make this claim—for example, Hooykaas [1972] and M. B. Foster [1934], [1935], [1936].

[27]As examples see Kelly Clark [1988]; McGuire [1968] sections 5-6; Brooke [1991] 75-76, 122, 130-29; Torrance [1989] 150-51.

[28]Ratzsch [1986] esp. chap. 4. Whitcomb seems to hold the priority ordering indicated; see McIver [1989] 548.

[29]Beck [1982] 739. John A. Moore [1983b] contains a nearly identical position.

[30]McCollister [1989] 56-57. There are other examples in McCollister as well. A variant is contained in NAS [1984] 26.

[31]In addition to those quoted in the text, see also Scott [1993] 41; Pine [1983] 10-11; Abell [1983] 34. See also Morris [1982a] 140; Wieland [1989] 47-48.

[32]Eldredge [1982] 134.

[33]Futuyma [1983] 169. Similar remarks are found in John A. Moore [1983b] 4.

[34]Ruse [1988d] 301. For a creationist statement of essentially the same view, see Kofahl [1990] 41. Tinkle [1970] 86 responds that to take something "out of the realm of science [is] not so bad as to take it out of the realm of truth."

[35]Fezer [1991] 17. The NCSE's Eugenie Scott is reported as saying that "science has to pretend that God doesn't exist" (Bethell [1992]). Pine [1983] 10. See Plantinga [unpublished] section 2 for further criticism of this view.

[36]Pine [1983] 6; Scott [1993] 43; Asimov [1981] 12.

[37]A similar criticism is contained in Gingrich [1993] 215 and passim. For a variant version of the problem, see the American Humanist Association statement in Singer [1977] 11.

[38]Bradley and Thaxton [1994] 197. Hedtke [1986] 10 makes a similar blanket claim concerning religious belief being immune to the empirical.

[39]See, for example, Provine [1982] 506; Newell [1974] 208; Denton [1985] 66; Birx [1991] for example, 40, 98; Milner [1990] 99; Kenneth Baker [1987] 17, 18; Provine [1987] 51-52; McKown [1993] 25. (And as Plantinga points out, "many hypotheses mentioning God are eminently testable: for example the hypothesis that God has created rabbits that weigh a ton and a half and live in Cleveland" [unpublished] 26 n. 44.) Some creationists do seem to see this—for example, Kofahl [1989] 13.

[40]Since the separation of church and state is a key weapon for anticreationists, the case for creation science actually being religion is foundational to legal strategy. The charge is thus contained in most NCSE documents, in over twenty of the documents collected in McCollister [1989] and has been accepted by federal courts—see, for example, the Overton decision. See also, for example, Ruse [1982] 322-23; Birx [1991] 257; Eldridge [1982] 146; Moyer [1980] 4 (speaking for the NABT); Cracraft [1983] 189; Godfrey [1983b] xiii.

[41]Scott [1990] asserts that " 'intelligent design' is an intellectually discredited idea that has *never* been science" (her emphasis).

[42]This again is a nearly universal objection. For example, Price [1983] 25-27; Bailey [1993] 166-67; Walsh and Demere [1993]; Overton [1982] 217; Birx [1991] 102; Shapiro [1993] 15; Kitcher [1982] 140; NCSE, "Evolution and Creationism"; John

A. Moore [1983b] 128; Godfrey [1983b] xiii; McKown [1993] 41-42; Tiffin [1994] 134-35; Ruse [1988d] 294-95; Futuyma [1983] 219; Beck [1982] 740.

[43]A similar point is made in Kemp [1988] 76. Quinn [1984] contains a very nice related discussion.

[44]NCSE, "Keeping Creationism out of Education"; Shapiro [1993] 16; John A. Moore [1983b] 4-5; Patterson [1983a] 151. This also may be what Levinton [1982] 496 has in mind. See also Eve and Harrold [1991] 191.

[45]See, for example, Newton's December 10, 1692, letter to Bentley in Cohen [1958] 280.

[46]Walsh and Demere [1993]. See also Harold I. Brown [1986] 21; Overton [1982] 217. See also several of the statements in McCollister [1989]. See Giddings [1987] 74.

[47]Laudan [1983] contains similar points, as does Quinn [1984] 377-78.

[48]John A. Moore [1983a] 7; Cloud [1983] 139; Ruse [1988d] 305.

[49]This point is also made in Laudan [1983] 352-53 and in McIver [1988/1992] xiv. See, for example, *ExNihilo Technical Journal* 1 (1984) for some lively creationist in-house fights.

[50]Ruse [1988c] 360 makes this claim.

[51]Harris [1981] 22-23.

[52]Skehan [1986] 26.

[53]Overton [1993] 217.

[54]NCSE, "Keeping Creationism out of Education." See also Strahler [1987] 75. The "abrupt appearance theory" is found primarily in Bird [1989].

[55]It is not surprising that opponents of creationism should think that its concepts are ultimately religious, since leading creationists frequently define the very idea of creationism in theistic terms. See, for example, Gish [1983b] 176; Gish [1973b] 24-26, 34; Gish [1978] 40; Gish [1985b] 11, 35-36, 44; Parker [1987] 68; Steele [1983] 192; Bliss, Parker and Gish [1980] 1, 23; Rusch [1991] 15; Rusch [1984] 26; Anderson and Coffin [1977] 80; Wysong [1976] 219; and Slusher [1974] 253.

[56]Ruse [1988c] 359.

[57]Morris [1974c] 246.

[58]Walsh and Demere [1993]; NAS [1984] 9. Of course, that a religious text is taken as an authority is also a source of objection; see Rhondda Jones [1989] 247.

[59]NCSE, "Keeping Creationism out of Education."

[60]Livingstone [1987] 102.

[61]R. W. Lewis [1981] 8. McKown [1993] 51 simply stipulates that any "theory of everything" must be mathematical and rules Genesis creationism to be nonscience on that basis. On the other side, Ettari [1988] 4 claims that to be scientific a theory "must be capable of being rigorously reduced to mathematical formulations" and criticizes evolution on that ground.

## Chapter 12: Theistic Evolution: Catching It from Both Sides

[1]Morris and Morris [1989] 9, 66-67; Morris [1946] 30-31; Morris [1980a] 83-84; Morris [1984a] 113-14. William Jennings Bryan thought that theistic evolutionists were more dangerous than atheistic evolutionists; see James Moore [1994] 128. See Lubenow [1992] 184; Lubenow [1983] 157-62. See also Anonymous [1988] 4. Some criticisms involve misrepresentations of theistic evolution. See Berghoef and DeKoster [1988] 77, 93, 131, 172-73; Criswell [1957] 14ff.

²Morris and Parker [1987] x, 190-96, 299; Gish [1973b] chap. 2; Gish [1993] 259, 305; Morris [1966] chap. 10, also 13, 136; Morris [1967] 66-67; Morris [1970] 15; Whitcomb and Morris [1961] 440-41; Morris [1984b] 18, 328; Morris [1963b] 14; Ham [1987] v, most of 1-54; Morris [1985a] 47; Huse [1983/1993] 5; Ankerberg and Weldon [1993] 5, 21-22; Moore and Slusher [1970/1974] xvii-xxiii; McGhee [1987] 139. Essentially all recent popular creationist works take this position. Morris, Boardman and Koontz *(Teacher's Handbook)* [1971] 12; Frair and Davis [1983] 55; Chittick [1984] 27, 29ff., 62, 97. See also earlier discussion in chapter six of this book. Definitions vary to the point that some—for example, Hoover [1981] 67—would consider theistic evolution to be creationism.

³For example, Morris [1974e] 8-9, 19, 33; Morris [1985a] 48; Morris [1973] 65, 69-70; Morris [1974a] 109; Morris [1974c] 271; Morris [1974f] 188; Ham [1987] chaps. 1-2; Morris and Parker [1987] 191; Morris [1967] 18; Frair and Davis [1983] 21; Bliss [1983] 195; Whitcomb and Morris [1961] xxi; Whitcomb and DeYoung [1978] 64; John N. Moore [1983] 128-29; Boardman, Koontz and Morris [1973] 6, 12. See also Morris [1970] 190; John N. Moore [1985a] 193. This is a standard creationist claim. Since the problems that creationists cite—no observers present, inability to reproduce the actual events, etc.—would not by themselves rule out hypothetico-deductive, falsificationist or other such approaches, the claim that those problems prevent *scientific* investigation of origins suggests that inductivism of some sort is what many creationists have in mind as true science.

⁴See Gish [1990] 32 and [1993] 126-27; Gish [1986] 64; Gish [1973b] chap. 1.

⁵Morris [1977d] 13; Crofut and Seamon [1990b] 56; Myers [1989] 15. For points of this general type, see Ankerberg and Weldon [1993] 21-22; Morris and Parker [1987] 191; Gish [1973b] 8-14; Whitcomb [1973] 100; Kofahl [1977] 13ff.; Gish [1972] 35-36; Morris [1974e] 9; Morris [1980a] 10; Morris [1967] 21-22; Wieland [1994] 4; Morris [1974g] 80-81; Morris [1988b] 35; Morris [1977c] 49; John N. Moore [1983] 130-34, 208. Some creationists believe that evolution does better with some data than does creationism—for example, John Klotz [1968] 50-51; Klotz [1985] 139; Rusch [1984] 29.

⁶Morris [1974e] 13, 20-23, 37-47, 196-205; Ankerberg and Weldon [1993] 31-32; Myers [1986] 5.

⁷Gish [1973a] 134; Morris [1974e] 19; Chittick [1984] 95; Boardman, Koontz and Morris [1973] 6; Rusch [1991] 19. See also Hedtke [1981] 11.

⁸Morris [1984b] 18; Morris [1974g] 3, 24; Morris [1988b] 15; Whitcomb and Morris [1961] 329-30; Boardman, Koontz and Morris [1973] 13. Also Whitcomb [1986] 74; Morris [1977a] 12. See also Morris [1976c] 348.

⁹For an explicit creationist distinction between the two models and biological theories, see Paul Taylor [1992] 9.

¹⁰Lewontin [1983b] introduction in Godfrey [1983b] xxvi. See also Kenneth Baker [1987] 17.

¹¹Eve and Harrold [1991] 108-19, 173-74, 176ff., 183, 190, 192.

¹²Chittick [1984] 101-2, 122. See also Ham [1987] 74; Morris [1972c] 269; Morris [1984b] 328; Morris [1985a] 93; Morris [1966] 149; Morris and Parker [1987] 300; Lubenow [1992] 194, 199; Huse [1983/1993] 121-25. Indeed, some take evolution with or without theism to be incoherent—see Morris [1967] preface and Huse [1983/1993] foreword.

¹³See Huse [1983/1993] 121 and John Morris [1991c] d for other examples of this

type of mistake.

[14]Matrisciana and Oakland [1991] 15; Berghoef and DeKoster [1988] 86; Ankerberg and Weldon [1993] 31-32; Huse [1983/1993] 59-60; Gish [1993] 305; Bliss [1988] 71; Morris and Parker [1987] x, 191, 197, 299; Morris [1984b] 18, 328; Morris [1967] 66-67; Chittick [1984] 29ff., 62, 145, 267-68.

[15]Morris [1966] 165-66.

[16]Morris [1988b] 13.

[17]Ibid. 14.

[18]Ibid.

[19]Morris and Parker [1987] 191.

[20]Ibid. 193.

[21]Ibid. 196.

[22]Morris [1974e] 9-12 is another good example. The move also can be found elsewhere, although possibly in less explicit form; see, for example, Morris, Boardman and Koontz *(Teachers' Handbook)* [1971] 12; Whitcomb [1984a] 32; Morris [1990b]; Lindsey [1985] i; Boardman, Koontz and Morris [1973] 13-14. Bird (vol. 2) [1989] 171 commits a variant version. See also Morris [1977d] 3-4 and Thaxton and Buell [1993] 23. See also Bliss [1988] 9, but especially 71; John N. Moore [1984] 115-16; John N. Moore [1985a] 193. See also John N. Moore [1976a] 46, 49. Ancil [1982] comes close to this, as does Gish [1993] 305; Bliss in Hyman [1988-1988] 30. Bliss [1976] defines theistic evolution in terms of guidance (3), argues against random chance evolution (47-49) and leaves the impression that the evolution model, which by his definition includes theistic evolution, has been dealt with.

[23]Kofahl and Segraves [1975] appendix C; Denton [1985] 66; Ian Taylor [1984] 369. That is also an implication of the views of some evolutionists. See, for example, Ruse [1982] 12-13; Asimov [1981] 11; Dawkins [1987] 5. Others, such as Futuyma [1983], also seem to hold similar views.

[24]Although I will not pursue it here, creationists sometimes misconstrue Darwin's concept of *chance,* for which Darwin—a determinist—had a special definition. For an example of such misconstrual, see Rushdoony [1967] 48-49.

[25]Gingrich [1993] 222, 224 contains similar points and related discussion.

[26]Johnson [1993a] 168 seems to hold this. Johnson also takes naturalism to be inherent in Darwin; see, for example, 116, 127, 153, 163.

[27]See, for example, Morris [1972c] 271.

[28]Creationists virtually without exception hold this position—for example, Morris [1967] 58-59; Morris [1966] 34; Ham and Taylor [1988] 59-60. Morris and Morris [1989] even claim that the earth's being "very good" required that it be fully functioning and thus that it had an appearance of age.

[29]Morris [1984a] 113-14; Morris [1971] 80; Morris [1974c] 278; Morris [1984c] ii; Morris [1985a] 27, 42; Morris [1974g] 11, 132, 185, 188; Morris [1993] 164; Morris [1966] 35; Whitcomb and Morris [1961] 345; Ham and Taylor [1988] 67; Davis and Kenyon [1993] 137; Morris [1984b] 328; Morris [1956] 34; Morris [1972b] 73; Morris [1967] 58; Wieland [1994] 6. Oddly enough, some evolutionists take this same line—for example, Kitcher [1982] 139; Hull [1991] 486; Provine [1987] 51-52. See also Morris [1970] 23-24; Morris [1946] 30-31; Morris [1966] 142; Morris [1972a] 55. Creationists also frequently cite Is 11:9 and 65:25 in this connection.

[30]Is 55:8-9.

31Ps 104:21; 145:15; Job 38:39. Oddly enough, on one occasion Morris, Boardman and Koontz claim that the *balance of nature* is part of the divine plan for creation—and their example involves wolves and deer. See *Living World* [1971] 18-20. But see also Morris [1976c] 78.

32One anonymous author [1993] claims that "efficiency is simply part of God's nature."

33Ham [1987] appendix 1; Morris [1974e] 219, 229; Huse [1983/1993] 121-25; Morris [1972b] 73.

34Dawkins [1987] 141.

35Ibid. 316.

36Ibid.

37Ibid. 316-17.

38Ibid. 287; see also 317.

39Ibid. 141. Whitcomb [1973] 100 makes a similar charge in the opposite direction: "Since uniformitarians do not really know where even an original molten mass of rock and metal could have come from, there is no truly rational alternative to the creationist model [of the earth's origin]."

40This is one thrust of several of the essays in Moreland [1994]—for example, those of Meyer, Dembski, and Bradley and Thaxton.

41For example, Pine [1983] 10; Albert [1986] 27; Walsh and Demere [1993]; Patterson [1983b] 137. See also Thaxton, Bradley and Olsen [1984] 205. On the other hand, some creationists argue that it is evolution that has impeded science—for example, Parker [1994] 6; Ankerberg and Weldon [1993] 25-28; Enoch [1966] 96ff.

42Scott [1990] 18. See also Nancey Murphy [1993].

43For discussion of attempted cases, see again chapter eleven, section entitled "Naturalism as Essential to Science."

44Hartwig and Meyer [1993]. See also Plantinga's discussion of God-of-the-gaps views. Plantinga takes "fear and loathing of God-of-the-gaps theology" as a major reason for the popularity of stipulations that science must be pursued as if naturalism were true.

45Thaxton, Bradley and Olsen [1984] and others attempt to make such cases. See also Denton [1985] 264-67. Behe's forthcoming *Darwin's Black Box* (Free Press) attempts to make a rigorous biomolecular "irreducible complexity" case.

46Moreland and others in Moreland [1994]. See also Hartwig and Meyer [1993] 157-59. See also n. 40 above.

47This claim has been recently defended by, for example, Howard Van Till.

48Such objections are standard in most popular creationist works. See, for example, Morris [1966] 33-34, 90-93; Morris [1984a] 119-20; Ham [1987] appendix 1; Ham and Taylor [1988] 56-57; Huse [1983/1993] 121-24.

# Bibliography

Abbott, Patrick L. [1984] "The Stratigraphic Record and Creationism." In Awbrey and Thwaites [1984] 164-88.

Abell, George O. [1983] "The Ages of the Earth and the Universe." In Godfrey [1983b] 33-47.

Ackerman, Paul. [1982] "Psychology as a Science." *Creation Social Science and Humanities Quarterly* 5, no. 1 (Fall): 13-17.

———. [1986] *It's a Young Earth After All.* Grand Rapids, Mich.: Baker Book House.

Albert, Leon. [1986] " 'Scientific' Creation as a Pseudo Science." *Creation/Evolution* 18 (Summer): 25-34.

Alexander, Richard. [1983] "Evolution, Creation and Biology Teaching." In Zetterberg [1983] 90-111.

Allen, Keith, and Derek Briggs, eds. [1989] *Evolution and the Fossil Record.* Washington, D.C.: Smithsonian.

Ancil, Ralph. [1982] "Is Creation More Than a Biological Model of Origins?" *Creation Social Science and Humanities Quarterly* 5, no. 2 (Winter): 3-13.

———. [1985] "On the Importance of Philosophy in the Origins Debate." *Creation Research Society Quarterly* 22 (December): 114-23.

Anderson, J. Kirby, and Harold Coffin. [1977] *Fossils in Focus.* Grand Rapids, Mich.: Zondervan/Richardson, Tex.: Probe.

Anderson, Wilfred. [1991] Letter. *NCSE Reports* 11, no. 1: 6.

Andrews, E. H. [1986] "Biblical Creationism and Scientific Creationism: Is There a Conflict?" In Andrews, Gitt and Ouweneel [1986] 46-47.

Andrews, E. H., W. Gitt and W. J. Ouweneel. [1986] *Concepts in Creationism.* Avon, U.K.: Bath.

Ankerberg, John, and John Weldon. [1993] *The Facts on Creation vs. Evolution.* Eugene, Ore.: Harvest House.

Anonymous. [1988] "Ten Years of the *CSSH Quarterly.*" Creation Social Science and Humanities Quarterly 10, no. 4 (Summer): 1-6.

Anonymous. [1991a] "On Darwin and the Eye." *Creation Ex Nihilo* 14, no. 1 (December-February): 39.

Anonymous. [1991b] "Science Spot." *Creation Ex Nihilo* 13, no. 4 (September—November): 50.

Anonymous. [1993] "Glorify the God of Details." *Bible-Science News* 31, no. 6: 3.

Appleman, Philip. [1994] "Darwin's Ark." *Creation/Evolution* 35 (Winter): 13-21.

Arduini, Francis J. [1987] "Design, Created Kinds and Engineering." *Creation/Evolution* 20 (Spring): 19-23.

Armstrong, H. L. [1980] "Evolutionistic Defense Against Thermodynamics Disproved." *Creation Research Society Quarterly* 16 (March): 226-27, 206.

Arndts, Russell. [1989] "The Logic of Evolutionary Reasoning." *Contrast* 8, no. 2 (March/April): 1-4.

———. [1991a] "Prediction and the Fossil Record." *Bible-Science Newsletter* 29, no. 2 (February): 8-9.

———. [1991b] "Scientific Explanation." *Bible-Science Newsletter* 29, no. 7-8 (July/August): 8.

Arries, Terry. [1991a] "Origins: Point/Counterpoint." *Bible-Science Newsletter* 29, no. 2 (February): 1-2, 4.

———. [1991b] "Mount St. Helens: God's Living Primer of Catastrophism." *Bible Science Newsletter* 29, no. 4 (April): 5-7.

Asimov, Isaac. [1981] *In the Beginning.* New York: Crown.

———. [1984] "The 'Threat' of Creationism." In Montague [1984] 182-93.

Austin, Steven (Stuart Nevins, pseud.). [1970] "A Spiritual Groundwork for Historical Geology." In Patten [1970a] 77-101.

———. [1971] "Stratigraphic Evidence of the Flood." In Patten [1971] 33-65.

———. [1976] "Interpreting Earth History." In Morris and Gish [1976] 201-8.

Austin, Steven. [1984] *Catastrophes in Earth History: A Source Book of Geologic Evidence, Speculation and Theory.* El Cajon, Calif.: Institute for Creation Research.

———. [1986] "Did Noah's Flood Cover the Entire World? Yes." In Youngblood [1986] 210-29.

———. [1989] "A Lesson from Mount St. Helens." *Creation Ex Nihilo* 11, no. 3 (June-August): 36-37.

Awbrey, Frank, and William Thwaites, eds. [1984] *Proceedings of the Sixty-third Annual Meeting of the Pacific Division, AAAS.* Vol. 1, pt. 3. San Francisco: AAAS Pacific Division.

Bacon, Francis. [1620/1955] *Novum Organum.* Chicago: Britannica.

Bailey, Lloyd. [1993] *Genesis, Creation and Creationism.* New York: Paulist.

Baker, Kenneth. [1987] "Creation Evolution as an Inevitable Conflict Between Two Contradictory Worldviews." *Creation/Evolution Newsletter* 7, no. 4 (July/August): 17-18.

Baker, Sylvia. [1976] *Bone of Contention.* Queensland, Australia: Creation Science Foundation.

Barrow, John D., and Frank J. Tipler. [1986] *The Anthropic Cosmological Principle.* Oxford: Clarendon.

Bartz, Paul. [1984] "Abusing Science—by Redefining It." *Contrast* 3, no. 1 (January/February): 3-4.

————. [1984b] "Luther on Evolution." *Ex Nihilo* 6, no. 3 (February): 18-21.

————. [1988] Editorial. *Bible-Science Newsletter* 26, no. 8 (August): 3.

————. [1989] "Death Before Adam?" *Bible-Science Newsletter* 27, no. 1: 14.

————. [1992] "Proof by Parable." *Bible-Science News* 30, no. 7: 4-5.

————. [1993a] "After Their Kinds." *Bible-Science News* 31, no. 5: 3. Reproduced nearly verbatim from *Bible-Science News* 27, no. 10 (October): 14.

————. [1993b] "Survival of the Kinds." *Bible-Science News* 31, no. 6: 6-8.

Bauman, Michael. [1993] *Man and Creation.* Hillsdale, Mich.: Hillsdale.

Beck, Stanley. [1982] "Natural Science and Creationist Theology." *BioScience* 32, no. 9 (October): 738-42.

Berghoef, Gerard, and Lester DeKoster. [1988] *The Great Divide.* Grand Rapids, Mich.: Christian Library.

Bergman, Jerry. [1983] "What Is Science?" *Creation Research Society Quarterly* 20 (June): 39-42.

————. [1991] "Mammals Present Some Milky Problems." *Creation Ex Nihilo* 13, no. 2 (March-May): 39.

————. [1992a] "Is There Any Such Thing as a 'Higher' Creature?" *Creation Ex Nihilo* 14, no. 2 (March-May): 10-11.

————. [1992b] "Some Biological Problems of Natural Selection Theory." *Creation Research Society Quarterly* 29 (December): 146-58.

————. [1993] "The Problem of Extinction and Natural Selection." *Creation Research Science Quarterly* 30 (June): 93-106.

Bergman, Jerry, and George Howe. [1990] " 'Vestigal Organs' Are Fully Functional." Terre Haute, Ind.: Creation Research Society Books.

Bethell, Tom. [1976] "Darwin's Mistake." *Harper's* (February). Reprint [1977] *Christianity Today* 21, no. 18 (June 17): 12-15.

————. [1978] "Burning Darwin to Save Marx." *Harper's* (December): 31-38, 91-92.

————. [1986] "Deducing from Materialism." *National Review* 38, no. 16 (August 29): 43-45.

————. [1992] "Darwin in the Dock." *The American Spectator* (June): 14-16.

————. [1994] "E-Mail Evolution." *The American Spectator* 27, no. 7 (July): 16-18.

Bird, W. R. [1989] *The Origin of Species Revisited.* Vols. 1-2. New York: Philosophical Library.

Birx, H. James. [1991] *Interpreting Evolution.* Buffalo, N.Y.: Prometheus.

Bixler, R. Russell. [1986] "Does the Bible Speak of a Vapor Canopy?" *ICC Pro-*

*ceedings* 1: 19-21.

Blake, Ralph, Curt Ducasse and Edward Madden. [1960] *Theories of Scientific Method: The Renaissance Through the Nineteenth Century.* Seattle: University of Washington Press.

Bliss, Richard. [1983] "The Two-Model Approach to Origins." In Zetterberg [1983] 192-98.

———. [1988] *Origins: Creation or Evolution.* El Cajon, Calif.: Master.

———. [1992] "Good Science." *Bible-Science Newsletter* 30, no. 7: 9.

Bliss, Richard, and Gary Parker. [1979] *In Search of the Origin of Life.* San Diego, Calif.: Creation-Life.

Bliss, Richard, Gary Parker and Duane Gish. [1980] *Fossils: Key to the Present.* San Diego, Calif.: Creation-Life.

Boardman, Donald. [1986] "Did Noah's Flood Cover the Entire World? No." In Youngblood [1986] 210-29.

Boardman, William, Jr., Robert Koontz and Henry Morris. [1973] *Science and Creation.* San Diego, Calif.: Creation-Science Research Center.

Bowler, Peter. [1989] *Evolution: The History of an Idea.* Rev. ed. Berkeley: University of California Press.

Brackman, Arnold. [1980] *A Delicate Arrangement: The Strange Case of Charles Darwin and Alfred Russel Wallace.* New York: Times Books.

Bradley, Walter, and Charles Thaxton. [1994] "Information and the Origin of Life." In Moreland [1994] 173-210.

Brinton, Crane. [1963] *The Shaping of Modern Thought.* Englewood Cliffs, N.J.: Prentice-Hall.

Brooke, John Hedley. [1991] *Science and Religion: Some Historical Perspectives.* Cambridge: Cambridge University Press.

Brown, Colin. [1982] "Variation and the Fourth Law of Creation." *Creation Research Society Quarterly* 19, no. 2 (September): 100-103.

Brown, Harold I. [1986] "Creationism and the Nature of Science." *Creation/Evolution* 18 (Summer): 15-25.

Brown, Walter T. [1983] "The Scientific Case for Creation: 108 Categories of Evidence." In Zetterberg [1983] 208-32.

Brush, Stephen G. [1981] "The Case Against 'Equal Time.' " *The Science Teacher* 48, no. 4 (April): 29-33.

———. [1982] "Finding the Age of the Earth by Physics or by Faith?" *Journal of Geology Education* 30, no. 1 (January): 34-58.

———. [1983] "Ghosts from the Nineteenth Century: Creationist Arguments for a Young Earth." In Godfrey [1983b] 49-84.

Bryan, William Jennings. [1922] "God and Evolution." *The New York Times,* February 26. Reprint in G. Kennedy [1957] 23-29.

Burgess, Stanley, and Gary McGee. [1988] *Dictionary of Pentecostal and Charismatic Movements.* Grand Rapids, Mich.: Zondervan.

Burien, Richard. [1986] "Why the Panda Provides No Comfort for the Creationist." *Philosophica* 37, no. 1: 11-26.

Burke, Derek, ed. [1985] *Creation and Evolution.* Leicester, U.K.: Inter-Varsity Press.

Burkhardt, Richard W., Jr. [1977] *The Spirit of System.* Cambridge: Harvard University Press.

Carson, Clarence. [1988] "Naturalistic Outlook." *Creation Research Society Quarterly* 25 (June): 16-24.

Cassirir, Ernst. [1951] *The Philosophy of the Enlightenment.* Boston: Beacon.

Chaffin, Eugene. [1982] "The Oklo Natural Uranium Reactor Examined from a Creationist Viewpoint." *Creation Research Society Quarterly* 19 (June): 32-35.

———. [1985] "The Oklo Natural Uranium Reactor: Evidence for a Young Earth." *Creation Research Society Quarterly* 22 (June): 10-16.

Chittick, Donald. [1970] "Dating the Earth and Fossils." In Patten [1970a] 57-74.

———. [1984] *The Controversy.* Portland, Ore.: Multnomah Press.

Clark, Arnold. [1987] *Understanding Science Through Evolution.* Springfield, Ill.: Charles Thomas.

Clark, Kelly J. [1988] "The Religious and Philosophical View of Sir William Herschel." *Astronomy Quarterly* (Pachart Foundation).

Cloud, Preston. [1983] " 'Scientific Creationism'—a New Inquisition Brewing?" In Zetterberg [1983] 134-49.

Cohen, I. Bernard. [1958] *Isaac Newton's Papers and Letters on Natural Philosophy.* Cambridge, Mass.: Harvard University Press.

Cole, John. [1981] "Misquoted Scientists Respond." *Creation/Evolution* 2, no. 4 (Fall): 34-44.

———. [1983] "Scopes and Beyond: Anti-evolutionism and American Culture." In Godfrey [1983b] 13-32.

Coleman, William. [1971] *Biology in the Nineteenth Century.* Cambridge: Cambridge University Press.

Colson, Charles. [1993] "Arguing with Evolution." Breakpoint Series. Washington, D.C.: Prison Fellowship.

Coppedge, James. [1973] *Evolution: Possible or Impossible?* Grand Rapids, Mich.: Zondervan.

Cowan, George A. [1976] "A Natural Fission Reactor." *Scientific American* (July): 36-37.

Cox, Douglas. [1976] "Cave Formation by Rock Disintegration." *Creation Research Society Quarterly* 13 (December): 155-61.

Cracraft, Joel. [1983] "Systematics, Comparative Biology and the Case Against Creationism." In Godfrey [1983b] 163-91.

Crick, Francis. [1988] *What Mad Pursuit.* New York: Basic.

Criswell, W. A. [1957] *Did Man Just Happen?* Grand Rapids, Mich.: Zondervan.

Crofut, Bill. [1992] "The Family Blattidae: An Example of 'Evolutionary Stasis.' " *Creation Research Society Quarterly* 28 (March): 149-55.

Crofut, Bill, and Raymond Seaman. [1990a] "Evolutionism: A View Through Rose-Colored Blinders." *Creation Research Society Quarterly* 26 (June): 35.

———. [1990b] "Evolutionist, Contradict Thy Ownself." *Creation Research Society*

*Quarterly* 27 (September): 56.

Crombie, A. C. [1959] *Medieval and Early Modern Science.* Garden City, N.Y.: Doubleday.

Darwin, Charles. [1859] *The Origin of Species.* Reprint London: Penguin, 1968.

———. [1867] *Variation of Animals and Plants Under Domestication.* Reprint New York: Appleton, 1896.

———. [1871] *The Descent of Man and Selection in Relation to Sex.* New York: Modern Library, n.d. (Bound as pp. 387-920 with *The Origin of Species.*)

Darwin, Francis, ed. [1892] *The Autobiography of Charles Darwin and Selected Letters.* Reprint New York: Dover, 1958.

———. [1897] *The Life and Letters of Charles Darwin.* Vol. 2. New York: D. Appleton.

Davidhuiser, Bolton. [1971] *Science and the Bible.* Grand Rapids, Mich.: Baker Book House.

Davis, Percival, and Dean Kenyon. [1993] *Of Pandas and People.* 2nd ed. Dallas: Haughton.

Dawkins, Richard. [1985] "What Was All the Fuss About?" *Nature* 316 (August 22): 683-84.

———. [1987] *The Blind Watchmaker.* New York: Norton.

———. [1988] "Universal Darwinism." In Ruse [1988b] 202-21.

———. [1989] "Put Your Money on Evolution." *The New York Times Review of Books* (April 9): 34-35.

Dawson, John William. [1873] *The Story of the Earth and Man.* New York: Harper.

Denton, Michael. [1985] *Evolution: A Theory in Crisis.* Bethesda, Md.: Adler and Adler.

Desmond, Adrian, and James Moore. [1991] *Darwin: The Life of a Tormented Evolutionist.* New York: Warner.

Diamond, Jared. [1985] "Voyage of the Overloaded Ark." *Discover* (June): 82-92.

Dijksterhuis, E. J. [1961] *The Mechanization of the World Picture.* London: Oxford University Press.

Dillow, Joseph. [1979] "Scripture Does Not Rule Out a Vapor Canopy." *Creation Research Society Quarterly* 16 (December): 171-73, 175.

Dirac, P. A. M. [1971] *The Development of Quantum Theory.* New York: Gordon and Breach.

Dobzhansky, Theodosius. [1962] *Mankind Evolving.* New Haven, Conn.: Yale University Press.

———. [1973] "Nothing in Biology Makes Sense Except in the Light of Evolution." *American Biology Teacher* (March): 125-29. Also contained in Zetterberg [1983] 18-28.

Draper, John William. [1874] *History of the Conflict Between Religion and Science.* New York: Appleton.

Dressler, Harold. [1990-1991] "Evolution: Still an Option?" *Creation Ex Nihilo* 13, no. 1 (December-February): 18-21.

Duhem, Pierre. [1954] *The Aim and Structure of Physical Theory.* Princeton, N.J.:

Princeton University Press.

Ecker, Ronald. [1990] *Dictionary of Science and Creationism.* Buffalo, N.Y.: Prometheus.

Edey, Maitland, and Donald Johanson. [1989] *Blueprints: Solving the Mystery of Evolution.* New York: Penguin.

Edwords, Frederick. [1983a] "An Answer to Dr. Geisler." *Creation/Evolution* 13 (Summer): 6-12.

_____. [1983b] "Decide: Evolution or Creation?" In Zetterberg [1983] 162-72.

_____. [1983c] "Is It Really Fair to Give Creationism Equal Time?" In Godfrey [1983b] 301-16.

Eldredge, Niles [1981] "Creationism Isn't Science." *New Republic* 184, no. 14 (April 4).

_____. [1982] *The Monkey Business.* New York: Washington Square.

_____. [1987] *The Natural History Reader in Evolution.* New York: Columbia University Press.

Enoch, H. [1966] *Evolution or Creation.* London: Evangelical Press.

Ettari, Vincent. [1988] "The Philosophy of Science." *Contrast* 7, no. 2 (May/June): 1-4.

Eve, Raymond, and Francis Harrold. [1991] *The Creationist Movement in Modern America.* Boston: Twayne.

Ferst, Barry. [1983] "What Bible-Scientists Can Learn from Bible-Science." *Creation Research Society Quarterly* 21 (September): 116-20.

Fezer, Karl. [1984] Editorial. *Creation/Evolution Newsletter* 4, no. 1 (January/February): 12-13.

_____. [1985] "In Defense of the Draft CC Position Statement." *Creation/Evolution Newsletter* 5, no. 2 (March/April): 7.

_____. [1988] "Response." *Creation/Evolution Newsletter* 8, no. 5 (September/October): 19-20.

_____. [1990] "Is the Concept of Natural Selection Tautolous [sic]?" *NCSE Reports* 10, no. 4 (July/August): 14-16.

_____. [1991] "Why Resorting to Scripture Isn't Done in Science." *NCSE Reports* 11, no. 3 (Fall): 16-17.

_____. [1993a] "Creation's Incredible Witness: Duane T. Gish, Ph.D." *Creation/Evolution* 33 (Winter): 5-21.

_____. [1993b] "Creationism: Please Don't Call It Science." *Creation/Evolution* (Summer): 45-49.

Forman, Paul. [1971] "Weimar Culture, Causality and Quantum Theory, 1918-27." *Historical Studies in the Physical Sciences* 3:1-115.

Foster, M. B. [1934] "The Christian Doctrine of Creation and the Rise of Modern Natural Science." *Mind* (October): 446-68.

_____. [1935] "Christian Theology and Modern Science of Nature, I." *Mind* (October): 439-66.

_____. [1936] "Christian Theology and Modern Science of Nature, II." *Mind* (January): 1-27.

Frair, Wayne, and Percival Davis. [1983] *A Case for Creation.* 3rd ed. Chicago: Moody Press.

Frangos, Apostolos. [1991] "The Correct Approach to Scientific Theories." *Creation Research Society Quarterly* 28 (June): 17-18.

Futuyma, Douglas. [1983] *Science on Trial.* New York: Pantheon.

Geisler, Norman. [1989] *Knowing the Truth About Creation.* Ann Arbor, Mich.: Servant.

Geisler, Norman, and Kirby Anderson. [1987] *Origin Science.* Grand Rapids, Mich.: Baker Book House.

Giddings, Luther. [1987] "Scientists on Creationism." *BioScience* 37, no. 1 (January): 70-74.

Gillespie, Neal C. [1979] *Charles Darwin and the Problem of Creation.* Chicago: Chicago University Press.

Gingrich, Owen. [1993] "Where in the World Is God?" In Bauman [1993] 209-30.

Gish, Duane. [n.d.] "Have You Been Brainwashed?" Seattle: Life Messengers. (Gish has reportedly denied writing this, but see Gish [1933] 124.)

———. [1970] "Challenge to Neo-Darwinism." *American Biology Teacher* 32, no. 8 (November): 495-97.

———. [1972] *Speculations and Experiments Related to Theories on the Origin of Life: A Critique.* ICR Monograph no. 1. San Diego, Calif.: Institute for Creation Research.

———. [1973a] "Creation, Evolution and the Historical Evidence." *American Biology Teacher* 35, no. 3 (March): 132-40.

———. [1973b] *Evolution: The Fossils Say No.* 2nd ed. San Diego, Calif.: Creation-Life.

———. [1974a] "Creation-Evolution." In Morris, Gish and Hillestad [1974] 130-39.

———. [1974b] "Petroleum in Minutes, Coal in Hours." In Morris, Gish and Hillestad [1974] 15-19.

———. [1977] *Dinosaurs: Those Terrible Lizards.* El Cajon, Calif.: Master.

———. [1978] *Evolution: The Fossils Say No.* Public school ed. San Diego, Calif.: Creation-Life.

———. [1979] "A Consistent Christian-Scientific View of the Origin of Life." *Creation Research Society Quarterly* 15 (March): 185-203.

———. [1981] "Thermodynamics and the Origin of Life." In Morris and Rohrer [1981] 39-46.

———. [1983a] "Creating a Missing Link." *Impact* 123 (September): i-iv.

———. [1983b] "Creation, Evolution and Public Education." In Zetterberg [1983] 175-91.

———. [1984] "The Scientific Case for Creationism." In Awbrey and Thwaites [1984] 25-37.

———. [1985a] "A Consistent Biblical and Scientific View of Origins." In Burke [1985] 139-63.

———. [1985b] *Evolution: The Challenge of the Fossil Record.* El Cajon, Calif.: Master. (This is a revision of Gish [1973b] and [1978].)

————. [1986] "The Origin of Life." *ICC Proceedings* 1: 57-64.

————. [1989] "Is It Possible to Be a Christian and an Evolutionist?" *Creation Ex Nihilo* 11, no. 4 (September-November): 21-23.

————. [1990] *The Amazing Story of Creation*. El Cajon, Calif.: Institute for Creation Research.

————. [1993] *Creation Scientists Answer Their Critics*. El Cajon, Calif.: Institute for Creation Research.

Gish, Duane, Richard Bliss and Wendell Bird. [1983] "Summary of Scientific Evidence for Creation." In Zetterberg [1983] 199-207. Also in Morris and Rohrer [1982] 129-38.

Godfrey, Laurie. [1983a] "Creationism and Gaps in the Fossil Record." In Godfrey [1983b] 193-218.

Godfrey, Laurie, ed. [1983b] *Scientists Confront Creationism*. New York: Norton.

Gould, Stephen J. [1965] "Is Uniformitarianism Necessary?" *American Journal of Science* 263 (March): 223-28.

————. [1977a] "The Problem of Perfection." *Natural History* (January): 32-37.

————. [1977b] "The Return of the Hopeful Monster." *Natural History* (June/July): 22-30.

————. [1978] "Bathybius Meets Eozoon." *Natural History* 77, no. 4 (April): 16-18, 22.

————. [1981] "Evolution as Fact and Theory." *Discover* (May): 34-37.

————. [1983] "Darwin's Untimely Burial—Again!" In Godfrey [1983b] 139-46.

————. [1985] "Nasty Little Facts." *Natural History* (February).

————. [1987a] "Darwinism Defined: The Difference Between Fact and Theory." *Discover* (January): 64-70.

————. [1987b] "The Verdict on Creationism." *Time* (July 19): 32-34.

————. [1994] "Common Pathways of Illumination." *Natural History* (December): 10-20.

Greene, John C. [1959] *The Death of Adam*. Ames: Iowa State University Press.

————. [1963] *Darwin and the Modern World View*. New York: Mentor.

Hale, W. G., and J. P. Margham. [1991] *The HarperCollins Dictionary of Biology*. New York: Harper.

Hallonquist, Earl. [1987-1988] "The Bankruptcy of Evolution, Part 2." *Creation Ex Nihilo* 10, no. 1 (December-February): 25-27.

Ham, Ken. [1985] "The Gap Theory." *Creation Ex Nihilo* 7, no. 4 (June): 25-29.

————. [1986] "Genesis and Evolution Don't Mix." *Creation Ex Nihilo* 9, no. 1 (December): 32-34.

————. [1987] *The Lie: Evolution*. El Cajon, Calif.: Master.

————. [1989] "Is God an Evolutionist?" *Back to Genesis* (March): a-b.

————. [1991a] "Billons, Millions or Thousands—Does It Matter?" *Back to Genesis* (May): a-c.

————. [1991b] *Genesis and the Decay of the Nations*. El Cajon, Calif.: Master.

Ham, Ken, Andrew Snelling and Carl Wieland. [1990] *The Answers Book*. El Cajon, Calif.: Master.

Ham, Ken, and Paul Taylor. [1988] *The Genesis Solution.* Grand Rapids, Mich.:
Baker Book Hosue.

Hamilton, H. S. [1985] "The Retina of the Eye—an Evolutionary Roadblock."
*Creation Research Society Quarterly* 22 (September): 59-64.

Hankins, Thomas. [1985] *Science and the Enlightenment.* Cambridge: Cambridge
University Press.

Hanson, Earl D. [1980] Letter. *BioScience* 30, no. 1 (January).

Harper, G. H. [1978] "Darwinism and Indoctrination." *Creation Research Society
Quarterly* 15 (September): 83-87.

Harris, C. Leon. [1981] *Evolution: Genesis and Revelation.* Albany: State University
of New York Press.

Hartmann, William K. [1989] "Birth of the Moon." *Natural History* (November):
68-77.

Hartwig, Mark, and Stephen Meyer. [1993] "A Note to Teachers." In Davis and
Kenyon [1993] 153-63.

Hasker, William. [1992] "Mr. Johnson for the Prosecution." *Christian Scholar's
Review* 22, no. 2 (December): 177-86.

Heckenlively, Donald. [1993] "Scientists Who Keep the Faith." In Bauman [1993]
231-46.

Hedtke, Randall. [1979] "An Analysis of Darwin's Natural Selection-Artificial Se
lection Analogy." *Creation Research Society Quarterly* 16 (September): 89-91,
131.

————. [1981] "The Episteme Is the Theory." *Creation Research Society Quarterly*
18 (June): 8-13, 26.

————. [1986] "We Are Teaching a Religion in Our Public Schools." *Creation
Social Science and Humanities Quarterly* 9, no. 2 (Winter): 8-11.

Heinz, Thomas. [1970] *The Creation vs. Evolution Handbook.* Grand Rapids
Mich.: Baker Book House.

Hempel, Carl. [1965] *Aspects of Scientific Explanation.* New York: Free Press.

————. [1966] *Philosophy of Natural Science.* Englewood Cliffs. N.J.: Prentice-
Hall.

Himmelfarb, Gertrude. [1959] *Darwin and the Darwinian Revolution.* Garden City,
N.Y.: Doubleday.

Hoover, Arlie. [1977] *Fallacies of Evolution.* Grand Rapids, Mich.: Baker Book
House.

————. [1981] *The Case for Teaching Creation.* Joplin, Mo.: College Press.

Hooykaas, Reijer. [1972] *Religion and the Rise of Modern Science.* Grand Rapids,
Mich.: Eerdmans.

Howe, George F. [1985] Letter. *Creation Research Society Quarterly* 22 (December): 141-42.

Howe, George F., ed. [1975] *Speak to the Earth.* Nutley, N.J.: Presbyterian &
Reformed.

Hull, David. [1991] Review of Johnson [1991]. *Nature* (August 8): 486.

Hummer, Chris. [1980] "The Human Lineage: Demurs and Disarray." *Creation*

*Research Society Quarterly* 17 (June): 26-27.

Humphries, Colin. [1985] *Creation and Evolution*. Oxford: Oxford University Press.

Huse, Scott. [1983] *The Collapse of Evolution*. Grand Rapids, Mich.: Baker Book House. (2nd ed. 1993.) Except as noted, all citations are from 1983.

Hyman, Clark. [1987-1988] "An Interview with Dr. Richard Bliss." *Creation Ex Nihilo* 10, no. 1 (December-February): 28-30.

ICC. [1986] *Proceedings of the First International Conference on Creation*. Vol. 1. Pittsburgh: Creation Science Fellowship.

Irvine, William. [1959] *Apes, Angels and Victorians*. Cleveland, Ohio: World.

Johnson, Phillip. [1991] *Darwin on Trial*. Downers Grove, Ill.: InterVarsity Press.

_____. [1993a] *Darwin on Trial*. 2nd ed. Downers Grove, Ill.: InterVarsity Press.

_____. [1993b] "God and Evolution: An Exchange." In Bauman [1993] 286-93.

_____. [1993c] "What Is Darwinism?" In Bauman [1993] 177-90.

Jones, Arthur. [1971] "The Nature of Evolutionary Thought." *Creation Research Society Quarterly* 8 (June): 44-49.

Jones, Bradley, and Esther Leise. [1987] *Science* (June): 1681.

Jones, Jonathan. [1990] "Hands Up for Creation." *Creation Ex Nihilo* 12, no. 13 (June-August): 11.

Jones, Rhondda E. "Evolution, Creationism and Science Education." In Allen and Briggs [1989] 242-55.

Jukes, Thomas. [1984] "The Creationist Challenge to Science." *Nature* 308, no. 5958 (March 29-April 4): 398-400.

_____. [1986] Letter. *Creation/Evolution Newsletter* 7, no. 5 (September/October): 22.

Kalthoff, Mark. [1993] "God and Creation: An Historical Look at Encounters Between Christianity and Science." In Bauman [1993] 5-30.

Kehoe, Alice B. [1983] "The Word of God." In Godfrey [1983b] 1-12.

Kemp, Kenneth W. [1988] "Discussing Creation Science." *American Biology Teacher* 50, no. 2 (February).

Kennedy, D. James. [1986] "The Crumbling of Evolution." In Walsh, Brooks and Crowell [1986] 239-40.

_____. [1988] *The Case . . . for Creation*. Ft. Lauderdale, Fla.: Coral Ridge Ministries.

Kennedy, Gail, ed. [1957] *Evolution and Religion*. Boston: Heath.

Key, T. [1985] "Does the Canopy Theory Hold Water?" *Journal of the American Scientific Affiliation* 37 no. 4: 223-25.

Kitcher, Philip. [1982] *Abusing Science*. Cambridge: MIT Press.

_____. [1993] *The Advancement of Science*. New York: Oxford University Press.

Klotz, Irving. [1980] "The N-Ray Affair." *Scientific American* 242, no. 5 (May): 168-75.

Klotz, John W. [1966] "The Philosophy of Science in Relation to Concepts of Creation vs. the Evolution Theory." *Creation Research Society Quarterly* 3 (July): 3-12.

_____. [1968] "Creationist Viewpoints." In Morris [1968b] 35-52.

————. [1980] "Is the Destruction of Plants Death in the Biblical Sense?" *Creation Research Science Quarterly* 16 (March): 202-3.

————. [1985] *Studies in Creation*. St. Louis: Concordia.

Koestler, Arthur. [1959] *The Sleepwalkers*. New York: Grosset and Dunlap.

Kofahl, Robert. [1973] "Entropy Prior to the Fall." *Creation Research Society Quarterly* 10 (December): 154-56.

————. [1977] *Handy Dandy Evolution Refuter*. San Diego, Calif.: Beta.

————. [1986] "Correctly Redefining Distorted Science: A Most Essential Task." *Creation Research Society Quarterly* 23 (December): 112-14.

————. [1989] "The Hierarchy of Conceptual Levels for Scientific Thought and Research." *Creation Research Society Quarterly* 26 (June): 12-14.

————. [1990] "Reply to McGhee." *Creation Research Society Quarterly* 26 (June): 40-41.

Kofahl, Robert, and Kelly Segraves. [1975] *The Creation Explanation*. Wheaton, Ill.: Harold Shaw.

Kuhn, Thomas [1962] *The Structure of Scientific Revolutions*. Chicago: University of Chicago. (2nd ed. 1970.)

————. [1970] "Reflections on My Critics." In Lakatos and Musgrave [1970] 231-78.

————. [1977] *The Essential Tension*. Chicago: University of Chicago.

Lakatos, Imre, and Alan Musgrave, eds. [1970] *Criticism and the Growth of Knowledge*. Cambridge: Cambridge University Press.

Lang, Walter. [1972] *Five Minutes with the Bible and Science*. Grand Rapids, Mich.: Baker Book House.

Larson, Edward J. [1985] *Trial and Error*. New York: Oxford University Press.

Laudan, Larry. [1983] "Science at the Bar: Cause for Concern." In Ruse [1988b] 337-55. Also appendix B in J. Murphy [1982] 149-54.

————. [1988] "More on Creationism." In Ruse [1988b] 363-66.

Leitch, Addison. [n.d.] *The Creation of Matter, Life and Man*. Christianity Today Fundamentals of the Faith Series 5.

Levin, Malcolm. [1992] "Life—How It Got Here." *Creation/Evolution* (Summer): 29-34.

Levinton, Jeffrey S. [1982] "Charles Darwin and Darwinism." *BioScience* 32, no. 6: 495-500.

Lewin, Roger. [1981] "A Response to Creationism Evolves." *Science* 214, no. 6 (November): 635-38.

Lewis, Ralph W. [1981] "Why Scientific Creationism Fails to Meet the Criteria of Science." *Creation/Evolution* 5: 7-11.

Lewis, Ricki. [1992] *Evolution of Life*. Dubuque, Iowa: Wm. C. Brown.

Lewontin, Richard. [1978] "Adaptation." *Scientific American* 239, no. 3 (September): 213-30.

————. [1981] Response. In Cole [1981] 34-36.

————. [1983a] "Darwin's Revolution." *The New York Review of Books* 30, no. 10 (June 16): 21-27.

———. [1983b] Introduction. In Godfrey [1983b].

Lindberg, David, and Ronald Numbers. [1986] "Beyond War and Peace: A Reappraisal of the Encounter Between Christianity and Science." *Church History* (September): 55.

Lindsell, Harold. [1977] Editor's Note. *Christianity Today* 21, no. 18 (June 17).

Lindsey, George. [1985] "Evolution—Useful or Useless?" *Impact* 148 (October): i-iv.

Lippard, Jim. [1994] Review of Gish [1993]. *Perspectives on Science and Christian Faith* 46, no. 3 (September): 193-95.

Livingstone, David. [1987] *Darwin's Forgotten Defenders.* Grand Rapids, Mich.: Eerdmans.

Lubenow, Marvin. [1983] *From Fish to Gish.* San Diego, Calif.: Creation Life.

———. [1992] *Bones of Contention.* Grand Rapids, Mich.: Baker Book House.

Maatman, Russell. [1993] *The Impact of Evolutionary Theory.* Sioux Center, Iowa: Dordt.

Macbeth, Norman. [1971] *Darwin Retried.* Boston: Gambit.

McCollister, Betty. [1989] *Voices for Evolution.* Berkeley, Calif.: National Center for Science Education.

McGee, J. Vernon. [1981] *Thru the Bible.* Nashville: Thomas Nelson.

McGhee, Lawrence. [1987] "The Metaphysics of Modern Science." *Creation Research Society Quarterly* 24 (December): 138-41.

McGowan, Chris. [1983] *In the Beginning . . . : A Scientist Shows Why Creationists Are Wrong.* Toronto: Macmillan.

McGuire, J. E. [1968] "Force, Active Principles and Newton's Invisible Realm." *Ambix* 15: 154-208.

McIver, Tom. [1988] *Anti-evolution: A Reader's Guide to Writings Before and After Darwin.* Baltimore: Johns Hopkins University Press. (2nd ed. 1992.)

———. [1989] "Creationism: Intellectual Origins, Cultural Context and Theoretical Diversity." Ph.D. dissertation, University of California—Los Angeles.

Mackay, John. [1984] "Interview with Dr. Henry Morris." *Ex Nihilo* 7, no. 1 (August): 14-18.

McKown, Delos. [1993] *The Mythmaker's Magic.* Buffalo, N.Y.: Prometheus.

McMullin, Ernan. [1993] "Evolution and Special Creation." *Zygon* 28, no. 3 (September): 299-335.

Malcolm, David. [1988-1989] "Can Water Flow Uphill?" *Creation Ex Nihilo* 11, no. 1 (December-February): 33-34.

Marsden, George. [1980] *Fundamentalism and American Culture.* New York: Oxford University Press.

———. [1984] "Understanding Fundamentalist Views of Science." In Montague [1984] 95-116.

———. [1991] *Understanding Fundamentalism and Evangelicalism.* Grand Rapids, Mich.: Eerdmans.

Marsh, Frank Lewis. [1933] *Evolution, Creation and Science.* Washington, D.C · Review and Herald.

Matrisciana, Caryl, and Roger Oakland. [1991] *The Evolution Conspiracy*. Eugene, Ore.: Harvest House.

Mehlert, A. W. [1987] Review of McGowan [1983], pt. 1. *Creation Research Society Quarterly* 24 (June): 3-33.

Milne, David. [1981] "How to Debate with Creationists—and 'Win.' " *American Biology Teacher* 43, no. 5 (May): 235-45.

Milner, Richard. [1990] *The Encyclopedia of Evolution*. New York: Facts on File.

Mirsky, Steven. [1988] "Standing on the Shoulders of Midgets." *Humanist* (January/February): 11.

Montague, Ashley, ed. [1984] *Science and Creation*. Oxford: Oxford University Press.

Moore, James. [1979] *The Post-Darwinian Controversies*. New York: Cambridge University Press.

———. [1994] *The Darwin Legend*. Grand Rapids, Mich.: Baker Book House.

Moore, John A. [1975] "On Giving Equal Time to the Teaching of Evolution and Creation." *Perspectives in Biology and Medicine* 16 (Spring 1975): 405-17.

Moore, John A. [1983a] "Creationism." In Zetterberg [1983] 115-33.

———. [1983b] "Evolution, Education and the Natural Sciences and Scientific Inquiry." In Zetterberg [1983] 3-17.

———. [1990-1991] "Is 'Creation Science' Scientific?" *Creation/Evolution* 27 (Winter): 6-15.

Moore, John N. [1973] "Evolution, Creation and the Scientific Method." *American Biology Teacher* 35, no. 1: 23-26.

———. [1974] "Some Definitional Formulations." *Creation Research Society Quarterly* 11 (June): 3-5.

———. [1976a] "On Methods of Teaching Origins: A Progress Report." *Creation Research Society Quarterly* 13 (June): 46-49.

———. [1976b] *Questions and Answers on Creation and Evolution*. Grand Rapids, Mich.: Baker Book House.

———. [1983] *How to Teach Origins (Without ACLU Interference)*. Milford, Mich.: Mott.

———. [1984] "Teaching About Origin Questions." *Creation Research Society Quarterly* 21 (December): 115-19.

———. [1985a] "Teaching About Origin Questions: Origin of the Universe." *Creation Research Society Quarterly* 21 (March): 189-94.

———. [1985b] "Teaching About Origin Questions: Origin of Life on Earth." *Creation Research Society Quarterly* 22 (June): 20-25.

———. [1986a] "Properly Defining Evolution." *Creation Research Society Quarterly* 23 (December): 110-11.

———. [1986b] "Was Evolution Involved in the Process of Creation? No." In Youngblood [1986] 86-109.

Moore, John N., and Harold Slusher. [1970] *Biology: A Search for Order in Complexity*. Grand Rapids, Mich.: Zondervan. (2nd ed. 1974.)

Moore, Robert A. [1983] "The Impossible Voyage of Noah's Ark." *Creation/Evo-*

*lution* 11 (Winter): 1-43.

Moreland, J. P. [1989] *Christianity and the Nature of Science*. Grand Rapids, Mich.: Baker Book House.

Moreland, J. P., ed. [1994] *The Creation Hypothesis*. Downers Grove, Ill.: Inter-Varsity Press.

Morowitz, Harold. [1982] Letter. *Physics Today* (February).

Morris, Henry. [1946] *That You Might Believe*. Chicago: Good Books.

_____. [1954] "Creation and Deluge." *His* (January). Reprinted with "minor revisions" as chap. 3 in Morris [1966].

_____. [1956] *The Bible and Modern Science*. Chicago: Moody Press. This is a revised version of Morris [1946].

_____. [1963a] "Biblical Catastrophism and Geology." *Grace Journal* 4, no. 2 (Spring): 9-14. This was also published in 1963 as a booklet with the same title by Presbyterian & Reformed, Philadelphia.

_____. [1963b] *The Twilight of Evolution*. Philadelphia: Presbyterian & Reformed.

_____. [1966] *Studies in the Bible and Science*. Philadelphia: Presbyterian & Reformed.

_____. [1967] *Evolution and the Modern Christian*. Grand Rapids, Mich.: Baker Book House.

_____. [1968a] "Biblical Catastrophism and Modern Science." *Bibliotheca Sacra* 125, no. 497 (January/March): 20-29.

_____. [1968b] *A Symposium on Creation*. Grand Rapids, Mich.: Baker Book House.

_____. [1970] *Biblical Cosmology and Modern Science*. Grand Rapids, Mich.: Baker Book House.

_____. [1971] *The Bible Has the Answer*. Grand Rapids, Mich.: Baker Book House.

_____. [1972a] *A Biblical Manual on Science and Creation*. San Diego, Calif.: Institute for Creation Research.

_____. [1972b] *The Remarkable Birth of Planet Earth*. Minneapolis: Dimension.

_____. [1972c] "Theistic Evolution." *Creation Research Society Quarterly* 8 (March): 269-72.

_____. [1973] Letter to W. V. Mayer (April 5). In Morris, Gish and Hillstad [1974] 69-70.

_____. [1974a] "Evolution, Creation and the Public Schools." In Morris, Gish and Hillestad [1974] 109-13.

_____. [1974b] "Evolution, Thermodynamics and Entropy." In Morris, Gish and Hillestad [1974] 123-29.

_____. [1974c] *Many Infallible Proofs*. San Diego, Calif.: Creation-Life.

_____. [1974d] *Science, Scripture and Salvation*. Rev. ed. Denver: Accent.

_____. [1974e] *Scientific Creationism*. San Diego, Calif.: Creation-Life.

_____. [1974f] "The Stars of Heaven." In Morris and Gish [1976] 184-92.

_____. [1974g] *The Troubled Waters of Evolution*. San Diego, Calif.: Creation-Life.

———. [1976a] "The Campus Debates." In Morris and Gish [1976] 3-67.

———. [1976b] "Creation and the Virgin Birth." In Morris and Gish [1976] 305-12.

———. [1976c] *The Genesis Record.* Grand Rapids, Mich.: Baker Book House.

———. [1977a] *The Beginning of the World.* Denver: Accent. This was a version of Morris [1974b].

———. [1977b] "Circular Reasoning in Evolutionary Geology." *Impact* 48 (June): i-iv.

———. [1977c] *Education for the Real World.* San Diego, Calif.: Creation-Life.

———. [1977d] *The Scientific Case for Creation.* San Diego, Calif.: Creation-Life.

———. [1978a] "Jesus' Doctrine of Creation." *Impact* (August): 5-6.

———. [1978b] *Sampling the Psalms.* San Diego, Calif.: Creation-Life.

———. [1978c] "Thermodynamics and the Origins of Life." *Impact* 57 (March): i-iv.

———. [1980a] *King of Creation.* San Diego, Calif.: Creation-Life.

———. [1980b] "The Tenets of Creationism." *Impact* 85 (July): i-iv.

———. [1981a] "An Answer for Asimov." *Impact* 99 (September): i-iv.

———. [1981b] "The Anti-creationists." *Impact* 97 (September): i-iv.

———. [1981c] "Revolutionary Evolutionism." In Morris and Rohrer [1981] 176-84.

———. [1981d] "Thermodynamics and the Origin of Life, Part I." In Morris and Rohrer [1981] 31-38.

———. [1982a] "The Anti-creationists." In Morris and Rohrer [1982] 139-44.

———. [1982b] "Bible-Believing Scientists of the Past." *Impact* 103 (January): i-iv.

———. [1982c] *Creation and Its Critics.* San Diego, Calif.: Creation-Life.

———. [1982d] "Evolution Is Religion, Not Science." *Impact* 107 (May): i-iv.

———. [1983a] "The New Meaning of Science." *Acts and Facts* 12, no. 6 (June).

———. [1983b] *The Revelation Record.* Wheaton, Ill.: Tyndale House/San Diego, Calif.: Creation-Life.

———. [1983c] "Those Remarkable Floating Rock Formations." *Impact* 119 (May): i-iv.

———. [1984a] *The Biblical Basis for Modern Science.* Grand Rapids, Mich.: Baker Book House.

———. [1984b] *History of Modern Creationism.* San Diego, Calif.: Master.

———. [1984c] "Recent Creation Is a Vital Doctrine." *Impact* 132 (June): i-iv.

———. [1985a] *Creation and the Modern Christian.* El Cajon, Calif.: Master.

———. [1985b] "Does Entropy Contradict Evolution?" *Impact* 141 (March): i-iv.

———. [1985c] "ICR, Fifteen Years in a Unique Mission: 1970-1985." *Impact* 147 (September): i-iv.

———. [1986a] *Science and the Bible.* Chicago: Moody Press. Revision of Morris [1956].

———. [1986b] "The Vanishing Case for Evolution." *Impact* 156 (June): i-iv.

———. [1987] "Is Creationism Scientific?" *Acts and Facts* 16, no. 12 (December): 1, 4.

——. [1988a] "The Gap Theory." *Creation Ex Nihilo* 10, no. 1 (December-February): 35-37.

——. [1988b] *The God Who Is Real.* Grand Rapids, Mich.: Baker Book House.

——. [1988c] "Is Creation Important in Education?" *Creation Ex Nihilo* 10, no. 3 (June-August): 29-31.

——. [1988d] "Looking at the Origin of Kinds." *Creation Ex Nihilo* 10, no. 4 (September-November): 15-16.

——. [1988e] *Men of Science, Men of God.* Rev. ed. El Cajon, Calif.: Master.

——. [1989a] "The Ice Age." *Creation Ex Nihilo* 11, no. 2 (March-May): 10-12.

——. [1989b] *The Long War Against God.* Grand Rapids, Mich.: Baker Book House.

——. [1990a] "How to Stop the Creationists." *Creation Ex Nihilo* 12, no. 2 (March-May): 40.

——. [1990b] "The Logic of Biblical Creation." *Impact* 205 (July): i-ii.

——. [1990c] "My Favorite Evidence for Creation." *Creation Ex Nihilo* 12, no. 1 (December-February): 35-37.

——. [1991] *Creation and the Second Coming.* El Cajon, Calif.: Master.

——. [1993] *Biblical Creationism.* Grand Rapids, Mich.: Baker Book House.

Morris, Henry, and Duane Gish. [1976] *The Battle for Creation.* San Diego, Calif.: Creation-Life.

Morris, Henry, and John Morris. [1989] *Science, Scripture and the Young Earth.* El Cajon, Calif.: Institute for Creation Research.

Morris, Henry, and Gary Parker. [1987] *What Is Creation Science?* Rev. ed. El Cajon, Calif.: Master.

Morris, Henry, and Donald Rohrer. [1981] *Decade of Creation.* San Diego, Calif.: Creation-Life.

——. [1982] *Creation: The Cutting Edge.* San Diego, Calif.: Creation-Life.

Morris, Henry, William Boardman Jr. and Robert Koontz. [1971] *Science and Creation Series.* San Diego, Calif.: Creation-Science Research Center.

Morris, Henry, Duane Gish and George Hillestad. [1974] *Creation: Acts, Facts, Impacts.* San Diego, Calif.: Creation-Life.

Morris, John D. [1980] *Tracking Those Incredible Dinosaurs and the People Who Knew Them.* San Diego, Calif.: Master.

——. [1986] "The Paluxy River Mystery." *Impact* 151 (January): i-iv.

——. [1989] "How Do the Dinosaurs Fit In?" *Impact* (May): d.

——. [1990] "Did Noah's Flood Cover the Whole Earth?" *Creation Ex Nihilo* 12, no. 2 (March-May): 48-50.

——. [1991a] "Are Plants Alive?" *Impact* (September): d.

——. [1991b] "Can Scientists Study the Past?" *Impact* (February): d.

——. [1991c] "How Can a Geology Professor Believe That the Earth Is Young?" *Impact* (May): d.

——. [1992] " 'Natural' Selection Versus 'Supernatural' Design." *Impact* 223 (January): i-iv.

——. [1995] "Does Scripture Require a Global Flood?" *Creation Ex Nihilo* 17 no. 2 (March-May): 37.

Moyer, Wayne. [1980] Letter. *BioScience* 30, no. 1 (January): 4.

Murphy, Jeffrie G. [1982] *Evolution, Morality and the Meaning of Life.* Totowa, N.J.: Rowman and Littlefield.

Murphy, Nancey. [1993] "Phillip Johnson on Trial." *Perspectives on Science and Christian Faith* 45, no. 1: 33.

Murris, Hendrik. [1986] "The Concept of the Species and Its Formation." In Andrews, Gitt and Ouweneel [1986] 175-207.

Myers, Ellen. [1986] "A Proof for Creation: The Hostility of Creation Denied." *Creation Social Science and Humanities Quarterly* 9, no. 2 (Winter): 4-7.

————. [1988] "The Story of Paul Kammerer: Or, Is Lamarckianism Dead?" *Creation Social Science and Humanities Quarterly* 11, no. 1 (Fall): 6-12.

————. [1989] "Evolution." *Creation Social Science and Humanities Quarterly* 12, no. 1 (Fall): 14-19.

NAS (National Academy of Science). [1982] "Statement on Creationism." In McCollister [1989] 33.

————. [1984] *Science and Creation: A View from the NAS.* Washington, D.C.: National Academy Press.

NCSE (National Center for Science Education). [n.d.] "Evolution and Creationism: What Can *You* Do?" Berkeley, Calif.: NCSE.

————. [n.d.] "Keeping Creationism out of Education: What Parents and Teachers Can Do." Berkeley, Calif.: NCSE.

Nelkin, Dorothy. [1992] *The Creation Controversy: Science or Scripture in the Schools.* New York: Norton.

Nevins, Stuart. *See* Austin, Steven

Newell, Norman. [1974] "Evolution Under Attack." In Eldredge [1987] 205-13. Originally published in *Natural History* 83, no. 4: 32-39.

————. [1982] *Creation and Evolution.* New York: Columbia University Press.

————. [1985] *Creation and Evolution: Myth or Reality?* New York: Praeger.

Niessen, Richard. [1980] "Several Significant Discrepancies Between Theistic Evolution and the Biblical Account." *Creation Research Science Quarterly* 16 (March): 203, 220-21.

————. [1983] "Starlight and the Age of the Universe." *Impact* 121 (July): i-iv.

Numbers, Ronald. [1982] "Creationism in Twentieth Century America." *Science* 218, no. 5 (November): 538-44.

————. [1992] *The Creationists.* New York: Knopf.

Ouweneel, Willem. [1971] "The Scientific Character of the Evolution Doctrine." *Creation Research Society Quarterly* 8 (September): 109-15.

Overton, William. [1982] Opinion in *McLean vs. the Arkansas Board of Education.* Appendix 15 in Bailey [1993] 206-33. Also in Ruse [1988b] 307-31.

Parker, Gary. [1984] "Creative Design." *Ex Nihilo* 6, no. 3 (February): 6-9.

————. [1987] *Dry Bones.* Rev. ed. El Cajon, Calif.: Master.

————. [1994] *Creation: Facts of Life.* Colorado Springs: Master. This is a reworking of parts of [1980] *Creation: The Facts of Life.* San Diego, Calif.: Creation-

Life.

Patten, Donald, ed. [1970] *A Symposium on Creation II.* Grand Rapids, Mich.: Baker Book House.

———. [1971] *A Symposium on Creation III.* Grand Rapids, Mich.: Baker Book House.

———. [1975] *A Symposium on Creation V.* Grand Rapids, Mich.: Baker Book House.

———. [1977] *A Symposium on Creation VI.* Seattle: Pacific Meridian.

Patterson, Colin. [1978] *Evolution.* London: British Museum.

Patterson, John W. [1983a] "An Engineer Looks at the Creationist Movement." In Zetterberg [1983] 150-61.

———. [1983b] "Thermodynamics and Evolution." In Godfrey [1983b] 99-116.

Pearcey, Nancy. [1987a] "Everybody Can Know: The Most Powerful Evidence Against Evolution." *Bible-Science Newsletter* 25, no. 6 (June): 7-10.

———. [1987b] "Running Down and Falling Apart: Thermodynamics and the Origin of Life." *Bible-Science Newsletter* 25, no. 9 (September): 6-8.

———. [1989] "Creation Is the Basis: An Interview with Ken Ham." *Bible-Science Newsletter* 27, no. 4 (April): 7-11.

———. [1990] "Anti-Darwinism Come to the University: An Interview with Phillip Johnson." *Bible-Science Newsletter* 28, no. 6 (June): 7-11.

———. [1993] "Teaching Creationism." *Bible-Science News* 31, no. 1: 1-2.

Pearcey, Nancy, and Charles Thaxton. [1994] *The Soul of Science.* Wheaton, Ill.: Crossway.

Peterson, Everett H. [1981] "The Necessity of the Canopies." *Creation Research Society Quarterly* 17 (March): 201-4.

Pine, Ronald. [1983] "But Some of Them *Are* Scientists, Aren't They?" *Creation/Evolution* 15 (Fall): 6-18.

Plantinga, Alvin. [n.d.] "Methodological Naturalism?" Unpublished.

Pollitzer, William. [1980] "Evolution and Special Creation." *American Journal of Physical Anthropology* 53: 329-31.

Poole, M. W., and G. J. Wenham. [1987] *Creation or Evolution—a False Antithesis?* Oxford: Latimer House.

Pope, Geoffrey G. [1989] "Bamboo and Human Evolution." *Natural History* (October): 48-57.

Popper, Karl. [1959] *The Logic of Scientific Discovery.* New York: Harper.

Price, Robert. [1980] "The Return of the Navel: The 'Omphalos' Argument in Contemporary Creationism." *Creation/Evolution* (Fall): 26-33.

———. [1983] "Creationist and Fundamentalist Apologetics: Two Branches of the Same Tree." *Creation/Evolution* 14, no. 4 (Fall): 19-31.

Provine, William. [1982] "Influence of Darwin's Ideas on the Study of Evolution." *BioScience* 32, no. 6 (June): 501-6.

———. [1987] Review of E. J. Larson, *Trial and Error. Academe* 73, no. 1 (January/February): 50-52.

Quinn, Philip. [1984] "The Philosopher of Science as Expert Witness." In Ruse

[1988b] 367-85.

———. [1988] "Creationism, Methodology and Politics." In Ruse [1988b] 395-99.

Randall, John Herman. [1926] *The Making of the Modern Mind*. New York: Columbia University Press.

Ratzsch, Del. [1986] *The Philosophy of Science*. Downers Grove, Ill.: InterVarsity Press.

Raup, David M. [1983] "The Geological and Paleontological Arguments of Creationism." In Godfrey [1983b] 147-62.

ReMine, Walter. [1993] *The Biotic Message*. St. Paul, Minn.: St. Paul Science.

Rice, S. [1985] "Botanical and Ecological Objections to a Pre-flood Water Canopy." *Journal of the American Scientific Affiliation* 37, no. 4: 225-29.

Riemen, William. [1987] "The Non-material Hypothesis and Its Implications for Modern Society." *Creation Research Society Quarterly* 23 (March): 141-45.

Riley, W. B. [1922a] "The Christian Fundamentals Movement." In WCFA [1922] 7-24.

———. [1922b] "Is It an Evolution or an Inspiration?" In WCFA [1922] 131-45.

Rimmer, Harry. [1937] *Modern Science and the Genesis Record*. Grand Rapids, Mich.: Eerdmans. Reprint [1973].

———. [1947] *Lot's Wife and the Science of Physics*. Grand Rapids, Mich.: Eerdmans.

Root-Bernstein, Robert. [1984] "Ignorance Versus Knowledge in the Evolutionist-Creationist Controversy." In Awbrey and Thwaites [1984] 8-24.

Rusch, Wilbert H. [1984] *The Argument: Creationism vs. Evolutionism*. Creation Research Society Monograph 3. Terre Haute, Ind.: Creation Research Society Books.

———. [1991] *Origins: What Is at Stake?* Creation Research Society Monograph 5. Terre Haute, Ind.: Creation Research Society Books.

Ruse, Michael. [1982] *Darwinism Defended*. Reading, Mass.: Addison-Wesley.

———. [1988a] "The Academic as Expert Witness." In Ruse [1988b] 386-94.

———. [1988b] *But Is It Science?* Buffalo, N.Y.: Prometheus.

———. [1988c] "Pro Judice." In Ruse [1988b] 356-62.

———. [1988d] "Witness Testimony Sheet." In Ruse [1988b] 287-306.

Rushdoony, Rousas. [1967] *The Mythology of Science*. Nutley, N.J.: Craig.

Saint, Phil. [1993] *Fossils That Speak Out*. 2nd ed. Phillipsburg, N.J.: Presbyterian & Reformed.

Salmon, Wesley. [1989] *Four Decades of Scientific Explanation*. Minneapolis: University of Minnesota Press.

Savage, Jay M. [1963] *Evolution*. New York: Holt, Rinehart and Winston.

Schadewald, Robert. [1983a] "The Evolution of Bible-Science." In Godfrey [1983b] 283-99.

———. [1983b] "Six 'Flood' Arguments Creationists Can't Answer." In Zetterberg [1983] 448-53.

———. [1985] "Gish at the University of Minnesota." *Creation/Evolution Newsletter* 5, no. 2 (March/April): 15-16.

———. [1989a] "Baconian Bible-Science." *NCSE Reports* 9, no. 5 (September/ October): 9.

———. [1989b] "The 1989 National Creation Conference." *NCSE Reports* 9, no. 5 (September/October): 19-23.

Schadewald, Robert, and Ronnie J. Hastings. [1990] "The 1990 International Conference on Creationism." *NCSE Reports* 10, no. 5 (September/October): 1, 18-23.

Schafersma, Steven D. [1983] "Fossils, Stratigraphy and Evolution: Consideration of a Creationist Argument." In Godfrey [1983b] 219-44.

Schoepflin, Gary. [1972] "On Assumptions and Their Relation to Science." *Creation Research Society Quarterly* 19 (September): 125-29.

Scott, Eugenie. [n.d.] " 'Scientific Creationism,' Evolution and Race." Berkeley, Calif.: National Center for Science Education.

———. [1988] Abstract of " 'Creation Science' and Philosophy of Science: Reflections." *American Journal of Physical Anthropology* 75, no. 2 (February): 268-69.

———. [1990] "Of Pandas and People." *NCSE Reports* 10, no. 1 (January/February): 16-18.

———. [1993] "Darwin Prosecuted." *Creation/Evolution* 13, no. 2 (Winter): 36-47.

Scott, Eugenie, and Henry P. Cole. [1985] "The Elusive Scientific Basis of Creation 'Science.' " *Quarterly Review of Biology* 60, no. 1 (March): 21-30.

Scott, Eugenie, and Thomas Sager. [1992] Review of Johnson [1991]. *Creation/ Evolution* (Winter): 47-56.

Segraves, Kelly. [1973] *Jesus Christ Creator.* San Diego, Calif.: Creation-Science Research Center.

Sereno, Paul C. [1995] "Dinosaurs and Drifting Continents." *Natural History* 104, no. 1 (January): 40-47.

Shapin, Steven. [1982] "History of Science and Its Sociological Reconstructions." *History of Science* 20: 157-211.

Shapiro, Arthur. [1993] "God and Science." *Creation/Evolution* 13, no. 1 (Summer): 10-19.

Shmaefsky, Brian R. [1991] "Teaching New Science Teachers How to Advocate Evolution." *NCSE Reports* 11, no. 1: 23.

Siegel, Harvey. [1981] "Creationism, Evolution and Education: The California Fiasco." *Phi Delta Kappan* 63, no. 2 (October): 95-101.

Singer, David. [1977] "What Christian Colleges Teach About Creation." *Christianity Today* 21, no. 18 (June 17): 8-11.

Skehan, James. [1986] *Modern Science and the Book of Genesis.* Washington, D.C.: National Science Teachers Association.

Slusher, Harold. [1974] "Clues Regarding the Age of the Universe." *Impact* 19 (November). Reprinted in Morris and Gish [1976] 253-59.

Smith, Hobart M. [1989] "The Myth Is Not Evolution." *Evolution* 43, no. 3: 699-700.

Snelling, Andrew. [1989] "Growing Opals—Australian Style." *Creation Ex Nihilo* 12, no. 1 (December-February): 10-15.

———. [1990] *The Revised Quote Book.* Brisbane, Australia: Creation Science Foundation.

———. [1991] "Where Are All the Human Fossils?" *Creation Ex Nihilo* 14, no. 1 (December-February): 28-33.

———. [1993] "Yet Another 'Missing Link' Fails to Qualify." *Creation Ex Nihilo* 15, no. 3 (June-August): 40-44.

Sonleitner, Frank J. [1990] "Molecular Nonsense in Bible-Science Newsletter." *NCSE Reports* 10, no. 2 (March/April): 14-15.

———. [1991] *What's Wrong with Pandas?* Norman, Okla.: Author. Distributed through NCSE.

Stambough, James. [1989] "Death Before Sin?" *Impact* 191 (May): i-iv.

Steele, DeWitt. [1983] *Science of the Physical Creation in Christian Perspective.* Pensacola, Fla.: A. Beka.

Steinhauer, Loren. [1975a] "The Case for Global Catastrophism." In Patten [1975] 99-109.

———. [1975b] "Tracing the Past: Is Uniformity Meaningful?" In Patten [1975] 85-97.

Strahler, Arthur N. [1987] *Science and Earth History: The Evolution/Creation Controversy.* Buffalo, N.Y.: Prometheus.

Sunderland, Luther. [1988] *Darwin's Enigma.* Rev. 4th ed. Santee, Calif.: Master.

Suppe, Frederick. [1977] *The Structure of Scientific Theories.* 2nd ed. Urbana: University of Illinois Press.

Synan, H. Vincent. [1988] "Fundamentalism." In Burgess and McGee [1988] 324-27.

Taylor, Ian. [1984] *In the Minds of Man.* 3rd ed. Toronto: TFE.

———. [1989] "Creatures That Time Forgot." *Creation Ex Nihilo* 11, no. 3 (June-August): 10-15.

Taylor, Paul S. [1992] *The Illustrated Origins Answer Book.* 4th ed. Mesa, Ariz.: Eden Productions.

Teeple, Howard M. [1978] *The Noah's Ark Nonsense.* Evanston, Ill.: Religion & Ethics Institute.

Thackray, Arnold. [1970] *Atoms and Powers.* Cambridge, Mass.: Harvard University Press.

Thaxton, Charles, and Jon Buell. [1993] "Why All the Fuss About Creation and Evolution?" *Creation Social Science and Humanities Quarterly* 15, no. 3 (Spring): 23-25.

Thaxton, Charles, Walter Bradley and Roger Olsen. [1984] *The Mystery of Life's Origin.* Dallas: Lewis and Stanley.

Thwaites, William. [n.d.] "The Evolution of Creationism." Berkeley, Calif.: National Center for Science Education.

———. [1984] "Design: Can We See the Hand of Evolution in the Things It Has Wrought?" In Awbrey and Thwaites [1984] 206-13.

Tiffin, Lee. [1994] *Creationism's Upside Down Pyramid.* Amherst, N.Y.: Prometheus.

Tinkle, William J. [1970] *Heredity: A Study in Science and the Bible.* Rev. ed. Grand Rapids, Mich.: Zondervan.

Torrance, Thomas. [1989] *The Christian Frame of Mind.* Colorado Springs: Helmers and Howard.

Torrey, Reuben A. [1907] *Difficulties in the Bible.* Lincoln, Neb.: Back to the Bible.

Toulmin, S., and J. Goodfield. [1965] *The Discovery of Time.* New York: Harper & Row.

Toumey, Christopher. [1994] *God's Own Scientists.* New Brunswick, N.J.: Rutgers University Press.

van Inwagen, Peter. [1989] "Genesis and Evolution." Kraemer Lectures at University of Arkansas, Fayetteville, March 31.

Wallace, A. R. [1855] "On the Law Which Has Regulated the Introduction of New Species." In Brackman [1980] 311-25.

──────. [1858] "On the Tendency of Varieties to Depart Indefinitely from the Original Type." In Brackman [1980] 326-37.

Walsh, Robert, Christopher Brooks and Richard Crowell, eds. [1986] *Proceedings of the First International Conference on Creation.* Vol. 2. Pittsburgh, Penn.: Creation Science Fellowship.

Walsh, Steve, and Thomas Demere. [1993] "Facts, Faith and Fairness." Berkeley, Calif.: National Center for Science Education.

Ward, Peter Douglas. [1992] *On Methuselah's Trail.* New York: Freeman.

WCFA (World's Christian Fundamentals Association). [1922] *Scriptural Inspiration Versus Scientific Imagination.* Introduction by T. C. Horton. Los Angeles: Biola Book Room. (Addresses at the Fourth Annual Convention of the World's Fundamentals Conference, 1922.)

Webb, George E. [1994] *The Evolution Controversy in America.* Lexington: University of Kentucky Press.

Weiner, A. M., and N. Maizels. [n.d.] "Unlocking the Secrets of Retroviral Evolution." *Current Biology* 4: 560-63.

Whitcomb, John, Jr. [1966] *Creation According to God's Word.* Grand Rapids, Mich.: Reformed Fellowship.

──────. [1973] *The World That Perished.* Grand Rapids, Mich.: Baker Book House.

──────. [1979] *The Origin of the Solar System.* Phillipsburg, N.J.: Presbyterian & Reformed.

──────. [1984a] *The Bible and Astronomy.* Winona Lake, Ind.: BMH.

──────. [1984b] "Creation Science and Biblical Creation." *Creation Social Science and Humanities Quarterly* 7, no. 2 (Winter): 22-23.

──────. [1986] *The Early Earth.* Grand Rapids, Mich.: Baker Book House. Revised [1972].

Whitcomb, John, Jr., and Donald De Young. [1978] *The Moon: Its Creation, Form and Significance.* Grand Rapids, Mich.: Baker Book House.

Whitcomb, John, Jr., and Henry Morris. [1961] *The Genesis Flood.* Grand Rapids, Mich.: Baker Book House.

White, A. D. [1896] *A History of the Warfare of Science and Theology in Chris-*

*tendom.* New York: Appleton.

Whitelaw, Robert. [1975] "The Testimony of Radiocarbon to the Genesis Flood." In Patten [1975] 39-50.

Wieland, Carl. [1989] "Science: The Rules of the Game." *Creation Ex Nihilo* 11, no. 1 (December-February): 47-48.

———. [1993a] "A Big Purple Frog Behind the Moon." *Creation Ex Nihilo* 15, no. 4 (September-November): 46-48.

———. [1993b] "Pagan Panic." *Creation Ex Nihilo* 15, no. 1 (December-February): 18-21.

———. [1994] *Stones and Bones.* Queensland, Australia: Creation Science Foundation.

———. [1995] "Bones Overthrown." *Creation Ex Nihilo* 17, no. 4 (September-November): 17-19.

Wilder-Smith, A. E. [1981] *The Natural Sciences Know Nothing of Evolution.* San Diego, Calif.: Master.

———. [1986] "Creation and the Appearance of Age." *Creation Ex Nihilo* 9, no. 1 (December): 14-15.

Willey, Basil. [1940] *The Eighteenth Century Background.* Boston: Beacon.

Williams, Emmett. [1975] "Thermodynamics: A Tool for Creationists." In Howe [1975] 447-63. Reprinted from [1973] *Creation Research Society Quarterly* 10, no. 1 (June).

Wysong, R. L. [1976] *The Creation-Evolution Controversy.* Midland, Mich.: Inquiry.

Young, Davis. [1982] *Christianity and the Age of the Earth.* Grand Rapids, Mich.: Zondervan.

Youngblood, Ronald. [1986] *The Genesis Debate.* Grand Rapids, Mich.: Baker Book House.

Zetterberg, J. Peter, ed. [1983] *Evolution vs. Creationism: The Public Education Controversy.* Phoenix, Ariz.: Oryx.

Zimmerman, Paul. [1968] "Can We Accept Theistic Evolution?" In Morris [1968b] 55-78.

Zindler, Frank. [1989] "John Morris vs. the Truth Patrol." *NCSE Reports* 9, no. 5 (September/October): 7-9.